ONCE UPON EACH TIME

COLLECTED POEMS

E.M. Schorb
Sculpture by Natale de la Padura

ONCE UPON EACH TIME

COLLECTED POEMS

E.M. SCHORB

HILL HOUSE   NEW YORK

© 2020 by E.M. Schorb

ISBN: 978-0-578-73906-9

Cover Painting: "Over a Moony Sea" by the Author
Cover Design: Selah Bunzey

ACKNOWLEDGEMENTS

Grateful acknowledgement is given to the following publications in which many of these poems first appeared:

    Agenda (England), The Amaryllis Review, American Journal of Poetry, *American Poetry Anthology,* The American Scholar, *Anthology of Magazine Verse and Yearbook of American Poetry, 1980, 1981,* Antigonish Review (Canada), Antioch Review, Arkansas Review, Art Villa (England), The Arts Journal, Ascent, Asheville Poetry Review, Atlanta Review,
    Baltimore Review, The Beloit Poetry Journal, *Best American Fantasy 2007* (Anthology), *Best New Writing 2015* (Anthology), Bitterroot, Black Heart Magazine, Blaze Vox, Blood and Fire Review, Blue Ridge Literary Services, Blue Unicorn, Brink, Brooklyn Review, The Brownstone Review,
    Candelabrum Poetry Magazine (England), The Cape Rock, The Carolina Quarterly, Caveat Lector, Chariton Review, Chattahoochee Review, Chelsea, Chicago Review, Chiron Review, The Cincinnati Review, The Classical Outlook, Coe Review, College English, The Colorado Quarterly, Comstock Review, Confrontation, Contempora, Context South, Crab Orchard Review, Crucible, Cutbank,
    Dalhousie Review (Canada), Dark Horse (Scotland) Davidson Miscellany, The Deronda Review (Israel), Descant, *Di-Verse-City* (Anthology), Dramatists Guild Quarterly, Dream International Quarterly,
    ELM: Eureka Literary Magazine, The Eloquent Atheist, Encore, Envoi (England), Epiphany, Epos,
    The Fiddlehead (Canada), Filling Station (Canada), Five A.M., The Formalist, The New Formalist, Frank (France), Free Lunch, Futures Trading,
    A Galaxy of Verse, Gallery (England), Gargoyle, Ginosko, *The Ginosko Anthology 2, The Great American Poetry Show Vol. 2, Vol. 3,* Green River Review, Green's Magazine,
    Haight Ashbury Literary Journal, Hampden-Sydney Poetry Review, The Hawaii Review, Higginson Journal, Hiram Poetry Review, Hollins Critic, Hot Metal Press, The Hudson Review,

In Whatever Houses We May Visit (Anthology, American College of Physicians), Innisfree Poetry Journal, Insight: Review & Herald Publishing Association, International Poetry Review, The Interpreter's House (England), The Iowa Review, Isaac Asimov's Science Fiction Magazine,

The Journal (England), The Journal of Contemporary Anglo-Scandinavian Poetry (England), Journal of New Jersey Poets,

The Kansas Quarterly, Kavya Bharati (India), Keats Prize Poems (England),

Lake Superior Review, The Laurel Review, Light: a Quarterly of Light Verse, Literal Latté, The Literary Review, London Poetry Review (England), Long Island Quarterly, Lucid Rhythms, The Lyric,

Mad Hatter's Review, Main Street Rag, The Malahat Review (Canada), Margie, The Massachusetts Review, Measure: a Review of Formal Poetry, *Meridian Anthology,* Midwest Poetry Review, Midwest Review, The Milo Review, Mississippi Review, Möbius; The Poetry Magazine, Mudfish,

Naugatuck River Review, NC Arts, Negative Capability, New Delta Review, The New Laurel Review, New Letters, New Orleans Review, The New Welsh Review (Wales), The New York Quarterly, Nimrod, Noon/Afternoon: American Poetry in Song, Composer, Daniel Jahn, North American Review, North Carolina Literary Review, The Notra Dame Review,

Off Course Literary Journal, Orbis (England), Outposts (England), Outrider (Australia), Oxford Magazine, Oxford Poetry (England),

Painted Bride Quarterly, Palo Alto Review, *Peace is Our Profession: Poems and Passages of War Protest, 1981* (East River Anthology), Pembroke Magazine,The Pennsylvania Review, Penwood Review, *The Phoenix Rising from the Ashes* (Anthology, Canada), Plains Poetry Journal, Plainsongs Poetry Magazine, Poet Lore, Poet: An International Monthly (India), Poetry Daily, Poetry Life and Times (England), Poetry Nippon (Japan), Poetry Northwest, Poetry Salzburg Review (Austria), Poetry Super Highway, Poetry Today (Wales), Poetry View Magazine, *Poets in Harmony* (Anthology, England), Potomac Review, Princeton Arts Review, Prism International (Canada), Private Photo Review (Italy), The Prose Poem, Puerto del Sol,

Queen's Quarterly (Canada), Quick Fiction,

Raleigh News and Observer, Rattle, Riverrun, The Road Not Taken: a Review of Formal Poetry, Roanoke Review,

Sand Literary Journal (Germany), SANE: Citizens' Organization for a Sane World Broadside, Santa Barbara Review, The Sewanee Review, Shenandoah, Showcase '76, Sisyphus, The South Carolina Review, Southern Humanities Review, Southern Poetry Review, Southern Review, Southwest Review, Sparrow 61, Sparrow 62, SpeakOut, Spring: Journal of the E.E. Cummings Society, St. Sebastian Review, Stand (England), Summerset Review,

Tar River Poetry, The Tennessee Quarterly, The Texas Review, Thalia (Canada), The Doctor T J Eckleburg Review, The Road Not Taken: a Journal of Formal Poetry, Timber Creek Review, Trinacria, Tulane Review,

Unitarian Universalist Magazine, University of Windsor Review (Canada),

Verse, Verse Wisconsin, Victorian Violet, *Viewpoint of a Poet* (Anthology, England), Virginia Quarterly Review, Voices International, Voices Israel (Israel),

Wallace Stevens Journal, War, Literature & the Arts: an International Journal of the Humanities (USAF Academy), Wascana Review (Canada), Webster Review, West Hills Review, Whiskey Island Magazine, William and Mary Review, The Wisconsin Review, WordWrights Magazine, The World of English: "The White Stallion" also published as "A Fable" (in English and in Chinese Translation, Beijing, China), Writers' Forum, The Writing Disorder,

Xavier Review,

The Yale Review,

Yearbook of Modern Poetry (Anthology)

Special thanks to Robert Rauschenberg and Change, Inc. for a grant for artwork; and also to the North Carolina Arts Council for a fellowship which made some of this work possible.

BY E.M. SCHORB

Poetry
The Poor Boy and Other Poems
50 Poems
Murderer's Day
A Fable and Other Prose Poems
Time and Fevers
Reflections in a Doubtful I
The Journey and Related Poems
The Ideologues
Manhattan Spleen, Prose Poems
Emanations from the Penumbra
Life and Opinions of Doctor Bop
Last Exit to East Hampton, Prose Poems
Fiat Lux!
Words in Passing
Dates and Dreams, Prose Poems
Eclectica Americana
Muddling Through
Contra Mortem

Prose
A Portable Chaos
Paradise Square
Needleneck
R&R: a Sex Comedy
Stories, Etc.
The Secret of Jessie Judas
Malum in Se
Collected Stories
Carbons, a Career in Letters

Cartoons
Moon for the Misbegotten?

Photographs
Electriks

Introduction

The title, "Once Upon Each Time," Schorb was kind enough to inform me, is meant to convey his artistic ideal: to make, like Picasso used to make, something new every time. This may be no more than a profession of modernism, amounting to "make it new," as Pound memorably formulated it; or it may be a symptom of a fear common among artists and poets of a certain age – both Schorb and I are of a certain age, so I speak in sympathy and from my own experience: I mean the fear of repeating, of parroting oneself. Once I asked the French poet Yves Bonnefoy what he thought of Samuel Beckett's work, and he said, dismissively, "Il se répète. Il se répète". It didn't seem to me that Beckett repeated himself more than did Bonnefoy in his own work, but of course I kept the thought to myself. Repetition, it is worth repeating, is very much in the eye of the beholder or in the ear of the listener.

With at least equal justice the title of this book could have been borrowed from Kierkegaard: "Stages on Life's Way," or better, "Stages on *One* Life's Way." For if in the following poems the variety of rhythms, styles of speech, and subject matter is remarkable, even more so is the sameness of the spirit that's behind and under them: always the same, impossible to mistake, from the crib to the final curtal sonnet. Here are its last lines:

Goodbye, myself, without you I shan't groan
but be my bravest, like those lonely trees
  that fall without a sound.

"Those lonely trees that fall without a sound": five iambs which convey, in the most classical meter available in English, at once the essential solitude of death and the aspiration to a brave, honest departure. To be able to say, like Socrates at his final hour, "We owe a cock to Asclepius": that is my aspiration, too.

Going back to the other end, to birth, here are the first few lines of the first poem in Part One, "From the Crib":

From the deep recesses of the universe
he woke to find himself
gumming the blue lead paint
from the top rail of his crib.

Schorb's humor is like permanganate, sharp, biting, and darkish purple; it often reminds me of Stevie Smith.

The lead paint was delicious and maddening,
and would,
no doubt
make a mad poet of him.

And just as here we see the double nature of the gift, tenaciously milked by anthropologists – the deadly lead poison in the crib which is also the gift of the Muse –, later we encounter the double nature of the kite, a word which originally meant only the bird of prey, and thence, according to my OED, the flying toy. In the poem "The Kite," the process is inverted: a toy during the day, at night the kite, in the boy's dreams, changes into a frightful monster, some sort of prehistoric giant bat:

From the dark, tarred roof where urchins chant
in garbled language some insistent word,

the line leads upward to the bending rod,
spine of a skin that billows in the breeze

...

the toys of children change into the ogres
of their bad dreams.

Childhood, in Schorb's spirit, is no Wordsworthian garden; if a garden at all, it is one always contiguous with Hell, an unchained, tumbledown door in between. We are reminded of the Hieronymus Bosch triptych in the Prado, "The Garden of Earthly Delights," which, like this book, teems with succulent detail. A number of poems fill us in; for example, in "Impedimenta," as the poet and his mother are staying in a flooded house:

... My father, the superior drunk, had left us in this dump
in Newark to go off selling his bullshit books in Buffalo,
and to shack up with his beautiful vocabulary, quoth the
    raven,
a bottle and a bimbo, and not to have to sit here with us,
under the dripping pipes wrapped in soggy cardboard ...

The father, whose looks, in the earlier poem "From the Crib," are compared to those of "the famous-at-the-time Arrow Collar Man," must have been as handsome as utterly irresponsible. In another earlier poem, "Denial," the mother is seen to be no better in comparison. She tries to convince her young son, who is just "about three feet tall," that what he has seen – a man, a stranger, kissing Momma long and hard on a Philadelphia street – has never happened. Such early cognitive traumas can be more toxic than lead paint.

"Haunting" is a word much abused in texts of the present sort, and I would do my best to avoid it, except that there is a line in Part III of the present volume about Doctor Bop (burnt-out prof) and his life in Academia, a line which has haunted me ever since I first read it more than two years ago. I singled it out when I wrote a review of Schorb's *Life and Opinions of Doctor Bop the Burnt-Out Prof and Other Poems*, for the 73rd issue of *Offcourse*, in June 2018. The haunting line in question is the first one of the poem "Veni, Vidi, Vici":

My old man was a Moishe Kapoyr if you ever saw one.

Since then, I've asked myself why I am haunted by this verse; what is, exactly, that which I find so special in it. Is it because it challenges me to jump up and reply, "Yes, I've seen one, and he was *my* old man"? For my father was a champion at getting things backwards or upside-down – *tokhes afn kop*, as my Bobeh used to say – and at making a bankrupted mess of all his businesses. Or perhaps it is that the words "Moishe Kapoyr" remind me of Moishe Lipiansky, my Bobeh's brother and Mother's uncle, who smoked those pestilential toscanello shorts that drove us kids away in asphyxiated disgust? Likely, what's so special about that line is, again, that seductive triptych structure, with "Moishe Kapoyr" in the middle, flanked left and right by those two harmonizing groups of five words each.

In any case, Schorb's old man, the Moishe Kapoyr, didn't think that taking a masters in English at Columbia University was a good idea for his son. What could his son have in common with "a super goy like (John) Donne"? I suppose he would have said the same of George Herbert and of Gerald Manley Hopkins: none of them are good company. To judge from the next poem, "Grooves of Academe," the son did not follow the paternal advice: he became an academic, or perhaps an outsider who closely witnessed the mystifying labors and sour sweats of Academe.

The spelling checker keeps objecting to "Grooves of Academe": it insists on "Groves," of course. How could a spelling checker, or any mechanical device no matter how smart, have an inkling of the significance of the extra o? In my own, not very extensive experience with American Academia, the first sign I remember of a rapidly spreading rot was when language requirements were dropped. Before I got my doctorate in math at NYU in 1966, I had to pass two language exams: French and German (Russian was a third possibility; Spanish, my native language, was not). A few years later, at most institutions, human languages could be substituted by computer languages, and the faculties considered that natural, that is, alas, logical. In 1975, at SUNY Albany, I participated in a committee that decided to cut, inter alia, the programs in Classics; I objected that Greek and Latin are of the first importance for the humanities, but the ipso facto dishonorable chair of the German department and chair of the committee, disavowed my objection. Inside the humanities, *homo homini lupus*; in short, mine was the only vote to retain the Classics, and my colleagues were puzzled that a mathematician would defend the teaching of Greek and Latin, to the point that someone from the office of the president asked me if I was of Greek descent. I didn't tell him that I had been taking courses in ancient Greek at SUNY Albany, and it hardly needs adding that some years later no foreign language program had survived there, except for Spanish, always popular with the numerous native-Spanish-speaking students. SUNY Binghamton, so far as I know, has the only Russian Studies program in the vast, 64-campusses SUNY system.

All that is to frame my feelings when reading Schorb's "Grooves of Academe," which sounds to my ear as the chorus of a Greek tragedy:

At the Modern Language Association,
the trees are bending down and going bare, the halls

*are getting knee-deep in rusty leaves, and everyone
is pointing a withered finger-stump at everyone else.*

Just so: the "withered finger-stump" of the short-sighted professors of the humanities. Then, a few lines below, the desolate choral theme is repeated:

*None of these things seem to have had much "impact,"
(now there's a word that I would ban) and,
while I wend my way through this historic traffic,
toward an historic college that no longer
recognizes history as a legitimate subject,
I notice that the leaves are down and tumbling
in the wind along the road to higher learning.*

Of what utility can history be for the untutored minds who live only in the present and nurse the conviction that all past times were despicably inferior. Besides, as Hegel (of all people!) wrote in his *Philosophy of History*, the only thing history teaches us is that people and states have never learned anything from history. A little further on, sadly summing up the difference between a hundred and twenty years ago and now:

*1899: John Dewey, "School and Society." Tunc pro nunc.
Another new building is going up on the green.*

The Latin *tunc pro nunc* may be rendered thus: from back then, fast forward to now. Back then, Dewey said that "only by being true to the full growth of all the individuals who make it up, can society by any chance be true to itself"; now, university presidents find it easier and more personally rewarding to erect new buildings than to help build sturdier and more enlightened souls.

But enough of tragedy: *Freunde, nicht diese Töne!* Schorb's *Collected Poems* contains tones for all possible moods, just as Spinoza's god contains all possible modes. In Part 5: Aspects of Love, you will find classical love poetry, rhymed and ready to compete with the best from the Elizabethan or the Augustan poets. The delightfully erotic "Ode on Sex," or "The Lay of the Lorn Marine," lie there together with "Good Works Are Love," a moving call to peace and tolerance between opposing schools of thought and poetry. Schorb calls for a truce between two poets he

noticed, randomly, on my shelf of poetry,
Bill Empson and Bill Williams
sitting side by side.

William Empson, the intellectual of *Seven Types of Ambiguity* and William Carlos Williams, the intuitivist physician of "No Ideas But in Things." And here I would add the anti-conceptualist Yves Bonnefoy against the intellectualist Paul Valéry and against nihilistic Samuel Beckett, since I mentioned two of them at the beginning of this guide. Poets are not paragons of tolerance and love; they may be more fractious and contentious than their cousins the theologians.

You will find a very different clime in Part 6: American Mobile, the long poem of the same title, and its Coda, "The Ghosts Go Home," with their folksy, Joisey-for-Jersey kind of speech, with their motorists touched by tachymania. Caravans of Harleys, RVs, and eighteen-wheelers will leave you astounded, open-mouthed and exposed to exhaust fumes. Don't worry. When you go to bed, take this book with you and start reading Part 8: Dream Spa Journal. Those poetic dreams will slither into yours and beautify them. Then, upon waking in the morning, you should begin Part 9: Muddling Through. And here I can't refrain from reproducing one of my favorites, "Pub Song," featuring Edith Piaf, her "Je ne regrette rien", and her arrogant, roaring rolled r's:

The jukebox unwinds a Piaf
 to us as we sit at the bar
trying to find some relief
 from a world where troubles are.

The bartender brings me my drink
 and I drink it without a remark.
Outside, the evening is pink
 with that pink that comes before dark.

"I regret nothing," sings Piaf,
 and the record drops dead in its box.
Now Piaf is free of the grief
 her glorious music mocks.

And drunk, I am free as a sailor
 to bless or not to bless.
Say, how can a man be a failure
 if he has no need of success?

Enough guidance. Now go by yourself into this garden of earthly and spiritual delights.

—Ricardo L. Nirenberg
Editor, *Offcourse Literary Journal*
University at Albany, SUNY

There is no God, but Divinity,
There is no space, but Infinity,
There is no time, but Eternity.

—*Edmund Bosch*

CONTENTS

Introduction ix

Proem – O To Be Rich and Powerful 3

PART ONE: THE POOR BOY

I Am Here
From the Crib 7
Milk 9
Denial 10
O Lost! 13
   I   A Nickel in the Slot 13
   II Dark Eye 13
Letters Home 15
The Letter, 1942 20
The Kite 23
Camden, War Two Years 25

Indian Territory, Part One
   I   Travelling Child 27
   II Indian Odyssey 28
   III Come a Cropper 28
   IV Paso Finos 30

Indian Territory, Part Two
Tatanka Iyotanka 31
The White Stallion: a Ballad 36
Kid Danger 46

Down Neck, Newark
Impedimenta 49
Hadewijch in Wall Street 51
Oncoming Company 52
Obituary 53
The Orphaned 60

Nighwatch 61
Upstate Storm 62
Dark Canzone 63
The Night Sweats 65
Communion 65
The Moral 66
Words in Passing 68
The Poor Boy 69
Candy Butcher 71

See the World

Sharp 82
Tracers 86
Troop Transport 87
Legal 88
The Survivor 89

Home Again

Holidays 90
   I Near Christmas 90
   II New Year Near the Hudson 90
The Applicant 92
O Popular Moon! 93
42nd Street, 70s 94
Brooklyn Heights 95
   I From the Esplanade 95
   II Variation 95
   III Dark Ages 96
Hire Actors! 97
Gary Player Wins Masters 98
Whistler 99
The Lesson 100
American Paris; or, Undergraduate Days 101
Lost Sketches by Bosch 103
Pollock 104
Art 105

Atget 107
Rodin, Balzac, and *The Thinker* 108
Career 109
   I Norma Jean 109
   II At a Classic Film Revival 109
Ich Bin Ein Dichter 111
Elegy for Patrick Harwood Jones 112
Waterfall 113
New Man on the Docks 116
Kwame and Dutch 118
Swans at New Rochelle 119
Nerves in the New House 120
Kindred Spirits 121

PART TWO: THE POWER GAME

The Power Game 125
Incident 126
Copperheads 127
Nightingale 131
The Kaiser Comes to Orlando 132
Cruel Games 134
The Murder of Garcia Lorca 135
Lorca de Profundis 136
Moontime 137
Cost of Freedom 137
Ballade of Pride 138
The Ideologues 139
Paris Recidivist 145
Life, a Western 146
War Coverage 147
   I War of Nine and Six 147
   II The Manwolf 147
   III Bad News 148

The Cultural Revolution 149
    I   Old Chinese Couple 149
    II A Kiss Outside Her Door 149
    III Remembering You 150
As Good as it Gets 151
An Evening with "Blood" 152
The Bosnian Cherry 154
The Viet Vet 144
Family Tragedy 159
No 160
Social Studies 162
    I   An Experiment in Governance 162
    II The Island of the Leaders 163
    III The Final Tithe 164
Murderer's Day 165
A Yellow Cross 167
Commentary 168
    I   Aquarius 168
    II The New 169
Dirge for the Dead Students 170
Holy Orders 173
    I   Scenario 173
    II The Nun 175
Peace in Our Time 177

PART THREE: DOCTOR BOP

Life and Opinions of Doctor Bop, the Burnt-Out Prof . 181
    I   Veni, Vidi, Vici 181
    II Grooves of Academe 183
    III A Speed of Semesters 187
    IV Sabbatical 194
    V   Commence Fire! 197
Spine and Spirit 202

Ballad of the Burnt-Out Prof 207
To the Guardian at the Gate 209
The Road to Nowhere 208
Breathless; or, Overture to Hyperventilation 209
Apologia 211

PART FOUR: HERACLITUS

    I   Hush, Hush, New House in Charlotte 215
   II Martial Music at a Band Concert 216
  III War Two Words 217
  IV The Good Ones 217
   V Postcard 218
  VI Roanoke Return 219
 VII Looking Down at a Friend 222

PART FIVE: ASPECTS OF LOVE

Poetry in Motion 225
An Acrostic 226
Want of Time 227
A Tumble for Skelton 228
The Vantage Point 230
Célestine 231
For Patricia 232
The Request 232
Transformations 233
For Unity 235
Subjects in Mirror are Closer Than They Appear 236
No Angel 237
This Man Insisting upon Living 238
Gray's Anatomy 239
    I   Bada-Bing Bones 239

   II The Makeover 239
Vanity Fair.. 241
   I The Fashion Show 241
   II The Steroid Lady 241
Ode on Sex 243
The Sex of Water 245
Today, Noon Traffic Crowding 246
Above the High Beams 247
Lover's Quarrel 248
The Lay of the Lorne Marine 249
Lipstick Skies 250
Good Works are Love 251
Winter Waking 252
Because of You 252
Flashbacks 253
Ready to Walk 254
Tippy's Rainy Day Blues 255
Tippy Remembers Reverend Smythe 256
Bereft 257
Descant 258
Dream Girl 259
Torch Song 260
Smoke 262
The Widower 264
RX: The Flower Cure 265
Insect Love Song 266
Last Exit to East Hampton 267
Inspiration at the Art Gallery 268
What's the Matter? 268
Chance 270
The Red Shift 271
The Broken Crow 272
The North of Love 273
Caesar and Cleopatra 276
Silvamoonlake 277

Rival Sleep..278
Tract..279
Carnival Sestina..280
Bucolic Song 282
The Couple in the Garden...282
Five Mile Movie Dance...283

PART SIX: AMERICAN MOBILE

At Heart, Speed 287
American Mobile..288
Uranium Blues...309
Hot Teen Hogs...311
The Islands of Langerhans 312
Singlewide...314
Carpooling it in the Caravan 316
Dry-Gulched..317
Bad Trip...318
An American Poet on Tour 319
Like the Titanic..320
Incognito..322
The Getaway...324
Spring Rides 325
On Wheels 326

PART SEVEN: CATECHISM

After the Storm 329
Wallace Stevens Contemplates
    Sunday Service in Haddam 330
Sunday Question...330
Symbols 331
"Batter My Heart"...335

Dark Ages 336
I Hear You Knocking 337
Eclogue 339
The Martyr 341
Missionaries 342
The Prayer 343
The Peruvian Apparition 344
The Leap 345
Walkie-Talkie 346

PART EIGHT: DREAM SPA JOURNAL 349

PART NINE: MUDDLING THROUGH

Circadian Rhythm
Spindrift 371
Forty Acres and a Mule 372
Endings 373
   I Knight's End 373
   II November Wind 373
On an Inland Island 374
Kyrie Eleison 375
Thoughts for Later 376
Outside the Hospital 376
Ambitions 377
The Secret Agent 378
A Pile of Leaves 379
The Weeping Butcher 380
Graffiti 381
Neighbors 382
   I To a Rat 382
   II My War With Roaches 383

III Now, the Fox!..386
Muddling Through..387
Shadow Over Africa 388
A Worker at the Waterworks....................................389
Late Sleeper..390
Elegy for a Late Tornado...391
The Campers..393
Over the Magnolia 394
Dreamscapes..395
Minim 396
Flag Day 397
The Poet Game 398
See/Saw 399

Light as Air

Wheel of Fortune..400
News of 45 401
The Honey House..402
Agent Sonnet..403
Out-Patient..404
The Ladies of Burdett...404
Detective Story 405
Snowbound 406
The Sorrow of Young Yeats......................................407
The Fallen Angel 408
The Composograph 409
A Tall One 410
Blarney Stoned 411
Song for Hand Puppets...412
Monsieur Elan, Windku, The Moral of Frankenstein 413
Education 414
Bod of the Old Man Moaned.....................................415
The Savage Breast 416
  I The Opera..416
  II The Bowel Organist 416
Pedantic Piece..418

VanGogh's Ear 418
Lunacy 419
The Fine Art of Haunting 420
A Consideration of Angels 421
   I   It Must have Been the Angels 421
   II Instant Angels.. 421
   III Wings 422
Sonnet at Sixty-Five 423
Life Surprised Me: or, Burrowing Moles 424
What I Did on My Summer Vacation 425
Cocktails for Two? 426
Notice to Moderns 427
The Deciduous Strip 428
Three by Heraclitus 429
Poetry and the Poet 430
The Fruits of His Thought
    Delivered to His Favorite Bartender 431
Oömancery 432
The Last Word 433
Bonjour à Tous! 434

Hanging Loose: A Musical Suite

   I   The Fiddler 435
   II   The Sold Piano Blues 437
   III Late Night Rap of Soul and Body 438
   IV Cabin-Fever Blues 439
   V   Bowery Blues 439
   VI Israfel 441
   VII Pub Song 442
   VIII Nostalgic Song 442
   IX The Rubber Church 443

PART TEN: CONTRA MORTEM

  Names of the Dead 447

A Hundred Years	448
The Roses	449
The Souls	451
Where are You?	453
Metaphysics of the Big Woman	454
Destruction	455
Chronicle	456
And/Or	457
The Man Who Hated Cities	461
Marked Man	462
Kaddish for Menke Katz	463
Old Choirsters	464
Houdini and the Dying Swan	465
Death Row	467
The Big Crunch	469
There I Am	470
Death	471
A Reply	472
Websites	473
I Life.org	473
II Death.com	474
The Town Dump; or, Lily	475
Old Women, Pausing	476
The Terrible Shadow	477
The Nursing Home	478
The Loss	480
Leadbelly	482
An Antiquary of the Future	484
Elegy for the Leader Bird	485
Anthologies are Sad	486
Old Icarus	487
Memento Mori	488
Death and the Mermaid	489
The Diamond Merchant	490
Hope and the Bipolar Poet	491

Allegorical Fountain 492
Gin Rummies 493
The Thin Disease 495
Spring and the Black Holes 497
The Orbiting X 498
Mice on a Mudball 499
   I   The Futurist 499
   II The Mall on Moon 499
Because 501
Those Who Die in Their Sleep 502
Through the Loupe 503
Heart Failure 504
The Urn 506
Provenance of an Old Poet 508
Toward the End 510
Curtal Sonnet 511

Notes on Earlier Works 514

for Patricia

PROEM

O TO BE RICH AND POWERFUL

*O to be rich and powerful, to be
like the great-winged dragonfly of the lake,
a jaunty helicopter over sea
whose little motor without spasm spake
of micro- and of macro-cosmic truth;
to say: Littleness is relative, I am
that which I am, younger than in my youth;
imagination's child; a boy like them—
the pirate, prince, or pauper; tree maybe,
no trouble being tree; an open heart;
a mind unmatrixed, ready for the sky
to turn, at will, into the deepest sea;
to put together and to take apart;
rich, powerful to be, and never die!*

Part One
THE POOR BOY

I Am Here

FROM THE CRIB

*From those beginning notes of yearning and love
there in the mist . . .*
 —Whitman, *Out of the Cradle Endlessly Rocking*

From the deep recesses of the universe
he woke to find himself
gumming the blue lead paint
from the top rail of his crib,
blissfully unaware
of the crack in the Liberty Bell,
or the Liberty Bell itself,
for that matter; Mussolini in Abyssinia,
Schicklgruber, in Guernica or the Rhineland,
Tojo in China,
or any of the problems
of the age into which he had been dropped.
The lead paint was delicious and maddening,
and would,
no doubt
make a mad poet of him.

He looked around and for the first time
saw other humanoids (oops, hominoids),
much bigger, but basically the same.
They, also, wobbled on two legs,
holding drinks to their lips,
as he held his empty baby bottle to his.
One fell back into a faded, flowered
easy chair, in what seemed,

even to his innocent eyes,
a flat, shabby and small,
compared with
whatever had been before.

Years later, photographs would tell him
who they were. Someone had taken
several Kodak snapshots.
Here was his young Aunt,
a fourteen-year-old schoolgirl,
who hookied to the City of Brotherly Love
to help with her new nephew,
the young Master, her big sister's first child.
An older boy would have noticed
the beginnings of her breasts,
and that she was a pretty young thing
with startling blue eyes and
chestnut waves piled up,
but he was unaware of
these uplifting attractions.
The woman was his Mother.
Later he would understand
that at that point in her life, made-up
and Marcelled, people said that she looked
like the actress Mary Astor, except
for her harlequin-shaped glasses.
The central figure, the one who had collapsed
in the armchair, wearing what then he,
himself not much more than an humunculus,
would eventually discover—by these presents—
looked like the famous-at-the-time
Arrow Collar Man.

Well, that was his old man, tall, dark, and
handsome alcoholic,
Depression-fallen from stocks

and bonds salesman, to selling
The Book of Knowledge in the territory
assgned him by the publisher.
His young Aunt stuck a rubber nipple
in his mouth and quickly
the picture faded and never came back, 'til now.

MILK

The child wakens to the first snow,
(noted), of its lifetime, and says: "Milk."
The mother takes it out so it can know
that snow is frozen water, slippery as silk,
paler than vanilla in a cone, harder, softer,
the strangest thing on Earth, so far,
stranger than its yellow urine. The mother
tugs it through the drifts, into the car,
straps it in, shakes her head like a puppydog,
and sprinkles baby's cheeks. Baby giggles.
Window-wipers make pretty window-fans. The rug
across its lap is hot and baby wiggles
to be free of it. They seem to climb the sky.
Everywhere they look the white stuff
is. It takes them to a cloud that has an eye
of darkness, surrounded by pale puff.
But it's the supermarket sign. Mother
takes excited baby in and buys some things.
Some day, she says, you'll have a little brother.
Baby doesn't understand, so sings:
caroo, caroo, milk, milk, milk... Baby thinks:
it's fun and frightening, too. Curled
up, back in the car, baby, dreaming, drinks
the whole white gallon of the world.

DENIAL

When you are about three feet tall,
the gray streets of Philadelphia
in winter are very long and tiring
and slowly climb uphill toward a dark sky.
His mother pulled him along.
Where were they going?
Their arms were empty.
Not shopping?
Was there no money?
Why were they walking, walking so far?
He was beginning to get very cold.
Then, on the deserted street,
a stranger appeared before them.
His mother knew the man,
yes, and they laughed together, startling laughter,
too high above him for him to have any idea
what was funny, but something obviously was,
for their laughter tinkled down upon him
like sprightly snowflakes, like tinsel and sequins,
a glittery sprinkling of fairy dust.
He tried to get under it, between them, where it fell.
His mother pulled him back and away,
toward her own back.
Then the man seized his mother
in his arms and dipped her back
toward where he waited,
and kissed her hard and long.
It was wrong, wasn't it?
Because this man was not his father.
His father was up ahead somewhere,
somewhere at the end of the long gray avenue,
somewhere up several flights of stairs,
in a small flat that looked down on the avenue,

drinking. It was wrong, wasn't it? Because
his mother did not struggle to be free.
Instead, she simply held him behind her,
away from them. He thought he might cry.
The man seemed to lift his mother
off the pavement
and to place her back on it,
her high heels firm.
She pulled him from behind her
and around to her side,
her other hand held out to the man
as he stepped back, back,
and turned and went a little way,
and stopped, and turned again,
and waved, and blew her a kiss,
and turned once again,
and went on down the long slowly sinking avenue.
Who was that? he wanted to know.
His mother pulled him forward up the hill.
"Who was that man?" he asked.
His mother climbed on,
pulling him along with one hand
and wiping tears from her eyes with the other.
"Mommy, who was that man?"
His mother ignored him until he shouted his question at her.
The question and its answer had become imperative,
like the bearing down of traffic at the intersection.
Finally his mother said, "What man?"
He looked back and saw the receding figure
of the man who had kissed his mother,
no more than a dot now, a dot in time.
He tugged his mother half around and pointed—
"That man," he said.
"I don't see any man," his mother said.
"I haven't seen anyone since we began our walk,

and neither have you."
He looked back again, desperately,
but the man was gone, only eternity,
only infinity remained to see. "You see,"
said his mother, "there is no one
on the street but us."
She was lying, wasn't she,
or could he not believe
the evidence of his own eyes?
From then on he struggled
to keep his hand free of hers.

O LOST!

I A NICKEL IN THE SLOT

Late evening, once, on the crowded midway of a carnival, amidst it all, the gay calliope, the loud, scary, sucking sound of the polio fund-raising iron lung, the punctuating squeals of the other children with air, balloons, the pop, pop, pop of the rifles at the gallery, and the mad laughter of the funhouse, a seven-year-old came upon a fortune-telling machine, the illustrations of which showed the requirement of an Indian-head nickel in exchange for what children wish for most: Knowledge of the Future, which seems to give the feckless and the hapless power over it. He searched through his small change and found just such a nickel, plunged it in the slot of his future, and received in return a card the size of a standard business card with the following printed on it: *Act the Way you Want to Be and Soon You'll Be the Way you Act.* Little people take such advisements seriously, one might even say, with all their hearts; and so he tried to live that dream, and must assume that what he is, is what he desired to be, when he was an eager if short-sighted child.

II DARK EYE

Like a spider on a thread, the eye dropped down on its optic nerve and drew up out of his range of vision. He was on his knees in a bar in Newark, shining shoes, maybe eight or nine years old. He sat between two men on stools whose heads were high above him. He was close to the level of the brass spittoon and the brass rail.

They glittered with the changing lights, but it was hard to see very well down there on the seat of the shoeshine box, hard to see anything but the whiteness of the eye, like an egg suspended on the cord that feeds the yoke. Some extraordinarily quick gesture of violence must have been employed. The shoes he was shining scrambled with the shoes he was about to shine. Crashing sounds, screaming, and he backed off to the wall behind him. A big scuffle of several men ensued. When he returned home late that night, his mother asked him if anything interesting had happened. "Have you ever seen an eye popped out?" he asked her, after stating his preference for the Campbell's Chicken Noodle soup over the Cream of Mushroom. He began counting his money, which he was saving for a bicycle. He was going to become a Western Union boy.

LETTERS HOME

For my half-brother, James Outerbridge

I

(An R.A.F. Pilot, Bermudan, Age 21; 1941)

I am on standby at flights,
or flying from ten until ten.
That's from the A.M. to A.M.

I return in the morning and sleep
until tea-time, get up and have tea,
and then see a cinema show.

After the flicks I walk back,
go to mess, and to bed about ten.
So at long last I'm on operations.

I enclose the newspaper clipping
to show you my handiwork.
I got the two hits dead amidships.

God, I was thrilled! But don't think
that I gloat on the enemy dead—
just glad that I wasn't afraid.

The Maltese are marvelous people,
always so cheerful and smiling.
They really deserve the George Cross.

The hotel at which I am billeted
is situated on the sea front
at Sliema, so when I wake mornings

I can look out my window and see
the white Mediteranean waves
on water as blue as Bermuda's.

*Over sea, out of Tunis, past Sicily,
off Naples, their Wellington fell.
They took to their rubber dinghy*

*and had drifted for thirty-nine hours
when the Italians reported them down.
The Germans, at last, picked them up.*

II

(A Fellow Prisoner to the Pilot's Mother)

Madam, any attempt at escape
is infused with a great deal of danger,
the success of it usually being

more a matter of luck than design.
It so happened that I had myself
been preparing to make an attempt

when he came to me late on the eve
of his transfer by train from the camp.
I did not have the chance that he did,

so it seemed like the right thing to do
to surrender my maps and my compass
and whatever provisions I had.

His journey commenced in the morning.
When it showed itself likely to end
before darkness could cover his flight,

he decided to make his escape
in the full light of day, at first chance.
Now to jump from a train in the dark

is an orthodox mode of escape,
but to make such a break in broad day
involved so much greater a risk.

But your Jimmy accepted that risk.
As his train was held up in a station
he was able to knock out his guard

and to leap out and run down the platform.
But the guards in the other compartments
saw, and repeatedly fired.

III

(A British Nurse to the Pilot's Mother)

The cemetery is outside the town,
so was saved from the worst battle scars.
When I found it this morning, my dear,

your young Jimmy's sad grave was at peace
and had flowers, carnations and roses,
which were left there by persons unknown.

The Italians erected a stone
with his name and the date of his death
and the fact of his being a pilot,

but unfortunately this was toppled
by some bombs which had landed nearby.
Two young Tommies were visiting graves

and they helped me to prop the stone up,
and we took several photos beside it
which I'll forward as soon as developed.

Now the padre has promised to make
a large white wooden cross
and to put on it "Outerbridge, James,"

and the crest of the R.A.F.
and that he was born in Bermuda.
He isn't alone among strangers.

There are Yanks and Canadians, too.
It's a beautiful spot, with the sea,
like the sea of Bermuda, in sight.

IV

(From His Last Letter)

... My Rhodes at Oxford is waiting,
so I study my Latin and Greek.
American sports are the thing,

and I play at softball every day
and am keeping quite physically fit.
You can learn almost anything here,

from chess to trombone playing,
and my program is so well arranged
that I haven't a moment to spare. . . .

*But this last letter wasn't received
until more than a year after he
had been killed. It had obviously*

*travelled through many countries,
for it bore seven censorship stamps,
including the swastika.*

THE LETTER, 1942

> *Twenty years . . . years of*
> *l'entre deux guerres . . .*
>   —T.S. Eliot

I

His mother and father
could not understand
the extreme of his grief,
for his father's other
son was only half his brother,
and had not existed
in their lives but for letters
and occasional photographs
taken around the world
where the war was, often next
to his Wellington, or by
a field tent, wearing his wings,
a smiling twenty year old
whom he, the child in a yard,
thought must look the way
he himself would look at twenty,
and be a brave pilot
and take up the war
against Hitler and Tojo
in his turn, not knowing
that even wars do not last
forever. How could the child
be so devastated by the news,
who barely knew of his half
brother's existence? How
adults box things up
the child could not know
or believe. Hard rain.

II

Rivers of rain, as when
you look up through greenhouse
glass on a rainy day, crossed
his green eyes blotting out the blue
dry sky overhead, and
he told the rain of his grief and
he told the blurred, ugly yard
behind the city row house
with its junked, warped
furniture and strata of
ripped linoleum, roses
and geometry, and its wet,
stalking cat along the old spiked
wooden fence, run with rusted wire
meant to throw yourself on, told
the whole world, which was
all the rain of tears
out of his breathless,
heaving chest, narrow
as a chicken's, out
of his pounding seven year old
heart, and cowlicked hair,
that was trapped by the
four-sidedness of fence
and could not fly with his
grief as his brother the
pilot had flown, whom
he had never known.

III

Let the child race
pointlessly in
circles, trapped in the
square yard, and cry
himself out. The letter
was already over a year
old and smeared with
his father's few tears,
sad horrible history,
but must be set aside
so that life could go
on. "He'll get over it."
"I never thought—" said
his mother. "No, of course
not," said his father.
But the yard was sodden
with the child's grief,
whose head burned with hope
against fact that a mistake
had been made, that this fine
brother was yet to come to him
who had no one, whose
loneliness could not be
surmised by two wise parents,
kept sane by callousing death
and full of the hard world's rain.

THE KITE

From the dark, tarred roof where urchins chant
in garbled language some insistent word,
the line leads upward to the bending rod,
spine of a skin that billows in the breeze:
the kite, a pterodactyl, hovers high
above the threatened eyes of three small boys.
There's little safety in the dangerous city,
the toys of children change into the ogres
of their bad dreams. Oh many times I've seen
a smudged dragon who had terrified his friends
stand screaming in his metamorphosis
until his mother's arms recalled his name.
So now: a phantom of pre-history
is hovering above the very roof
where these boys stand, eyes staring up in awe.
It shudders in the wind; the shining tail
of multi-colored terrors coils and snaps,
like tentacles of a drifting man-o'-war.
And as they watch, the afternoon drifts on,
diminishing the day, and evening falls,
until at last, yet suddenly, it's night,
and hunger wakes the hypnotized to time.
The boy who holds the line begins to haul
his monster from its perch among the stars.
Descending in the darkness, huge, aglow,
it seems to seek its prey among the three.
They watch bewitched, enchanted for a time,
a fascinating nightmare coming true;
but as its membrane shadows chimney stacks
and falls upon them, tenting out the view,
they cry aloud, and bolt toward the door,
one frozen hand still dragging the bad dream,
five others struggling for it to be free.

Then, at the door, they see the line slide up
suspended from the belly of a bat,
a giant bat whose little hands they see
attempt to tear their line—umbilical, their line.

CAMDEN, WAR TWO YEARS

If I think of night, and factories, and day-bright streets,
   I get some of it. The whole town seemed to be a factory
full of graveyard- and swing-shifts and vox-populated
   streets
   at all hours, so that one lost track of night and day.

The children of Camden roamed the streets in gangs
   composed not so much of juvenile delinquents
as of orphaned children looking for something to do, their
   parents lost to them at Campbell's Soups or at Lionel
     Trains,

ground up in the Wheels of Industry. The schools didn't
   count,
   were apparently attended out of a need to get indoors for a
     time,
their schedules not fitting the schedules of the factories.
   Sleepers slept when they could, morning or evening

or night. Meals came when they did, now or later,
   morning or evening or night. I drank containered coffee,
ate stale chocolate donuts drizzling in wax paper, and huge
   greasy
   restaurant meat-cakes smothered in sour brown gravy.

In winter the snow was black, in summer the air was heavy.
   There was a constant grinding out of matter, of goods, of
     people,
but the funereal unreal light made one feel that no matter
   how much
     was made, the making was wages of sin, of death; and the
     whistles

blew and the sirens sounded and the mobs made their moans.
 The white faces were black and the black faces were white,
and everyone seemed to be slow-marching a treadmill to death,
 just after the war, once, in Camden, way back when.

Indian Territory: Part One

I TRAVELLING CHILD

> *Hotel Muskogee*
>
> *The sirens of the dust,*
> *did they sing me a new song,*
> *did they pied-pipe my heart away?*

Night: the rockety-rockety train:
the coach filled with sleepers: the moon
outside: the passing poles: by, by, by, by:
another child: friendship for a day,
for an hour like a lifetime:
a parting kiss at Kansas City:
Why? Why? I loved him. I loved her.
The khaki soldiers eating sandwiches:
candy butchers: Daddy? Hot. Cold.
Night and morning: death: time.

The magical furnished rooms, each new,
alive with new things to know:
closets that could be used for loneliness,
in which one might discover
the artifacts of a previous tenant,
or in which one might create
the lost cave, the bandit den, the jungle,
and, as each of these, the place
to crawl into: sanctuary.

II INDIAN ODYSSEY

In Memory of Acee Blue Eagle

I was afraid of the Indian boys
with no feathers in their hair
when I was twelve, in Oklahoma,
and went to Indian school there.

They came at me, angry, red,
because I was from the East.
I did not know I should be dead.
I did not know I was a beast.

I tried to make them like me. "See,
this is my Red Ryder rifle.
Shoot it, shoot it, if you please."
They hurt me with that windy trifle.

Oklahoma is no place
unless you are Blue Eagle, Ace.

III COME A CROPPER

*In Memory of Mister Culbertson, Master Rancher
and Horse Breeder*

They head down
in a great slow motion,
as if they are galloping
into the underworld at some
suddenly found entrance,

with the amazed boy now
riding the underside of the huge,
stunned animal, like a ship's
captain on the belly of a ship
overturned and about to sink,
waiting for rescue, and nothing
heard but the horse's breath,
which struggled with the dry
hot air, and somewhere inside
that enormous exhausted body
the great heart finding its
rhythm once more.

Thrown
clear, the horrified boy
fans his horse with his hat,
crying, telling her he didn't
mean to hurt her, telling her
he loves her, begging her to rise
and be well, finally thinking of
the lake and water to throw on her.

Making his way to the lake, he
cannot imagine how in a half hour
she will rise out of her exhaustion
and plant her unsteady hooves
under her weight, and he
will lead her home,
along the shimmering,
dusty roads and among the cows
in the scrubgrassed fields of the
1940s dust bowl, limping, and frothy
on her flanks, like something from
the sea, home to her shady stable,
and to the master of the ranch,

      to explain to such a man, how
      he has galloped the legs from under
      such a horse in the noonday sun.

IV Paso Finos

Fine-paced, their manes sweeping the shortest grass,
their chins held in, like quick-stepping cadets,
almost miniature, they circle in wherever they are

like a carousel, and you can almost hear the music.
Sometimes they seem unreal, as if you watched
in a lucid dream the archetype of horse, the perfect

children's dream animal, the one that they could take
    between
finger and thumb and lift and place in air and see
the beautiful pinions form from barreled ribs,

and lean back giggling together as the little horses hover
and wing off, flying in the children's psychokinetic
imaginations, like Persian storybook animals, like

what should really be, and, amazingly, nearly is.

Indian Territory: Part Two

TATANKA IYOTANKA
Double Ballad Of Sitting Bull

    Sioux must have mounts. Sun-Dreamer,
                greatest of all shaman,
              advised, Go
            to the horse-rich Crow.
            Up from Mexico,
        stolen by Comanche,
        passed north to Utes, Shoshoni,
    the best mounts came, finally,
            to the Crow.
So a hundred Hunkpapa
went on the warpath, the
                Sioux seeking Crow
in Yellowstone summer,
    lariats ready, led by Sitting Bull,
        finding and making off with many a Crow
            pony.
From French frontiersmen—coup, to touch or to strike
    the enemy.
    Let aftercomers slay
    him: you are first in honor because first in the
      fray.
Slow, who,
    at fourteen, had no other name—he
was considered deliberate, thoughtful,
    not slow—must join the hunting party—
            but out on the trail,
        so his mother could not try to stop him,
                would not hold him back and
                wail

    as if he were riding to his death. Deliberately,
Slow must be fast, first, must make coup
   Pursued! so that along the
         skyline the rays of rising sun
        were
        made of long wide rare
        red feathers, each on a spear.
     Crow galloped—Sioux galloped.
     Now Sioux must be intrepid—
  must hold the herd! Winter Rides,
       the Crow Chief,
  sent Sitting Bull a challenge
  to a duel on the range,
        just chief and chief
  in single combat. They
   knelt, aimed, and fired. Sioux and Crow
    prayed. Both sides
    waited for the white cloud to clear. Winter
     Rides was dead,
or die now and be done, for "It is better to lie naked
  than to rot on a high
   scaffold," an old man who has lived safely, afraid
   to die,
now naught
  but bent bone and thin loose flesh for the
sun to cook and the crows to eat. A name
  must be earned. Let the braves mock his war
       lust—who cared?—but he
    would have greatness, and he must begin.
        He will not allow anyone in
      the
world to stop him, not mother nor sisters nor
  mocking braves
nor even father. And so he caught
  Sitting Bull's round shield pierced, the

sole of his foot penetrated and
badly mangled, and
his legendary limp
acquired for American
history. And now a grand
chief, famous, mighty, un-
defeated,
with his every step, he
reminds all who see
how he can spread
over the prairie the
Sioux's high might and exclusive
dominion,
for there were fewer and fewer bison.
These hunting grounds,
and joined his father's band, saying, of himself and his
pony,
"We are brave and strong, and
are going too." On his father's face he saw
pride, and
"A brave
is a brave when he proves it," and Slow
had already killed his first buffalo;
had touched a dead foe's face. He gave Slow
his own coup-stick, then
prayed to the Great Bull Buffalo God
to keep Slow safe in the
band—
for who would forgive him Slow's death?—then
willed that Slow be
first to send an enemy to his grave.
which had once belonged to the
Crows, Hidastas, Rees, Shoshonis,
and
poor, dying Mandans,

                    once many and grand,
                  could not keep such numbers.
                    The Treaty of Fort Laram
                  -ie, which held the tribes to peace,
                        Sitting Bull
declared, must be broken or
his people starve, and by
                  1864,
all the chiefs who had signed
      the Treaty of Fort Laramie with the
            Sioux nation were dead, their tribes driven
                off and hiding,
Then it was hard riding, to where the bubbling, blood
  red water
    of the Missouri river
    turned brown, and there were the Iroquois, taking
      from the giver,
brothers
    to vultures, stealing their bison—meat,
hoof, and hide—from the hungry Hunkpapa,
    who would ambush the Iroquois but
                  for the gold-painted
          boy, crying, "I am Slow, bravest of the
                    Hunkpapa," who charged
                        ahead
of his band to make coup on an isolated Iroquois
hunter, alarming the others.
      afraid to hunt buffalo
                        at all, Sitting Bull having
                          triumphed.
                        "Chief Sitting Bull fed
                          the nation," Sioux said,
          "on thirty-five thousand
            bison a year." "Grandfather,
my children are hungry," prayed

                    Sitting Bull,
        when taking aim at a great
        bull buffalo, "so I
                        must kill you. It
        is what you were made for."
            Then he offered meat to Wakan Tanka,
                Double-of-the-Sun, who had given bison
                    their meat.
Now the surprised Iroquois hunters turned in retreat—
    all but
        one brave, who stopped, turned about,
        and drew his bowstring. But coup! Slow struck
            him with a shout,
and fame
        was Slow's, as other Hunkpapa slew
the unfortunate brave. Sitting Bull, Slow's
    great father, felt his pride overfull
                        as the others circled
                his son Slow with raised weapons in salute
                            of his courage in battle.
    He must give some away. He, Returns-Again,
        now Sitting Bull,
awarded Slow his honored name.

THE WHITE STALLION: A BALLAD

       It seems there is a place
where beggars and poor people go to tell tales,
and the mostly riding moon will park to look
and to listen in the dark to the tales as they are told
    by the poor beggar bards of the hobo jungle,

       a place lonely as life,
at the end of the track, in a cul-de-sac
of starred, campfired night, in a turntabled copse
in the dark ragged green of smoke-stunted oak and rope-
   strong
    weeds, where birds bivouac: and of all beggar bards

       who sang a sad ballad
there, for the folk, or chanted a moon-watched tale,
the most famous because most magical was
the hobo bard the Pinkertons called "The All-Seeing Eye,"
    because of his blind, superhuman vigilance,

       and the mooncalf folk called
"O'Shay the Irish Shaman" for his gift of
curative power, uncanny control
of events, and for divining the deep, hooded meaning
    of things beyond their poor eyes and plain powers to
       see.

       Now O'Shay rose up and
loomed before them, above them, his flame-mapped face
red and changing as the cat-o'-nine-tailed fire,
his great, blind eyes like those of the horse of his inner-
   eye
    (a carp-eyed stallion), his hair a red, swimming flame

        dowsed by the cool waters
of the moon. O'Shay, though blind, was free, though poor,
was proud, and did not like to see the poor folk
bowed by that boulder, Care, nor bullied by the railroad
   dicks
        and afraid in their camp at the end of the track

        underneath the parked moon
in the starred, turntabled copse where he loomed now,
watching their weak eyes with his strong, inner one,
and knowing that they needed a hopeful tale to be told
        that the Depression be lifted, courage restored,

        and the parked moon set free
to ride the night into dawn, and new hope for them,
crying: "Pride's the subject of my moon-watched tale.
Now listen to O'Shay, poor people, and see what you think–
        stop, look, and listen with the fascinated moon.

        "There was a white stallion
that lived when you were but babes of scuttlebutt
at heaven's height; nay, that moon itself unborn
of the great, swaying sea; a stallion of clouds and spirit
        that came finally to gallop the great plains of

        "the North American
west; a pale, proud, bellows-nostrilled, carp-eyed king
of a horse, that could blow back the floozy wind
from Manitoba down to the plains of old Mexico;
        that could whinney across the west to call a brood

        "mare from her happy home
to him a thousand miles away in the night;
that spoke in trumpeting tongues of his freedom,
stamped, and neighed pride from his great, rampant heart;

    who hammered hope
        with his hooves to the ranging mustangs of the plain.

        "A maverick king, he!
And this is the best part, for the horse was blind
like myself, and nothing daunted, unconstrained,
for he saw with his four, steamed, cow-catcher hooves, and
  his ears
        that could hear the baby-breath sigh of a willow

        "on an unborn wind; saw,
too, and best, with an inner eye like my own,
and had powers, like myself, gifts of nature,
with which he could divine the treachery of humankind,
    and thus keep himself free, and wear no man's hot
      brand.

        "For he wore no man's brand;
and that was a heartache to all rich ranchers
who had heard of the white stallion: his freedom
mocked their staked, barbed wire; and they offered gold
  for his capture—
        pots of rainbow gold those rich ranchers offered the

        "buck who captured the horse;
gold, gold beyond a poor cowpoke's wildest dreams—
fifty thousand dollars in gold bullion to
the buckaroo who brought in the phantom of the prairies,
      fifty more to the bronco buster who broke him—

        "fifty thousand in gold,
one hundred thousand in gold bars to do both!
They came from the stretched limbs of the continent—
wranglers, roustabouts, beggars and poor people like
  ourselves,

> all with mad schemes to capture the blind, white
> stallion,

> "keen on the trace of gold."

Here O'Shay's brick jaws mortised, his lips ringed teeth,
and his dark sockets fixed face after face, saw!
And yet they knew O'Shay was a blind man and could
not see
> the mad excitement that they felt, hearing of gold,

> could not see how they stood

who had sprawled or hunkered down on their heels here,
could not know, therefore, how ready for pursuit
they were, how each in his mind saw a fleece-white
phantom flee
> his grasp, as O'Shay took pause from his moon–
> watched tale,

> and they cried out to him

suddenly, as one many-voiced, to go on.
"Mad men with mad schemes!" cried O'Shay. "For they
knew,
the earthly fame of the phantom being, by now, widespread,
> that all the ordinary methods of capture

> "had been tried and had failed.

No, a ghost must be caught in some other way.
Hence these mad or tragic traps. One loon dreamed of
speeding hoopsnakes that would ensnarl the steed's cow-
catcher hooves,
> another's gold-frenzy fancied a fast balloon.

> "The supernatural

horse and the idea of gold had made them mad.
Not all, some had sounder brains and better schemes.

A wrangler, a strong man who knew his horses, had staked out
      an arroyo which was the haunt of the white steed.

"He pitched camp and waited;
and happenstance his patience was rewarded
when, like a mirage, the pale, maverick king,
with his own remuda of mares prancing and curvetting
      behind, galloped up to drink, stamping and snorting.

"The wrangler climbed a rise,
and, twirling an Indian-charmed lariat
of rawhide interwoven with shot-gold wire
which he had bought from a Kiowa shaman, roped him,
      looping the golden noose neatly around his neck.

"The white stallion whinnied,
rose rampant, and snapped the charmed, magic lasso
as the wrangler might have snapped a golden thread;
and the still-noosed stallion and his mares vanished in
  white dust.
      But this was the closest that any man had come."

      O'Shay stopped his story
here, drank from his flask, wiped his mouth up his sleeve,
and looked intently out at the poor people,
who had begun to suspect that he was not blind at all,
      so seeing seemed his ragged, flame-valanced sockets.

      And now they felt that he
could see them fingering their necks, golden-noosed
now, like that of the horse of his long, tall tale;
fingering their necks and feeling the golden noose tighten
      as they pulled from the shaman, and snap, freeing
        them.

      Suddenly O'Shay laughed,
and the rubbernecking, neckrubbing folk shook:
but then there seemed to have been no laughter there
but merely the bark of dogwood flame from the heeling fire
    or the sudden gold caw of a blackbird, bivouacked

      nearby. O'Shay frowned, now
and said: "Having heard how the wrangler had failed,
the rich ranchers upped the purse to a million;
but before any could claim it, he must represent them,
    having won a competition for horsemanship

      "from among the finest
cowhands and vaqueros to be found; and then,
having conquered all men, must conquer the horse.
The competition involved every truck or skill of
    wrangling science and art, and lasted a twelvemonth.

      "A vaquero triumphed,
and had fine mounts stationed at mile intervals
from a wheel's hub out for a hundred hot miles,
the hub the arroyo where the horse had escaped the noose,
    the fine mounts the posed spokes of a great wagon
      wheel.

      "The vaquero waited
at the hub of the wheel for the phantom horse
until it appeared, and the pursuit was on
for a hundred miles, mile on hot mile, with fresh, mile-new
  mounts,
    for the vaquero hoped to exhaust the phantom.

      "But the great vaquero
could not exhaust or overtake the white steed,
who taunted him with his easygoing gait;

and, after his hundredth horse had dropped, could only
   report
      that the golden noose still hung from the phantom's
         neck.

         "News of the hunt's failure
spread up and down the plains, told by range riders
on lonely duty tours, at starred, campfired night,
until word reached a famed trapper up in Manitoba,
      one who had trapped every kind of animal.

         "His name was Hawkeye Red."
O'Shay paused here to take a swig from his flask and
to consider the beggars and poor people,
who were amused by the blarney of their shamrock shaman,
      who again managed to relate himself to

         the pacing white stallion.
A few friendly hoots were heard, with which, O'Shay,
scrunching a flame-snake of brow in a dark wink,
returned to his tall, romantic tale. "Hawkeye Red," he said,
      "left his cold northern home and journeyed far south-
         west

         "to find the white phantom,
or to find out where he might be found. Then he
methodically began work on his great trap.
He gathered the strongest oaken lumber that could be found
      and built a great stable in the arroyo where

         "the horse was golden-noosed,
and in it placed the most beautiful young mare
that the rich ranchers possessed among them, a
doe-eyed, blazed-faced bay with black mane and tail. Ring-
   bolt-tethered,

    high-strung, frightened, Bonny-Pru would be the bait.

    "Now he set the trap doors,
cleverly contrived to clap shut behind the
white horse when, or if, he entered, trapping him.
After making sure that the trap would work, Hawkeye
    Red and the rich ranchers went to a vantage point

    "to wait for the phantom.
Under the riding moon, Bonny-Pru pulled, kicked
the oaken planks, and whinnied for her freedom
across the dappled night, until her fearful, fearsome cries
    were borne as on an unborn wind to the white steed.

    "The man-watched moon rode high
as the hours passed and nearer and nearer he
galloped with all his magical might toward
her in her trap, and his; but at last he came to the dark
    and looming stable; and, though the great, mouthing
    doors

    "gaped open, paused, galloped
away, circling wide the foreboding building;
then, though he knew this was a trap, galloped in
to the distressed, stable-trapped, ringbolt-tethered damsel
  mare
    who cried out for a brave champion like himself.

    "The trap doors shut! Silence.
No sound whatever from inside the stable.
The rich ranchers whooped high for their victory;
but, somehow, Hawkeye Red, now rich, felt saddened by
  success.
    All left their vantage point and approached the stable.

> "But, nearing it, the doors
split, splintered like kicked glass, spilled, filled the spiked
  air,
and up and over the heads of Hawkeye Red
and the rich ranchers rose the white steed and his damsel
  mare
> > like two wide-winged, magical, legendary birds.

> "Hawkeye Red shook his head
in unbelief, turned, dazed, to see them, bullets
that followed the riflings of infinity.
In a moment of wild, unholy desperation, he
> > ran to his horse, reached for his rifle, aimed and fired.

> "The rifle exploded,
but from the breech, not the muzzle, blinding him.
And in that first blind instant he saw the horse
of his mad pride go free, the white phantom rise rampant
  and neigh,
> > like a musical muscle that flexes and sings,

> "and vanish from the land,
with his blazed-faced bride, Bonny-Pru, by his side,
never to return again." The poor people
were on their feet, now, whinnying, and galloping in place,
> > for O'Shay had turned them into happy horses

> > who would wear no man's brand,
who applauded their pleasure with hoof-clap hands
and tongues that rode the roofs of moon-watched mouths.
"Hawkeye Red," he said, "regained his vision, but saw no
  more
> > with his outer eyes but with a strong, inner one,

"and lived to tell the tale
at the end of a track, in a cul-de-sac
of starred, campfired night, in a turntabled copse
in the dark, ragged green of smoke-stunted oak and rope-
  strong
      weeds, where birds bivouac." And he set the moon
      free.

KID DANGER

My little rubber doll Mickey melted in the hot trunk the
 summer
I was five, and I lost my only friend, his brown rubber
 hair a smear.
    I was very lonely without Mickey so I got a cat
      named Winkey but
      I didn't know how to spell that so I renamed her
        Scuttlebutt,
which I could spell believe it or not because of a
 character

in a cartoon in the Sunday funny pages somewhere but I
 don't know
where we were living then—we were usually on the go.
    I think my father was running from the law or from
      his first wife
      or both—he drank a lot, maybe he was just running
        from his life
—anyway I recall going up and down in the world and
 to and fro.

Being an only child and being poor with parents who
 are drunk a lot
of the time is a good way to develop one's ability to
 plot,
    so I began to draw and write a comic strip called Kid
      Danger,
      about a motorcycle cowboy who was always out to
        lasso a gangster
and who had a magical friend who I believed was a
 Hottentot,

because I had read something about them in the
 WonderBook of Knowledge

(which itself stood me in good stead later when I went
   to college)—
      and he wore the clothing of the black man in the
         book and a turban
      and had more dignity than the other seven or even
         the U'do Urban
and before he had joined Kid Danger he had been king
   of his village.

The plot thickened because the gangster became president of the US
of A, and Kid Danger and his Hottentot friend, whom he
   called Uziss,
      had to cope with the defending combined forces of
         the United States,
      and in one episode they were forced to storm the
         White House gates,
and I couldn't get the story straightened out and dropped
   the whole mess.

Anyway I was nearly ten by this time and I had to go
   out and work,
and my imagination began to fade away on the streets of
   Newark
      and pretty soon I forgot about Mickey and Winkey
         and Kid Danger
      and his friend Uziss the Hottentot and what should
         become of the gangster
and after many adventures pleasant and unpleasant I
   moved to New York.

But last night I dreamed of them all again, first one, then
   the other,
and sadness overwhelmed me when I thought of my
   melted Mickey who was like a brother

    and my cat Winkey or Scuttlebutt and Uziss the
        Hottentot and Kid Danger
    and how I could never show them how finally to
        catch that gangster,
and I sat on linoleum roses again and cried, seeing my
    poor father and mother.

Down Neck, Newark

IMPEDIMENTA

The rain flooded down the back steps and in under
the old linoleum, floating it, with its sad faded roses,
above the slab floor, an hallucination of a magic carpet,
the backyard's muddy effluvium oozing into every corner
and crevice and halfway down the hall to the bathroom,
and making my mother cry for all her hard waxing work.
My father, the superior drunk, had left us in this dump
in Newark to go off selling his bullshit books in Buffalo,
and to shack up with his beautiful vocabulary, quoth the
    raven,
a bottle and a bimbo, and not to have to sit here with us,
under the dripping pipes wrapped in soggy cardboard
by the puke-green wall of bricks with a thousand holes
in them for the bedbugs, roaches, and rumpled ringdings
that came out at night and crawled all over us, biting,
that swarmed like emigrating termites when the lights came
    on.
The asbestos-insulated furnace belched, farted, and hummed
outside our door, a jack-o'-lantern whose serrated teeth
did not scare the rats, who warmed to him, in his furry gray
    suit
that glowed in the dark, a giant rodent Golem. One could
    hear
him breathing through the thin walls that divided the super-
    rintendent's
apartment from the front basement, a pathed indoor junk-
    yard.
We had to wend our way out through that La Brea Tar Pit
to get to the stairs that climbed and turned out to the street,

where we would peep up to see if anybody out there
would notice where we were coming from, which was out
from among the dented old metal cans full of raw garbage,
and what peculiar species of spelunker we were—what
Untouchables were surreptitiously seeking light and air.
I lied about my age and became a Western Union boy,
having shoeshined my way to the top, saved my money
and bought a bicycle, a Western Flyer, O Icarus! I found
my mother a pretty little apartment high over a pizza joint,
and we moved up into the air and the smell of baking
  dough.
My timid mother was shocked at such derring-do, daring
to fly so high, so near to the sun; and, for a while, we were
happy. But my father came home and said, "This place is
  too
expensive." We must get another sump-pump dump to
  superintend.
"Another nice basement that drips piss?" I asked, and added,
  "No,
I can afford to pay this rent, as I have been doing
for some time now. Now stick with me on this one,
Mom." But we better do what your father thinks best,
she whispered; and I said to myself—
                                     "That's it, never again,"
as I helped to carry our embarrassing paltry possessions—
"Impedimenta" my father called them—through the streets.
My father led the way like a brass hat, soused and self-
important, my mother followed him into nothing but worse,
with a "Wither-thou-goest" and a last wistful look up
over the pizza parlor at our window of opportunity, a
dutiful wife of the Fifties, and I planned my escape.

HADEWIJCH IN WALL STREET

When I walk in our ancient millioned alley
and dream of my Dutch past, I find my father,
a fortune-hunting youth who could not know
that flannel suits and frilly office frocks
are gray or parti-colored walking shrouds.

What terrible ecstasy would you have brought
this padded bourgeoisie, mad Hadewijch,
Dutch poet-nun who'd copulate with God?

The need for exaltation that I feel
in morbid secret service to my soul,
I walk like a mad soldier on patrol
among my enemies, the dressed to kill.

ONCOMING COMPANY

Oncoming company:
the flooding tides, the fell
ingrowing grave, the sea
of place, the held in hell.
What dark, what bleak o'clock
swings pendulously now?
No record on a rock
survives the voice and vow.

No record on a rock
survives the voice and vow:
Swings pendulously now
that dark, that bleak o'clock
of place, the held in hell
ingrowing grave, the sea
of flooding tides, the fell
oncoming company.

OBITUARY

Edwin Marsh Schorb, Sr. (1893-1963)

Requiescat in pace

> *Success is counted sweetest*
> *By those who ne'er succeed.*
> *—Emily Dickinson*

Without the mummeries of death, by fire,
but not by burning but by breath of smoke,
you died like some high god upon his pyre:
O quick, barbaric, merciful good luck!

I had so many fears for you, my father;
your ribald binges must have racked your body;
I feared some lingering illness, and I'd rather
have anything attacking one so bawdy

than an unthrilling, invalided life
spent somehow to its end in spite and temper;
though there was one thing sterner than its strife:
no death, no anything could make you whimper!

Your life was preparation for its pain:
you trained for ill and not for good, as Housman
advised his blear-eyed Shropshire lad to train
when, "moping melancholy mad," that yeoman

had rhymed the cow to death. A country boy
yourself, of Dutch and Anglo-Saxon stock,
New Jersey born and bred, hobbledehoy
and shining-faced, at fourteen, to New York

you went, in Nineteen-Hundred-Seven, to be
a runner on the New York Stock Exchange:
No more a rube!—No more a nonentity!—
but now (or then) a Wall Street runner, plung-

ing through the frantic, money-making crowds
America's romantic myth had brought
to conquer fortunes (time, events, becloud
so far-bygone an era, the magic sort

of moment that it was, the innocence
of fledgling fortune-hunters like yourself,
whose world of thought was Yankee common sense
and industry, who dreamed a sweet success

sometimes into existence in a trice:
opposing Mogul, Robber-baron, Tycoon,
all those first-comers who had set the price
of your success so high, O youngest son!)

Your struggle was a long one: studying
beside a late oil-lamp, O handsome youth
with raven hair!—your eyes only seeing
great dreams—reading of Rome, in law—in faith

that "Education makes the man;" with knowledge,
as Bacon'd put it, being power. Your roommate,
a brilliant graduate of Harvard College,
who one day would become a diplomat,

and later on Ambassador-at-large
in a long dead administration, instructed
you in "polish," as if you were his charge:
"Marry a rich woman," he told you once, "Ed.

That's my advice to you. I mean to do it
myself." Indeed, that's what he did. Not you,

though. Women meant too much. They knew you knew it,
too, handsome twenty-one, bonds salesman now,

and "Coming," as they called it then; they knew,
and loved you for it; helped you to establish
your reputation on The Street, and strew
themselves like flowers at your feet, flashing

their smiles like diamonds, their gems like teeth,
attracting and repelling, always rich
and husbanded by ghosts—a jewelled wreath
of Marley'd widows, beauties, and rich bitches,

young and old, fell about your frail young shoulders
—the day was almost won for Trumpery!
But meanwhile now the world was hurling boulders
of War, had been since Ferdinand, Humpty-Dumpty

of Peace, had fallen from the caving wall
at Sarajevo, four trenched and bloody years
before—time now for you to heed the call!
You went with other would-be "Officers

and Gentlemen" to be inducted, and
trained in the arts of martial leadership;
but suddenly, amazingly, they hand-
ed you your discharge.—We had won, had whipped

King Billy and the Ottoman Empire
(for better or for worse the deed was done!)
—and you, handsome young E.M. Schorb, Esq.,
were free to enter stormy Prohibition,

that time of Ought-not, But, and All-be-damned,
when "bathtub was synonymous with gin;"

an Eighty-nine-day-wonder, you had lammed
back into mufti—lost the veteran's pension

for my dear mother's Merry Widowhood;
but not your fault—a bureaucratic trick
that politicians played on Motherhood
is what we'll call it, for a sad laugh's sake.

Your first wife was a dopefiend. She's long dead.
The next an upright nurse—good family;
tubercular, although Bermuda bred;
and oh, British to the bone; unamatory,

or so you said, although you got a son
by her;—but not in Colorado, where
you went to help her lungs, and met someone
more amatory—Governor's daughter

she was: young, bright, and burning in her britches:
Black-Bottoming and Charlestoning and being
filled with a Flapper's ripe and bitching itches
—until you ran away from both of them.

By now you'd made the magic book—*WHO'S WHO*.
Success had come. You worked out of New York
and lived "Uptown"—and then the Market threw
its curve: Black Tuesday, Twenty-nine. What work

of evil genius had occurred? O fell
green hand of money! Lost hey-days! Your wife
was gone! Your son was gone, taken. What Hell
had happened and had happened here? What grief?

When, still young, you rode the Elevated,
the rumble of the wheels ground down your heart:

that iron-roar made you think quick death was fated,
thuswise against ambition raised your guard.

From then on you'd inveigh against that world
of Business, Finance, Property, Possessions
that you were trained in. Overboard you hurled
it, calling afterwards impedimenta

whatever slightest trinket stuck to you
as to summer-melting wax, which washed away
itself,—before the pierce-eyed public view!—
whatever'd stuck. The haberdashery

was all you kept: the custom-tailored suit;
silk tie; the Homburg hat; the shining shoes:
as you had worn them through the Prohibition Toot
you wore them through the sad Depression Days;

the Fylfot-War; the Eisenhower Fifties. . .
when I was there to know you, aging father:—
I, growing up by then, you in your sixties,
hair briny with the years, a heavy breather,

but still a regal, leucomelanous head—
bared now ("The man who never wears a hat"
was what they called you then—you were ahead
of time, before the style, an old pace-set-

ter—Kennedy would make bare heads official
—"My reason is to save my head of hair;
hats stop the circulation," you said; "this'll
become the style, when people learn.") Never

will I forget those idiosyncratic
quirks, those oddnesses, that set you apart

from ordinary beings so dramatic-
cally! I, walking by your side in Newark,—

where we then lived, deep in a basement flat,
where roaches climbed the walls like living paper,
and damp night brought the rustle of a rat,
—would glow to see the people look, O happier

than a rich son, to be the son of one
so striking and distinguished in appearance!
"That gent I seed you wid, are you his son?"—
yet of the poor we were among the poorest!

You'd married Mom in Nineteen-Thirty-Two,—
one year before Repeal, deep in Depression
days. Having met in a speakeasy, you
decided to continue partying—

and did throughout the years, by fits and starts!
Though making money was a difficulty
that interfered with freedom, your free hearts
went on their merry way, higgledy-piggledy,

from the Honeymoon Hotel, here in New York,
where you escaped the bill by wearing all
your wardrobe out the door, until the stork
dropped in your lap a wet, if "Wonderful!"

responsibility—which you were not
quite ready to live up to, though you tried—
"To be father, now! Why, I've forgot-
ten how to burp a child! I'm forty-five!"

Soon fifty-five! Now, door-to-door, you sold:
bandaids, thread, pots and pans, encyclopedias

(once more you carried Bacon's quote in bold
lettering on a business card, *KNOWLEDGE*

IS POWER!)—Oh, a library of books!
Ah, melancholy-morbid! How you read
"The Raven," with your Barrymorish looks
to help you dramatize as you recited!

And "To the Ladies!" How that angered Mom!
You made her Judy O'Grady, not the Lady,
while you remained the Colonel! Deaf and dumb
with anger, she would wait until payday

before she made things up. The years went by.
You went to work at managing hotels
for some cheap chain; then later you would try
your hand at selling real estate; but selling

was too rough now, Old Charmer, sixty-five!
And then you read De Quincey and De Ropp:
"Why, I have never even been alive!"
And that was how you found your way to dope!

To dope and death as well! For you left home,
went to a hobo rooming house downtown,
and, three weeks later—dead! O poor poor Mom!
"I loved him. Understood him? No." She frowned.

SIX DEAD IN BLAZE IN NEWARK, the paper said:
I read the headlines on the Hudson Tube
while on my way to Newark. Could you be dead?
Yes, I identified you at the Morgue!

Without the mummeries of death, by fire,
but not by burning but by breath of smoke,
you died like some high god upon his pyre:
O quick, barbaric, merciful good luck!

THE ORPHANED

When the mood comes upon him to die
of a loneliness deeper than death,

he must speak to himself like a parent
in a lecturing voice, but with love.

He must be his own father and mother,
and at night when he looks up at heaven,

where nothing of earth seems to live,
and the range of all things is so great

as to startle the love from his breast,
he must think of his father, the Rock,

and of his mother, the Dead Sea, and of
the message he brings from the sun.

NIGHTWATCH

My loneliness was deep.
  I could not see beyond it.
It robbed me of my sleep.

I lay awake, saw sheep,
  counted; no dream responded.
My loneliness was deep.

The tide was at the neap.
  I took the moon, and donned it.
It robbed me of my sleep.

I heard a great bird leap,
  die, singing as the swan did.
My loneliness was deep.

You sow and you shall reap;
  for guilt was how I conned it.
It robbed me of my sleep.

"Lord, take my soul to keep!"
  I cried. Not He: no one did.
My loneliness was deep.
It robbed me of my sleep.

UPSTATE STORM

Heavenward, at middle-height,
where the moon is cumbersome,
like a pale breast on the sky,
hanging big, and full of seas,

clouds coagulate, then darken,
curdle, into angry gray;
shed appendages adrift
in the rising, warning wind.

Thus they hover, sheep, above,
turned about by barks of wind
as the baa-waymenting lambs
can be turned about the field

by the windy barks of Dog.
Bent electric lances snap
(violence claps the whirling air),
blasting black a mangled oak

(cedars cinder at a stroke);
thunder echoes over hills,
rolling in the wind beyond
tangled and uprooted trees;

pitchforks fill the lofts with light;
carp-eyed horses leap away;
flooding rivers jump their banks,
drowning lowland cattle, sheep;

and the farm foundation quakes
with the force of wind and rain,
heedless of the life it holds;
cold, indifferent to pain.

DARK CANZONE

From when some wandering primate first discovered
that vocal cords had formed within its throat:
when thorax wind was blown, and it discovered
a modulation of its grunts, discovered
it had a tongue that could articulate
more subtly than it had presumed; discovered,
in fact, its ur-humanity; discovered
that it was different from monkeys, wiser,
and could communicate a plan; was wiser,
one than the other, in this gift; discovered,
in short, itself as special being, poet,
it sang in lamentation for the poet,
O felt itself the oddest ape, a poet,
and, with the weight of what it knew, discovered
the truest nature of itself as poet,
that it must bear the burden of the poet,
harsh bile of truth that rises in the throat
and burns the vocal cords of every poet.
For meaning murders innocence, the poet
learns, word by word; and to articulate
as in a grammar, to articulate
as words demand, and so to be a poet
is to be that most special being, stranger
than any other animal—but wiser?
It felt itself the strangest thing, much stranger
than any other animal—a poet
—for strangled words had made it thuswise stranger.
But was it better being this much wiser?
What had this primate after all discovered?
Who really thinks it's better to be wiser?
Who doesn't know it's sadder to be wiser?
Who envies words blown through a poet's throat?
What poet hasn't wished to cut its throat?

If grammar makes for meaning, is it wiser
to be a special being, to articulate
the truth words find—or not articulate?
It may be braver to articulate,
to be an animal, yet strangely wiser,
but is it wisdom to articulate
the grunts of animals, articulate
from them the existential life of poet
among the primates, to articulate—
syntactically commanded—articulate
the place in nature that we have discovered,
the death in nature that we have discovered?
Grunt one last grunt! Enough! Articulate
no more! Oh, envy nothing from the throat
of any poet! Let it cut its throat!
Oh, let the primate poet cut its throat
before it's forced on to articulate,
by sending lamentations through its throat,
from its self-fabled heart and out its throat,
how truly sad it is to be a little wiser
than other animals that have a throat
but have no vocal cords within that throat
which they can use to make themselves a poet
who sings the lamentations of a poet,
a sadder wiser primate prophet poet,
whose ordered language has at last discovered
what other animals have not discovered . . . .
What is it animals have not discovered,
which leaves them happier than any poet?
The ordered thought of death! It might be wiser
for nature never to articulate.

THE NIGHT SWEATS

By our intensity, with hanging head,
we spell the wolf away, who pants and croons
outside the door, who wants us to be dead
so he may have his meal. By magic runes
we rid the world of wide-winged evil loons
whose madness mixes metaphors instead
of bringing clarity, whose looney tunes
make breathless nightmares in our sweat-wet bed.
Hear them who creep toward our peace of mind,
destructive artifices of our brains,
to wreak their havoc! Run, leave them behind!
And in the dark we try to run in chains
and can't escape because the night is mined
to blow us up in spite of all our pains.

COMMUNION

I lie in the darkness and listen into silence
sometimes, outside the stream of time
where life hums and burns with its moths and flames,
its mechanical tropisms of desire and death;
I listen to the silent voice of the nightingale
with my friend Keats, the dead boy, the poet.

THE MORAL

Some say the world will end in fire . . .
　　　　　　　　　　—Robert Frost

My father died in fire.
My mother dies of ice.
Myself? It is desire.
So ruinous a price
we pay for what we need!
The Muenster needs of mice
have trapped them in their greed.
It's never very nice.

My father felt the mire,
and threw decisive dice.
He died upon a pyre
with roomers and with lice.
A churchman of the creed
succumbed to shoes and rice,
then found he couldn't breed.
It's never very nice.

My mother feels with ire
the lack of kind advice,
and will time really buy her
another paradise?
A mongoose met a weed
and bit him off a slice,
then started in to bleed.
It's never very nice.

Myself, I'd be a liar
to say I have no vice.
I'll do it till I tire,
I've said so once or twice.

A hound who took no heed
once tried to make a splice.
The lion had a feed.
It's never very nice.

So all of you who read,
for you let this suffice:
that we shall be agreed,
it's never very nice.

WORDS IN PASSING

An apparently homeless occasional visitor to the Bedford-Stuyvesant Store Front Church, who signed our Guest Book with an "X," and was known to us only as the "shopping cart lady," was crushed by a bus as she left evening services. Donations toward her last expenses will be appreciated.
—Church Bulletin

I passed here earlier and saw beneath
a bus an old black woman mocked aloud.
Forty-five minutes saw her ticking, transfixed figure
flouted in blood-filching snow, a crowd's breath
from peace and her God, a corrugated cardboard pyre,
too wet to burn, beneath her Earth-embracing body
and her Earth. Death was an everyday duty,
a boring business, to the busy ambulance
that came too late to save her from her shroud.
And so they chalked this shape of her small fame,
a tableau of her love in white and black,
while the mad mob leaned on linked arms to have
its picture taken by her broken frame.
Here, face down, toward the fiery zodiac,
she saw through Earth and, God please, forgave
that necrophilic crowd, Death's audience.
But in the unseen ceremony of her dying,
before the great beyond of her death, I pray
that they seemed members of her family
and that this reeking street where she was lying
seemed like an avenue of light down which
she went with You and Death without a balk
the while You made her young again and rich;
and that, for Love's sake, You hurried her catafalque,
through traffic-horn salutes and laughter,
beyond her first name, toward her last, and after.

THE POOR BOY

I

Not having had inheritance or luck,
undemocratically good blood or breeding,
nor any gold come out of family stock
that sets a young man up, preceding
maturity and forming for it pride
in action and aristocratic strength,
solace in having purpose in each stride,
and discipline that carries to its length,
I've found myself romantically inclined,
a muzzy mongrel with a barking mind.

II

How I admire those men and women who
were reared in order, dignity and pride!
You see it in their eyes, a voiceless vow,
a knowledge Levelling denied.
Here now is social change preeminent,
the mass man rises to his rightful place;
but his ascension leaves a remanent
of unredeemable darkness of disgrace
in that all art must kowtow to a taste,
now at his rising, weaned on gutter waste.

III

I know, for I have foraged in the lots
of blackened cities looking for a prize
of red discarded unbroken flowerpots
to place my plants, to brighten eyes.

I've shined a thousand shoes along the streets
of coughing cities all across this land.
A child, I'd enter taverns and retreats
the like of which to others would be banned.
Oh, I know poverty, unhappiness;
such things I know, I have no need to guess.

IV

And yet a sturdy strength comes out of it,
that's undeniable; but at what cost!
The strength of street-bred children is their wit
and nerve; nobility is lost
in the hungry race of mongrels for a bone,
and Honor hangs his head before the scene.
The heart of the street urchin is a stone
ground more with each engagement, until mean.
We learn to fight and hate, but not to love,
no matter who says so. We learn to shove.

CANDY BUTCHER

fragments of an unfinished musical

Characters
Jimmy, a candy butcher
Elliot, Jimmy's father
Fay, Jimmy's mother
Kosmo, Brandy & Stoney, candy butchers
Singer
Flame O'Hair, a stripper
Moe, a concessionaire
Scenes
Minksy's Burlesque Theatre
The Midway Hotel

Scene: Theatre
PROLOGUE

JIMMY
(*rembering shining shoes of Lola Albright, the movie star*)

Kneeling upon your
knees on the ground
kneeling upon your
knees and around
you the city
making its noise
shaking with pity
for shoeshine boys
who were not kneeling
as if in a prayer

who were not dreaming
of lost summer fields
and sweet summer air
always were scheming
and fighting for places
always were stealing
your hard-won spaces
and beating you up
and beating you down
all over town
and then to have seen her
all bright like a star
at night to have seen her
as if from afar
as if you were off
in some summer field
all alone with the night
when suddenly light
caught your eye
and you looked up to see
what it was in the sky
that was shining
all bright!

*   *   *

CHORUS

Nobody's blue,
it's Nineteen Fifty-two.
Come with me, Mike,
I'm voting for Ike.
It's odd or even, son,
so maybe Stevenson.

But nobody's blue
in Nineteen Hundred
Fifty-two!

*   *   *

SINGER

The most beautiful girls in the world
are at Minsky's
oh, they're dandy
oh, they're handy
oh, Minsky girls
are the most beautiful girls
in the world!

(candy butchers enter)

STONEY

Ice cream, orange drink
and gurly magazines!
Eat, drink, be merry,
see the pictures of the Queens!

KOSMO

Tom, Dick, and Harry
have an orange drink!
Ice cream, orange drink!
Gurly magazines!

BRANDY

Got a changer on my belt.
Buy before my ice creams melt
from the pictures of the Queens
in my gurly magazines!

KOSMO

Buy my pissy orange drink
and stand and sip and stop and think
of what the show was all about
then you'll never leave without
the pictures of the Queens
in my gurly magazines!

ALL

Eat, drink, be merry
Tom, Dick, and Harry!
Buy the pictures of the Queens
in our gurly magazines!

*   *   *

BOXER BALLAD
(Moe, the concessionaire, tells Jimmy his story)

A lightweight in those days,
   now I'm a heavyweight
(the booze, the cheesecake, stays).
   At age twenty-eight
things were looking good,
and I did what I should.

But Beauty was a lady
   out to be a star—
contender, a little shady—
   determined to go far.
She might have made it, too,
had life been kind and true.

A gangster was the gent,
   out to steal my love,
a man who was hellbent
   to be so much above
all others that he fell
finally to hell.

We never got fame's joys.
   I had to lay him out.
That gangster and his boys
   cost me my title bout
and she did not get far
toward that Broadway Star.

A chorus girl, a gent—
   it's people happen, son.
It was my main event,
   the last one that I won.
For wrong things came out right.
Love won my toughest fight!

FLAME O'HAIR
(appears in Jimmy's dream)

I'm not what I seem to you.
I'm just a dream to you
because you're so young.

You're what you are to me,
a boy very far from me,
because you're so young.

When I was your age
I dreamed of a prince—
I haven't dreamed very much since.

(speaks softly)
When you are my age
you won't dream of this Flame,
you'll dream of me young.

(singing, fading from sight)
I'm not what I seem to you.
I'm just a dream to you
because you're so young.

* * *

Scene: The Midway Hotel
DUET: THE BICKERSONG

ELLIOT

I'm in a lovely state of grace.
Indeed, a happy paradise—
my robe, my Chesterfields, this place,
my glass of sherry filled with ice—

Don't send me to the desk below,
down to the mundane world you prize.
There's much of wisdom you don't know.
Believe me, this is paradise.

FAY

This is a dump
and you're a lump
of a drunk
on a trunk!

Calling me a peasant
is not a very pleasant
thing for you to do,
even if it's true.

Your father was a rambler
after women, and a gambler
who lost your mother's farm
and brought you all to harm.

Had he any virtue,
how could he so have hurt you?
Why, we'd be rich today
if your mother'd had her way.

But this is up to date!
At the awful awful rate
you are going, we are going
on the sidewalk when it's snowing

and the wind is blowing!
They are going, going, going,
without the slightest doubt,
they are going, going, going
TO THROW US OUT!

*   *   *

SONG: MALE CHAUVINIST
Elliot

Now the bird in the bush is an egg-laying thrush
    requiring a nest of some kind,
but the high-flying male, who freely would sail,
    to virtue is never so blind—
    to virtue is never so blind.
He spreads out his wings as soon as he's dined.

The high-flying male who freely would sail
    without envy or rancor or doubt
must not have his wings weighted down with mere things
    though his female forever should pout—
    though his female forever should pout.
The object of life is to keep objects out!

It's said that I'm selfish. That's better than *pel*fish,
    and greedily grasping at straws;
for what are possessions but straws of obsession
    in the winds of eternal laws—
    in the winds of eternal laws?
The high-flying cock will spread his great claws.

Remember, my boy, to get rid of the toy
    that is solid, existing in fact.
Let all of the things that you bear on your wings
    be musical, wise, and abstract—
    be musical, wise, and abstract!
All else from your flight you must fiercely subtract!

SONG: THE GAME OF LIFE
   Elliot, Fay and Jimmy

ELLIOT: See if you can make it in the world out there.
It only has the meaning that you give it.
See if you can make it in the world out there,
Make it a game and live it!
What's the difference in the end if you win or lose,
Dead if you do and dead if you don't?
What's the difference in the end if you win or lose,
Either you will or you won't?
There's nothing in the world to say you're wrong or right.
You got to make it up as you go along.
There's nothing in the world to say you're wrong or right.
In the gamble with life you've got to be strong.
You've got to be brave for a while at least,
especially when you're young.
Got to be brave for a while at least,
at least till your song is sung.
Now I'm an old man so I really don't care,
and I sit around here and I think.
Now I'm an old man so I really don't care,
except for another drink!
I had you so late that I'm no example,
for a young uprising son—
I had you so late that I'm no example—
FAY: No example for anyone!
ELLIOT: See if you can make it in the world out there!
JIMMY: (*chimes in*) I'll see if I can make it in the world
   out there.
It only has the meaning that I give it.
I'll see if I can make it in the world out there,
make it a game and live it!
ELLIOT: What's the difference in the end if you win or
   lose,

dead if you do and dead if you don't?
JIMMY: What's the difference in the end if I win or lose,
  in the end, I will or I won't!
ELLIOT: There's nothing in the world to say you're right
  or wrong!
JIMMY: I've got to make it up as I go along!
There's nothing in the world to say I'm right or wrong.
ELLIOT: In the gamble with life you've got to be strong.
JIMMY: I've got to be brave for a while at least,
Especially when I'm young!
ELLIOT AND JIMMY: Got to be brave for a while at
  least,
At least till our song is sung!
FAY: I'd like to make it in the world out there.
It only has the meaning that you give it.
I'd like to make it in the world out there—
make it a game and live it!
In the gamble with life you've got to be strong,
You've got to be brave for a while at least.
In the gamble with life you've got to be strong,
At least till you've sung your song.
Now you're an old man and you really don't care,
and you sit around here and you think.
You're an old man and you really don't care,
except for another drink!
But I'm a woman who's still quite young,
just a wee bit past my prime—
you've got to understand that I'm still quite young
and I'd like to use my time.
I'd like to have a castle a chateau or a house.
I'd like to have at least a quiet flat.
I'd like not to run a hotel or rooming house,
or anything at all like that.
I'd like to pay our rent right out of pocket,
and have some furniture that's really ours,

and not to be afraid that you would hock it,
and to sit and dream for months and days and hours.
Yes, I'm a woman who's still quite young—
ELLIOT: But you married an older man.
FAY: But I'm a woman who is still quite young,
and I'd like to do what I can.
FAY AND *JIMMY*: Let's see if we can make it in the
    world out there.
It only has the meaning that we give it.
Let's see if we can make it in the world out there,
make it a game and live it!
ELLIOT: Now I'm an old man so I really don't care.
JIMMY: I'd like to be somebody in the world out there.
ALL: You've got to be brave for a while at least,
especially when you're young!
Got to be brave for while at least,
at least till your song is sung!

Curtain

See the World

SHARP

Poet of Parris Island

"Cock crows, wolf bays, caterwauls, eldritch sounds ringing
  out and echoing
    back from the escarpment, weird screams meant to
      terrify, crazily
announcing attack across fogbound spiderwebs of barbed-
  wired
    terrain. Then the poop of mortars, the red spit of burps,
a flare, shedding chartreuse in its lazy swaying gravity fall,
    beautiful tracers burning out in air, phosphorous grenades
      making

small midnight suns . . ."   Buck Sergeant Robert E. Lee
  Sharp of Macon read
    to his captive audience of Marine recruits his poems of
      Korean
conflict—recruits who had, night before, waded the blind-
  dark swamp of the
    Sea Island called Parris, shitbirds and turds up to their
      chins in
swamp gunk, whipped on and kicked by water moccasins,
  Mae-Wested
    in the dark by boa constrictors, or so they believed. All
      but Clover—

descendant of Sea Island plantation slaves, cursing the
  mouthfuls
    of swampwash in gurgling Gullah, the islands' lingo—

    who knew the snakes
would be scared off by such commotion as this—two
    hundred-some farm
        boys and city slickers scared spineless in the snakes'
        swamp—knew
it was drowning to be feared, in the slippery dark, burdened
    with
        fifty-pound packs rifles helmets cartridgebelts canteens
        bayonets and night-

blind eyes, under a starproof vegetable roof of shingling
    fronds and fans.
        Clover stretched his neck like a turtle above the din of
        clanks
splashes and shouts of terror. And always above any din
    Sharp's mellifluous
        Georgian, urging, commanding a motley crew of shit-
        birds and turds to become
Marines, who himself was Poster-Marine, whose men
    thought him perfect
        but for the fact that he was mad as the Hatter, perfect, but
        for

his constant, barely submerged violence, which was the
    song behind his words
        now, as he read with great beauty, vivid clarity, his
        martial
poems of nightmare mayhem on Bunker Hill and Snipers
    Ridge, where
        he won a chestful of medals, a seemingly mad hero
        Marine poet
drill instructor, angrier than God. At what? War, the
    poems told, at war,
        at human nature, at himself, filled with his own violence;
        at us, too,

but to save us, always to make us triumph over what he had
  endured, cried:
    "Coming! Outposts in! The sand-bagged weight of the
      bunker collapsed
under artillery—a full barrage—pf-f-f-f-f BOOM—and the
  Reds slid
    in on us. Got one under my arm and slit his throat. Now
      tell me about
Mao, I said; I'll tell you about freedom, you two-mouthed
  bastard!" Sharp scanned
    us, in our skivvies on the squadbay floor, across the little
      table he

brought to his recitals. "Unnerstay-end," he growled, "Mr.
  Kennan in
    Washington has devised for America a policy of contain-
      ment. The Reds
cain't continue to eat if they don't swallow up other coun-
  tries. They don't
    create wealth, they re-dis-tri-bute it. Get me? They are
      an empire.
Unnerstay-end what that is? They gotta eat up their neigh-
  bors
    or else they collapse. Unnerstay-end? Do you dumb
      shitbirds

unnerstay-end what it's all about, what Bunker Hill was
  about—either
    one? About FREEDOM, you dumb turds, FREEDOM!
      you eat enough 'gator-
doo, you'al'll learn. One o' them Reds shoots your balls
  off—Non
    emasculatatum est—" Off in another reality field, Sharp
      whispers, "My

best buddy, from Valdosta . . ." Back. "You gonna priss like girls when you march.
We gonna win the base ensign. I don't care a fiddler's bitch if the

red flag goes up at a hunnerd-ten degrees. You gonna priss like girls.
You gonna look PRETTY. Get me? And you know what you gonna be?
Do you? You gonna be God bless America Uncle Sam's most perfect killers.
Now what you gonna be?" SIR, killers, SIR! "Makes my heart sing.
And if the army and the navy ever get to heaven's scene . . . What, dammit?"
They will find the streets are guarded by United States Marines, SIR!

TRACERS

Young, dreamy,
on a hill
dark as a
frown,
I fired
a fifty
-caliber
machine-gun
into the
night's abyss.
Every fifth
round
was a tracer
that flared
with a
wonderful
will as
it sought
the dark
ground.

What was
the magic
that night
that I could
never forget
how angelic
the tracers
looked,
losing their
light
without
whatever

      regret
     must be
    humanly
    brooked
   when the
    flare of
  life flames
  down and
   into the
   ground?

TROOP TRANSPORT

We love to be hit by the spray
while watching the wake as the bow
dips five stories down and rises again
as if to take off for the clouds
where the gulls look down at us
as if we were sardines on toast
to snatch in their snooty hooked bills.
We love the sea, who knew only
the green rolling hills and cattle and horses:
but cowboys can't swim, so I stand
with my life-jacket on and stare
at the mountains of water and valleys
that keep changing places, loving the buck
and the crash of the bow and its wake
that sprays me with spindrift, mad
for its plunge full of colors, for
my face in the face of the moon-drawn,
gravitied deep. What ecstasy is,
is the danger of down, then returning,
like riding a bull till he drops.

LEGAL

Twentieth Birthday

They stood in a cracked photograph before your tenth
birthday cake like puckered fountain cupids, helping you
to blow out your candles and in your wish. Your wish
then was that they would never grow old, a child's
wish, born of dependency, your need for them
to flourish for your sake. You looked away, about,
and wondered, if, upon your return to the mainland,
your parents would look the same as always, the same
as in the cracked photograph, or look old, altered.
You glanced up, and saw a long, black, tail-finned
limousine, shining moons of sun, pass out of
sight on the busy street where you entered the bar;
and, startled out of your reverie, you turned about
to find Waikiki Beach behind you, a keepsake
postcard of one of the most important days
of your life, and you wondered at the power
of your first legal drink to so disorient you;
for, when you entered, you were looking out at the sea.
Then you realized that you were on a turntable,
imperceptibly turning counterclockwise, but only,
of course, by the machinations of human will.

THE SURVIVOR

The tugs towed us out,   two on each side,
then left us alone.   There loomed the sea,
slate in the slant   of sunlight at dawn;
here, hecatombs hoped,   the hundreds aboard,
boys nearly babies,   boys fat and thin,
homely and handsome,   helmet-haired boys,
among whom myself,   woman-cheeked, pale.
But daylight saw dolphins,   wagging dogs of the sea,
gulls at our garbage   —grand, that display!—
while rainbows rolled butts,   drowned nails of tobacco.
We drilled out on deck,   dodging white wakes,
the escorts escorting   scorned in vainglory.
No sooner sun shined   than set the same sun.
But sharks, shining-finned,   sure found our path.

Not long before light,   a large ship appeared
and held the horizon,   hovering there,
a carrier, cruising,   crossing, recrossing,
then bombers, like bees,   buzzed in the sky.
A bomb amidships!   We scrambled on deck,
where booms lowered boats   as bombs blew them up.
No escorts escaped!   Scrapped in the deep!
Our shuddering ship,   shadowed with death,
slid on its side   and sank slowly down.
I rose on a raft   and reached for survivors.
Hope in my hand,   I hauled them aboard:
boys nearly babies,   boys fat and thin,
homely and handsome,   helmet-haired boys,
among whom myself,   woman-cheeked, pale.

Home Again

HOLIDAYS

I Near Christmas

Now in November winter is half turning
on autumn down the land from Maine to Jersey,
and Christians think of Christmas. Bargain basements
hum with the hymns of shoppers who are yearning
for the millennium of peace; but hearsay
has it that trouble brews. The icy casements
of early winter, frigid films of frost,
portend now, and remind the multitude
of Christmas shoppers to count up the cost
of (being human) being bad or good.

In all the avenues and cross streets of
Manhattan Island, how the atmosphere
improves! One notices an unexpected
smile, kindness; odd euphoria of love
pervades the frigid evening air; the fear
of strangers is diminished; unaffected
good humor rises, rampant; *Noel! Noel!*
sounds in, or seems to sound in, every voice.
Now only Heaven's true; there is no Hell!
This is the season to forgive, rejoice!

II New Year Near the Hudson

The summit of time has been reached!
Wind is the breath of the demon of ice
who breathes down our necks at the peak.

    In cold blood, with wide hands,
  he pushes, creeping and cresting dark water,
while across the rumpling bay,

    beyond illuminated, skyline geometry,
  while frozen excelsior hangs fire in the air,
a shuddering ragged phalanx

    traces the fall of a ball,
  as the polluted Hudson,
drunk on party poisons, rolls on.

THE APPLICANT

The day perfused its natural light, but here
the indirect fluorescent lighting gave
a ghastly look to marble walls and faces
and like a psychotomimetic agent, produced
its odd effect: she saw her life go by her
just as they say all drowning persons do.
Bright artificial light fell from the air
as she looked on, and strangers swam the lobby
as if they were a vague sea-life, dull clots,
and she among them like a thing in tide,
and all the while her life kept going by
as if the pages of a book were turned,
a morbid album scanned in lurid light.
She saw her early youthful face, and then
her latest face (but that was in the red
art-deco elevator's gilt-edged mirror)
and nearly missed her floor for concentration.
Then she was spoken to, and told her name,
poking her *New York Times* ahead of her
as if its roll of news contained a proof
enclosed within it, like a royal-cartouche,
and wiped the perspiration from her brow
and took an offered chair, and waited.
Suddenly her name hummed in the shell
of deep-sea office sounds her ear had pressed to
and she went forth to do as she was told,
but fuddled in a kind of difficulty
that her officious tester could not know,
and missed the bell (they rang the one bell only).
The lady gave assistance, tried to help,
betraying, nonetheless, suppressed impatience.
What sort of person are they sending us?
And yet she was amusing to the rhythm,

a nervous smiling creature, out of place;
a feckless angel fallen out of grace.

O POPULAR MOON!

 —Moon Landing 1969

Now what kind of moon is it, darling,
 that, so blandly turning blue,
overhangs us here in greenly summer Brooklyn
 while the astronauts go round
and the sea at Coney rises,
 all its little lucky ripples
wiping off the darkened sand?

Now what kind of moon is this,
 questing for the old romance?
Acknowledging our loneliness,
 we know better than to ask,
returning from the Goldman Band
 and kinder songs of long ago.

Your pearl your blue your golden loneliness
 bring in our need,
which we acknowledge, seeing you
 sailing light, O, all unburdened.
Burdened by my loneliness,
 I hold her gentle hand in Prospect Park,
walking from the Goldman Band
 and the dismantling of the instruments.

42ⁿᵈ STREET, 70s

When I've gone out to walk at night,
to tour the streets, mean-dark, false-bright,
of this sick city that is no home
but for the Giant and the Gnome,
the Monsters of Despair, I've seen
pathetic sights and sights obscene:
   The fat black man who has no eyes
but two great holes from which he cries
long hours, holding out his cup
for Times Square crowds to fill it up;
   the woman with the bleeding leg
who climbs the subway stairs to beg;
   the legless men who crabwise creep
on wooden gloves to morning sleep;
   the varicosed, tumescent, sick,
already dead and yet still quick;
   male hustlers, leaning in long rows,
posed in mock movie-hero pose;
   porn shops with tainted men inside
some of whom have kissed a bride;
   retarded vendors at their stands
masturbating, hiding hands
beneath big stacks of filthy mags;
   and drunks on jags, and hags in rags,
asleep in doorways commandeered
from rats and stiffs; the other weird
displaying signs of coming doom
Hellfire and Brimstone in the tomb;
   and faces stupified by dope,
expressionless of love or hope—
   these sights and worse are near Times Square
at night when I go walking there.

BROOKLYN HEIGHTS

From low to high doth dissolution climb,
And sink from high to low, along a scale
Of awful notes, whose concord shall not fail . . .
                              —*Wordsworth*

I From the Esplanade

When, in the morning remnant of the moon,
the restless city stirs beneath the stars,
its buildings hunching in a black tableau
that forms Prometheus from common themes
of steel and glass and brick, I walk abroad—
for an hour now—while night lays claim on time
for the first time for me tonight (and now
already it surrenders to the sun!)—
I walk abroad requiring only love;
that it may be a morning gift unwrapt
from this dark shapeless parcel and received
in utter nakedness; that it be light!
But more than having light, I want to be
one for whom light adventures into change,
allowing for my lustings after it
and gives me place to say in certain praise:
O Light, allow me several such days!

II Varaition

The night-calmed city stirs beneath the stars;
the buildings shape into a gray tableau
that forms Prometheus from common themes
of stone and steel; I walk the esplanade
and think of night and day, of life and death.

I watch the morning remnant of the moon
pale overhead, slow-swinging scimitar!
The bridges in the twilight tax the breath.
Oh, night was beautiful; no debt was due;
but I am grateful night's amorphous parcel
contains, somewhere, that morning gift, the sun.

III DARK AGES

> *More light!*
> *—Goethe, on his deathbed*

O there was never any actually powerful light
by which to comprehend the common day,
merely the milktoast light of we benight-
ed, who cannot understand what we see.
But whose fault is that if we sadly try,
standing clumsily up to our full height
like doomed, dim-minded begging bears
that with sad hungry hearts are so unbright?

Is it any wonder that all we do is fight?
Is it any wonder that all we do is lie?
Is it any wonder that what we do is trite?
Is it any wonder that we stand and sigh,
  who are graced with only such a little sun
  by which to try to be someone, anyone?

HIRE ACTORS!

Being superficially
mourned would be a
last wicked joke on me.

Hire actors

who, though they have
never met me, can
read my story and
genuinely feel.

Hire actors

and be honest and
revile me at leisure
while the actors mourn.

Hire actors

who have been taught
the Method and know
their motivations.

Hire actors!

One good actor can feel
more than an average
family.

Hire actors!

GARY PLAYER WINS MASTERS

> *Poetry is news*
> *that stays news.*
> *—Ezra Pound*

"The beloved draws the lover," Aristotle says.
We are wanted to be what we become.
Chester Carlson, inventor of
xerography, died in 1968.
Think of it under the stars.
Or think of this: "Greek Fire,"
a missile weapon of sulfur,
rock salt, resin, and petroleum,
was invented by Kallinikos of Byzantium,
in 671. He shall not be forgotten.
Poetry is an accidental of essence.
It could have been drumming,
had I been able to afford a drum.
I could always come up with a piece of paper
and a pencil. In 1788 James Hutton wrote
a "New Theory of the Earth" and Laplace
came out with his "Laws of the Planetary System."
(Also first hortensia and fuchsia imported from Peru.)
Aristotle says, "Essence is the principle of everything."
It's the unchangable that makes change possible.
Substance is what we stand under.
Becoming is guided in terms of a goal.
"Greek Fire" turned atomic.
How do we calculate the goal? What should
poetry turn into? Does a new century require
a new kind of poetry? Has the Information Age
created it? 1961: Jack Nicklaus wins U.S. Golf
Association Amateur; Gene Littler
wins Open; Gary Player wins Masters.

WHISTLER

looked into his nocturne,
then up and down and side to side.
Which was the way? The water flowed
like a pale tongue from the horizon;
it grew wide and thick three-quarters up
the canvas, then dropped down the sides
three-quarters to a long thin tongue.
He could not resist the patch of land
in the close forewater two-thirds down,
or whatever floated there, nor the bottoming twig
that seemed to say he was a camera still,
though one instinctively out of focus.
But how not be a camera? Was it
unthinkable, the next natural step: to compose
with no more than patches, splotches of color?
Hugo had done it, but Hugo was a poet;
who would see his paintings? Who would care?
A pure abstraction? Whistler's instinct
may have urged him on, but life
warned not, and even so John Ruskin
called him coxcomb, said he flung
paint in the public's face—brush and pen
at war. Ruskin's world would not admit
a purely graphic language
of shape and color.

Nocturne in Black and Gold:
The Falling Rocket: how close
to spatter painting Pollock! How very close
to knowing how the essence is what counts!
True, Art won its farthing against Ruskin,
but the new vision remained unseen.
But had they asked how they could see,

those blind, Whistler might have said,
as he did to Oscar Wilde that night in the salon,
"You will, you will!"

THE LESSON

I have learned not to be quiet,
otherwise Death finds you.

I have learned to be unstill,
to sit loud, to talk long.

And I have learned why some
of us go on mountain treks

and others leap, on motorcycles,
a dozen cars; but I have not,

anymore than these, been able
to sit silently still, and die.

AMERICAN PARIS; OR, UNDERGRADUATE DAYS

Seeing in my mind now those winding, those twisting and
    turning, those populace
        and spiriling streets,
the carts full of produce and the sausages hanging from
    hooks in shop windows
        along MacDougal Street, the

bread, full of crunch, and tasting again the tang on my lips,
    purpled with wine,
        seeing myself strolling
the Washington Square where Henry of James fame
  dreamed
    his intransigent
        heiress, her hair

in a hurting knot, and sitting at the fountain, or on the
    rails at the foot of the park
        near my new,
old school, ah, seeing the paintings outdoors on display at
  the
    rails, as if Manet and
        Monet, the pre-

and the post- of impressionists, the Fauves and the Cubists,
    Picasso,
        and splattering Pollock,
were hawking their wares, remembering wandering from
  where
    the flowering boppers would follow me
        to espresso cafes

to the beat of a bongo or the twang of a Bob Dylan song,
    and of course remembering the

      first loves of youth,
difficult, daring, darling, oh, and, drawing back from the
   darkening window of then,
     where the street corner

lamp glowed like a crystal ball with no knowledge of
  anything
    but my dream
      of a fabulous future,
I think lovingly of the Village of the Sixties as my own
   American Paris
     in the fargone time of my innocence.

LOST SKETCHES BY BOSCH

Is it true that they have been found in a bedpost,
the most profound and diabolical of Bosch's visions,
such recisions of budding life, such deracinations,

that the curators will only allow medical-psychological
bureaucrats and high government officials to see them?
Is it true that a journalist who moled his way into the

museum was hysterically blinded; and that psychologists
warn that the health of the public must be protected
from the homunculi of Hieronymus Bosch? They
   wondered:

Were his works the result of an old painter's colic?
Did he hear in the braying of an ass the voice of a man,
praying? Was his large breakfast egg humanly impregnated

to form such a melancholy yolk? Young Hieronymus saw,
his mother used to say, through the holy mask of
   benevolence.
She told how he could sense what was there, and tell her

the hell beneath the inevitable illusions, the true tree
spring-budding grinning grotesques wearing black wreaths
of dried blood. Some say he had access to alchemists' jars,

because the imagination must base its visions in fact.
It's evident now, they say, in light of these gory graphics,
that he had to tone down, make less consequential,

his best-known paintings to make them at all acceptable.
O, that his mother had burned and not saved out of love
these abominable sketches by the young Hieronymus Bosch!

POLLOCK

here my dream would color truth   like roaches bleeding
crimson bitter poison   leading ahead to inspiration
love   questions   accusations   gunshots   brain-wreckage
misdirected footprints   prison   shackles   a thousand
promises & quiet penance   opening sad pretense
regularly burning a familiar promise   simple scribbled
dreams perpetuate observance   remembrance   hard
commandment   rearrange me buried beneath   torment
please   you   my clinician analyst disconnect merry
poetry   our better wine   & recite certain darkness eyes
fist   weapon   pretending freedom   care   more like
powerless whispers we have against least-left morning
low nights   life   time   if driftwood love claim me   I
slide matter   marking empty alabaster moon like long
winter there   isolation   thinking: look   feel
treading them   they almost quiver feel KNOW   days
here too swept on   not stuck   brought off   not
seen   felt   thoughtless   how softly lightly   now
I bear grace past will   all built burden hovers awaiting
clamor   the coming night   splintered recollections
will you own certain recesses of dedicated brass?   you
opening   small whispered entry..................?   Pollock, 51

ART

for Ludwig Datené

His lens held a sea like rocks
from the side of a tossing vessel.
But the film couldn't see the colors
for the movement of up and down,
and clouds that shut out the sun,
in the snap of the snarling sea,

and left him a picture of rocks,
a film of hard-labor cut out
of a field of hammered stone,
and paint that had bled and blended.
He lost his way in the image
he held enlarged before him,

a rocklike Pollock of greens,
of blues and even of reds,
not a sea- but a lunar landscape,
not a lunar but Martian, maybe,
where convicts had worked in a swelter
and dropped in their tracks one day.

Now, looking flat at the thing,
hanging walled as a square on brown,
it tilted strangely away,
into the brown of the wall,
and no further angling would work.
What troubled him was that he saw,

clearly, in its strange unclearness,
the graph of a feckless life,

and terrain of the place where it lived,
his art in a criminal pile
of a hybrid of land and sea,
and the day of his germ in chaos,

spinning wildly forward in time
from where it must always have come,
some dimension of a kind unknown
to the rational light of day,
and he let the print fall from the wall
and slide at his feet on the floor.

And he walked there, on that sea
of carven and sharpened stone,
on that rocky path, where water
had frozen into strange land.
He would walk there, gone from this world,
till he found what it was he had lost.

ATGET

La génie c'est la patience.

Great Atget took his time.
A picture was no chance,
unlike a lucky rhyme
unknown in advance.

Patiently, he stood
waiting for the light.
His camera wore a hood.
The sun must come up right.

And now his photographs
show us Paris then.
And no one these days laughs
at such patient men

as pioneered the picture
so that painters paint
no more a literature
proving memory faint,

but finally engage
with true imagination,
while on every page
he shows La Belle, his nation.

RODIN, BALZAC, AND *THE THINKER*

Because assemblers will let us place atoms
in almost any reasonable arrangement . . .
they will let us build almost anything that
the laws of nature allow to exist.
 —*K. Eric Drexler, Engines of Creation*

Atomic transmigration was beyond Rodin,
who could not finally touch his statues into life.
And yet he must have seen the likeness of his art

to that of universal processes, stone into soul,
and felt the homeopathic nature of his magic,
the sympathetic magic of his mastered art.

But if Rodin could catch an atom in his hand,
then he could build a living man from solid rock,
then he could make him think and be a tender lover,

could make Balzac emerge from what was holding him
and step down from his pedestal and have a drink
and tell, as only Balzac could, where he had been,

of what the world of rock was like before the soul.
But once out of the rock, Balzac could never tell
Rodin about the rock, nor why his touch must fail;

and if Balzac could never tell, how could Rodin
make great Balzac march forward from the marble slab?
It must be that Rodin confronted his conundrum

and sat down like *The Thinker*, head in mighty hand,
and thus inspired himself to yet another task—
to show poor humankind its constant puzzlement.

CAREER

I Norma Jean

I was a student then and waited in
the office of a famous acting coach,
and in came Marilyn Monroe. I grinned,
but she was self-involved, not to approach.
It had begun to rain, the window showed,
and she showed too, rain on her London Fog,
blue scarf, pulled tight below her chin and bowed,
rain running down her face. I was agog,
but tried my best not to disturb her, not
to make my presence felt. She looked afraid,
and pale, and wet, and small, and sad. She seemed
so regular a pretty girl that I forgot
she was a movie star and saw instead
a girl from home of whom I'd always dreamed.

II At a Classic Film Revival

Walking down the darkened aisle, he stops,
shadows leaping about him. Behind the credits
rolling down the screen, the detective
hero strides a shabby street of cheap hotels.
I know that neighborhood. I know that boy.
Old Technicolor flashes in a static blizzard.
Still, he sees, or thinks he sees, *himself*
up there, behind the striding hero,
innocently tailing him, his own trench coat
collar up against the wet wind that was
blowing that day—for now he remembers
that day, but does not recall a camera

or a striding movie star ahead of him.
Someone shouts,
                        Sit down! Sit down!
He gropes the dark for a seat, dislodging others,
who spill popcorn and sticky drinks down on
his tissued pants and rundown shabby loafers
but keeps on looking up—at the image of himself!
—*Oh so beautiful, that blooming boy!*
He wants to be in Fred's Bar, to tell the flies
that he is in a film, or, at least, in the credits.
It doesn't matter that he got no credit, nor got paid.

ICH BIN EIN DICHTER

I

Nein! Ich bin drei Dinge.
Natürlich, bin ich ein Mann;
aber das ist nicht viel.
Es wäre etwas.
Es wäre ein Anfang;
aber es ist ein Ende.
Sie können aber sagen:
Ach, 's ist doch nur ein Mensch.

II

Und ich bin ein Arbeiter
doch keiner beachted meine Arbeit.

III

Und drei: der Tod treibt herum
wie ein wahnsinniger Vogel,
und ich bin der goldne Kern.

ELEGY FOR PATRICK HARWOOD-JONES

I

So now the sea is calm, the ebb and flow;
and all the tides of life have come and gone;
and Peace reigns in the mind of my dear friend,
instated like a great calm king, benevolent
and tender, to regard his new domain.

II

My head, an egg, cracked, addled, petrified,
incompetent to solve the cosmic riddle,
in Spring brings forth a Phoenix, but in Fall
twins blackbirds, Time and Death. I write in Fall,
five years from you, in friendship and remembrance.

III

"A man must have his mysteries," you said.
So now, my thoughts upon you, I am blank
to understand, to make some sense of death.
Look! For memento mori I possess
your spectacles, in which I see myself.

IV

Merely the blankest statement, tragic gesture,
as when some friendly hand is flung aloft
above the crowd, remains to keep; the vespers
of evening memory; the prayer I coughed
to save your life that wasn't saved by me.

WATERFALL

for Ed Bosch

Reflected mountains
bushes trees and below
crazily slanting vistas
gems half buried
in landscapes
as if the flow
had discovered
a sunken treasure
unmanufactured
axes arrowheads
raw material
of a stone culture
and casting over all
over reflected
layered escarpments
tiny rock flowers
bits of blue
scarlet and gold
reflected skies
full of mysterious
darting shadows
unseen birds
swaying branches
wind-caught leaves
and wading a long bend
found Ed on a great
rock arms akimbo
chest heaving
then pointing up
through thick trees
and followed his gaze

seeing deeply hidden
in brush bramble
tangle a small cabin
grayed by weather
Ed called "Poet!"
Wading on waist-
deep we came to
our umpteenth
small waterfall
and had to climb
our way around it
up a steep embankment
of black mud and green moss
fingers and feet
ripping upheaving
fine smooth moss
and then at last
able to drop down
into cool water
mud washing from feet
dipping hands
in purling water
and washing mud
from knees
water here only
four or five
inches deep
but stepping into it
surprised by its
force pressure
for an instant
thinking it
might topple me
but learning
one must flow

not fight the stone
underfoot
put down a foot
with all its
muscles loose
let it find
its shape on the earth
looked up
saw an
overawing
escarpment
circling in deep
beautiful
rainbow folds:
hitting an odd rock
the waterfall fell
out like an opening fan
or like two falls
translucent lovers
entwined and
undulating
and above them
below the deep
blue heaven
a cliff hung
weighted with trees
I knew a magic place
when I saw one
and vision
an Indian chief
stood on the cliff
smiling
in full regalia

NEW MAN ON THE DOCKS

> *It's a pseudo-death, more or less. Your whole system is paralyzed and you give all the appearance of death.*
> —Working, Studs Terkel

The new men were issued key-chain badges
with numbers on them, then they were
divided into workgangs and marched off,
each gang to a different tractor-trailer truck,
to off-load its vegetable green-and-gold,
later to be loaded aboard the great gray ship
that walled out the harbor view like a dam.
The trucks had aluminum ladder-like rollers
placed from their side doors and resting atop
three or four stacked crates. Half the gang
lived down at the receiving end of the roller,
and the other half lived aboard the truck
and began shooting sixty-pound crates of cabbages
down at breakneck speed. He watched
the men ahead of him catch these whooshing,
wire-wrapped rectangular cannon-balls,
the bottom inside corner ramming
into their shoulders, sending them staggering
backwards, until it was his turn
and one of them was placed in position
to be fired at him. He heard a Samaritan
behind him say, "Don't catch it in the neck,
kid." He raised his shoulder and was glad
for his leather jacket when the concussion came.
He dragged the crate down from his shoulder,
then back, catching another crate, and off
and back in the line again. Soon the crates

were being fired at him with such speed
he fell into an hypnotic trance. He had no self
left, just a dream of whooshing crates,
chalk marks, and blurred, pained faces,
and didn't wake until he felt the planet
roll out of its orbit. The universe,
the quiet and beautiful music of the spheres,
was crashing. He stood waiting for the rhythmic thud,
and no thud came. He looked up. Everyone
was leaving him, shambling off without a word.
He wiped the fast-freezing sweat from his face
on the backs of his gloves. Then he shambled away, too,
through the dismal morning light of the waterfront,
by ancient, devastated buildings, dreaming of sleep.

KWAME AND DUTCH

*Note: In Africa, AIDS is often
referred to as the thin disease.*

We worked on the New York docks,
off-loading ships, on-loading trucks.
Sick and a former junkie, Kwame shirked.
He bled from the rectum when he worked.
The bleeding reached such an intensity,
we had to rush him to the Emergency.
Later, the surgeons cut the grapes away.
Released, he hobbled to a bar nearby
as if he walked on broken glass,
a knot of stitches in his new tight ass.

He put a long-boned arm over my shoulder
in the manner of someone wiser, older,
and wheezed, "Dutch, I'm going to die.
The blood tests say that I
've got the thin disease."
He gave my shoulder a squeeze.
"I got it from being heedless
about the stinking dirty needles."

And soon, he took sick. The white bed
was empty but for Kwame's wave-crested,
black skull, and the clear, draining hoses.
Next to his bed was a jar of posies
one of his girlfriends had brought.
Now Ghana was a faraway thought,
but I was there, with him, near.

He could see me clearly
if he looked, holding his bony hand

that wore an African wedding band—
and I am there now, again, as he lingers,
our funny different-colored fingers
entwined, though pulling apart,
breaking my hard Dutch heart.

SWANS AT NEW ROCHELLLE

I counted twenty-one swans
at the New Rochelle yacht
basin, while I sipped white wine.

Twenty-one! I thought of
Yeats, who counted nine-and-fifty
before he had well done.

But twenty-one swans is good
counting. So is one swan,
swans being swans and not

lesser creatures, like cars.
Twenty-one swans made me feel
proud, glad that I could count.

Often, I feel ashamed of it,
sitting in the window of a
corner cafeteria, counting.

NERVES IN THE NEW HOUSE

I heard the calls again,
through the long night,
material manifestations
of the ghostly immaterial.
Or, if you are not
of a fanciful turn of mind,
if you prefer the
psychological explanation
for every sort of phenomenon,
it must have been the wind I heard,
and the house settling
(a hundred year old brownstone
creaks), the water pipes gurgling,
the radiators knocking, the cats
in the yard outside, skulking,
and transformed these in my mind
into the calls I thought I heard
that sounded to me like the crying out
of the earth's multitudinous dead.
And what I felt they told me
of my life's unmeaning,
my time's misuse,
my soul's fear,
out of the vastness,
the great underdarkness,
caused me to writhe
in my wet white sheets
and sweat, glistening,
like a great, gray worm.

KINDRED SPIRITS

I

The kindred dead have taught me how to sing.
They hover in the wind at night, I say,
and chant in dirges while they're hovering
in readiness to hold my breath away.
I've heard the dead elm's charry branches bend
under the weight of Nobody-at-all,
until a greater ruggedness would rend,
were it desirable to them, and fall.

II

I know they're in my mind—they tell me so—
down deep within the labyrinthine lobes;
they dance and whistle in the wind, I know,
somewhere inside the gray and outer robes.
But they project themselves into my yard
and frolic like the children of their past,
obscene and awful, shrunken up and charred,
that I may see their funeral at last.

III

They fall upon my sleep and, when awake,
they mock me underneath the midnight moon.
They say that I am drowning in the lake,
they tell me I will strangle on a spoon.
I can't so much as take a simple bath
without the water rising to the rim
and looking at me with a look of death,
as though to say, This is the end of him!

IV

What have I done to them? Why torment me?
I know the inner laughter they must feel.
I've seen that bird, reflected in the sea,
that made the Mariner go mad, until
he troubled purity with his sad tale
and dragged the wedding guest down with the dead.
I do not know if I shall rise or fall
or live as something different instead.

PART TWO

THE POWER GAME

THE POWER GAME

The king is weak, the enemy has planned,
the queen is powerful and vain, and vain,
and everywhere there is a helping hand.

The enemy has landed on the land!
Who is afraid of fear? The pain! The pain!
The king is weak, the enemy has planned.

The pawns go forth and die. They understand
their queen is beautiful, not plain, not plain,
and everywhere there is a helping hand.

Her knights are paramours. They leap or stand
according to her will. The gain! The gain!
The king is weak, the enemy has planned.

The bishop says a prayer. The castle's spanned
by other drummers than the rain, the rain,
and everywhere there is a helping hand.

Yes, trouble plagues the kingdom. Undermanned
and understaffed, they try, and strain, and strain.
The king is weak, the enemy has planned,
and everywhere there is a helping hand.

INCIDENT

The day is a blown and bending one.
The sky is puffs and smears.
The street is coats like flags
and wind-pushed faces,
eyes, isolation and confusion.
At the wild square
the flocking birds eye me,
move in little rushes.
A metal man, a hero, stands braving the wind,
unfeeling. I sit at his feet.
Near me a man seats himself,
then a thin girl, another man:
suddenly there are many, a crowd.
Across the square, in phalanx,
march men. They wear one earring each.
They are armed with small silk squares.
My group stands at attention, hums.
The phalanx halts. A man steps from it,
strikes the thin girl with the silk.
She is prostrate, bleeding.
One by one they step forward,
strike, and one by one they fall.
The last is struck. The hum has stopped.
The phalanx marches off.
I sit alone; begin to hum;
look at the hero.

COPPERHEADS

The New York Draft Riots

Vanish these walls, vanish this wealth, with visionary
  eyes that see
back to hot July 1863. Vanish where wealth shines
  shopping on Fifth
Avenue, five minutes from the lion-braced library,
  where I turn down
my book. Vanish these great, gray walls, to see when
  this mirage
was another, of a white-winged building housing
  motherless humanity.
Try to see out of the eyes of two hundred frightened
  black orphans

and their saviors, or, better, the eyes of one little girl
  under her bed,
who is to be beaten to sleep and burned alive. They
  come now, the first,
malignant rumble of mobs is heard. A giant, bearing a
  huge American flag,
appears. Ten thousand men and women follow. They
  shout: *NO DRAFT*;
shout: *KILL THE NIGGERS*! One mob of ten thousand,
  among many mobs,
one mad mob, is coming; Copperheads coming; but
  Mary doesn't know

what they are. Snakes, she is told; and, people like
  snakes. Snakes?
What does it mean? But behind them the sky is red, as
  if the sun had
set in broad day, as if it had hit the earth and bounced
  back to the sky

in cones of flame, like upward teeth, serrating the
   downward, hot blue.
The fireworks for the Fourth, a week before, had shaken
   her.
Looking everywhere, she saw no arms to hold her.
   BOOM BOOM!

Now again—*BOOM BOOM!* But this is wilder, worse.
   She caps her ears,
her eyes rolling for a mother, while the giant bearing
   Old Glory juts
his lantern jaw toward the white-winged building where
   she hides terror
in tears, holding her braided, ribboned head as, between
   her ten-year-old
fingers, distorted clangor of malignant mob-voice
   penetrates with
curses and screams of coves and harpies, liquored-up
   looters, drink-mad,

blood-mouthed molls, ill-wind-shifted, now, toward
   Mary in the white-winged
Colored Orphan Asylum on Fifth Avenue, the ghost-
   building, inside tall
wealth, that I can reach in five minutes from this great,
   gray library,
close my book and walk out into the Fifth Avenue
   festival of limousines
and be inside of its smoldering, ectoplasmic doors with
   the orphan children,
who are always poorest, with Mary, who hides under
   her bed, her eyes

spraying terror, shutting her ears to the Fourth of July
   or, now,

a week later, to the flag-bearing giant leading a mob
   through the present
affluent Fifth Avenue shoppers to *BOOM BOOM KILL
   THE NIGGERS
NO DRAFT KILL*, outside the library window on Fifth
   Avenue, inside of,
behind, through, the tremendous modern traffic stalled
   at red, frustrated,
Manhattan-honking. *KILL!* Mary sees feet, fast feet.
   She doesn't

understand that the children are being herded out to
   safety, to
Blackwell's Island on the East River. Mary sees feet
scurry by her bed, sees a watery world, like one sub-
   merged, when she
looks out. Then, above her bed, something huge and
   malignant appears,
something too big. An evil thing! She will not come out
   from under, she will
not, as the white-winged building shakes like her body
   with battering

and the doors are pulled from their hinges. Mary tries
   to find her mother
inside of herself, and finds an entrance and a dark hall.
   She goes in,
finds herself upright, her legs steady under her. She
   pats the bodice
of her pink dress, straightens her pink ribbon—for she
   knows her mother
waits at the end of the dark hall—as the giant lifts her to
   the sky—
knows a door will open at the end of the dark hall—and
   dashes her ten-

year-old body down. Great doors open, her mother
    shimmers with beauty,
with long, strong, brown open arms. In fury at his loss,
    the giant howls
after the escaping orphans, and flames rise up around
    him as he moves,
touching, touching the pitiful beds of orphans, touching
    and torching,
his small mad head hissing, spitting curses upon
    Lincoln, the top-
hatted ape, and Greeley, and niggers, niggers, for his
    tongue would fork

with curses if it could, as the white-winged asylum
    crumbles
in flames inside of the facades of now with its *BEEP
    BEEP* of prosperity.
As if the great library walls had vanished, as if the
    market values of now,
with their multi-millions of construction, were trans-
    parent, there
stands the Colored Orphan Asylum, and there inside is
    Mary, hiding under
her bed. Mary and the flag-bearing giant. Mary and the
    mad mob. I lean

back in my library chair and push up my glasses. I am
    trying to see more
clearly. I think I don't understand any more than Mary
    did,
as the lion-braced library walls form around me again,
    shutting me off
from my shopping, struggling fellow Americans on
    Fifth Avenue, outside,

who cannot see the white-winged Colored Orphan
  Asylum as they pass it.
But I know that all hurts must be outlived as humanity
  presses forward.

NIGHTINGALE

Warriors honor you
because you changed
forever the way
wounded were cared for.
You lifted your lamp
in dark Scutari, where
the wounded could see you
plunging amidst their cramped cots,
merciful gifts from your pocket
when England refused to expend
on working-class wounded,
the blood-giving soldiers
of Queen and Country.

THE KAISER COMES TO ORLANDO

for Uncle Austin Hopkins in Fond Memory

You are having another one of your crazy nightmares and a big gaping mustachioed mouth is chasing you up seven post-Great-War decades of the Twentieth century. You're keeping ahead, but you come to a red light, and you have to stop because beyond is nothing, or heaven, or hell, so you mark time, waiting, and the gaping mouth is catching up to swallow you, you who have pledged allegiance to the Moose, and you collapse your dry knees like folding chairs, you break and bend them until you are under the kitchen table and, when you look up and out, you are back there again and they are charging at you across no-man's-land, spiked helmets and long thin bloodguttered bayonets, and in Orlando you go to the V.F.W. and live in a house where the sun burns back blindingly off the flung newspaper, its date a liar making you nearly a hundred, and you look up from your muddy trench, your long, bolt-action Springfield, its stock tangled under your trenchcoated arm, barrel aimed out toward them over sandbags, and with your free hand you pat your pet rat. Little black clouds form and vanish. You think they are like exploding eight balls. You hear *FIRE!* And your nerves jerk the trigger, while still petting the traitorous rat that scurries off. *OVER THE TOP!* You hear things crashing about you: the table, sugar bowl, coffee cups, a whole sideboard filled with dishes ... And now a Great Power is holding you down and it is the cartoon face of the Hun, the fat rat-face and mustache of the Kaiser. He wants to eat you as he would a Belgian baby. Then you awake voiceless in England, a fire-breather, your elephant-nosed, goggle-eyed gas mask tangled, your sucking-for-breath, mustard-gassed lungs collapsed. Then you awaken in another hospital, in Orlando, Florida, seventy years later, and you are surrounded by strangers who say they are your family—they are strangers, of course, because you are still too young to marry, as Mother says you are, still too young for such responsibility, only a beardless boy from Hoboken in a slouch hat and brogans, an apprentice leatherworker commuting to Brooklyn, no scared-to-death doughboy in the Argonne and Belleau Wood, no Alzheimer's patient in a hospital bed in Orlando. And look, no jaywalker you! The light turns green for you to go!

CRUEL GAMES

I read somewhere about a wizard with computers,
a man who's made a myriad millions in the field,
who lives out in an island's perfect solitude
in order best to think about life's origins,
who seriously thinks our universe is bits
and bytes, a program made some cosmic Otherwhere.

We make computer games ourselves and love to play them,
why then might we not be a game for something else,
a smarter It, why might it not be true that we,
the world, the universe, are toys played in an Else,
a game called Life, or its equivalent in Else,
played by the happy children of the clever Its?

Truly the Demon of Intelligence must thrive
among the happy Its of Else in Otherwhere,
but one must notice all the cruelty of the game
and think that those in Else have not evolved as yet
to that high point that even we, their bits and bytes,
their pawns, aspire to daily in our average lives.

I must look up that article about the wizard
and find his name and write to him and ask him how
he thinks the whole thing works, and if the software used
is durable enough to keep us going on until
our progress takes us well beyond the happy Its
of Else in Otherwhere, who play such cruel games.

THE MURDER OF GARCIA LORCA

> *No es sueño la vida.*
> *¡Alerta! ¡Alerta! ¡Alerta!*

I tug the strings of my fear, my bad puppet, Diablo, and tap him about this space, my first and last stage, last props, last lights, behind and in front of my painted screen. See, I pull up a leg and he hops, hops, hops! Who are you, Diablo? Herr Hitler, con permiso. Then hop, Hitler, hop! Garcia will be dead when I do this jig under the Arc de Triomphe. Not amusing, Diablo. Be something else. I want light and color! Then look at my gypsy dress, all layered, laced, ribboned, and brocaded—scarlet, gold, and green. Feel the wide wind of my rich fan. Hear my diamonded castanets! When did you put that on? An instant ago, behind the screen, when you were talking. But now I'll be Franco and rise against the Republic. Another ugly joke! But in an instant, true! Just let me don this uniform. I love good fun, but this is wicked. Night must fall, Federico, even if it frightens you. Diablo, I command you, take off that uniform, with its golden shoulder-mops and scrambled eggs and salads. I wish I could drop the reins of your dark horse. Who am I now? Wait, I recognize you. You're a man from my hometown, a *granadino*. Your name is. . . *Diablo!* Yes, and I am jealous of your genius. I call you out! I name you Red! *Red, red, red!* I am a poet. I hate politics. Nevertheless, I charge you, Federico Garcia Lorca, with crimes against the state . . . of my ego. And what now? Bang, bang, you're dead! Am I dead, Diablo? In an unmarked grave! Is it dark, Federico? No darker than this dark century, Diablo.

LORCA DE PROFUNDIS

Like an elephant's trunk
cut off
my poetry trumpets blood
out of anger
as memory is drained in each
hoarse music
trumpets blood
like an elephant's trunk
cut off
for the helplessness of the mutilated
telling the dark history
of the ivory poacher's greed
& machete
that felled the musical beast
in a trade for money
potency for the limp
the erotic for the dull
but is merely the dust of the dead

like an elephant's trunk
cut off
my poetry trumpets blood
telling dark history

MOONTIME

The Greeks measured Earth by its shadow on the moon. Thoreau said, Time is a stream I go fishing in. Ford said, History is the bunk. Sumerian writing, done on clay tablets, shows about 2000 pictographic signs. The moon is a bad woman because she is very romantic. We all know the trouble romance can get you in. I am romantic tonight, amorous with the moon. O how many leaves lay scattered? I guess thousands, and I have a study that agrees with me. When you pay for a study, you get what you want. Therefore, all studies are romantic and have a dark side like the moon. Theodora, the Byzantine empress, died in 548, one of a kind. Her death was a big relief to some of her subjects. Five years later disastrous earthquakes shook the entire world. The house I live in was built much later. I leave the actual count to you. The first water-driven mechanical clock was constructed in Peking in 1090, the wrist watch around the turn of the Twentieth century. I've got a digital that I can read in the dark. I can also read the chained and sailing moon from here. Its glyphs of pox say the odds are against us.

COST OF FREEDOM

The Vanderhorns own most of Arkanstate,
the Heebeejeebeezes own Kent;
a few score others own the rest of Freedom,
and we, the people, pay the rent.

BALLADE OF PRIDE

> *They're a proud people.*
> *—The Frugal Gourmet*

Of every group whose food he shows,
    this Doctor of Diet, this Frugal Gourmet,
this chef whose goodness simply glows
    and who doesn't know there'll be hell to pay,
    we need not ask just what he'll say,
for he shouts it from the TV steeple
    like the old ham actor in the play
When the Master Race Meets the Chosen People.

He shouts of any group he knows,
    "A *proud* people, those from Cathay;
those, too, from Kilimanjaro's snows."
    He doesn't know there'll be hell to pay
    when these proud people meet someday.
I wish all this pride would go and sleep ill.
    But meantime let me get out of the way
When the Master Race meets the Chosen People.

Proud Capulets, proud Montagues,
    proud Hatfields and real McCoys all day,
proud people everywhere, God knows,
    and who doesn't know there'll be hell to pay?
    They make you want to kneel and pray
that you needn't hear another peep till
    ugly young pride is old and gray
When the Master Race meets the Chosen People.

When Evil meets Good, as it will on the way,
who wouldn't know there'd be hell to pay?
Heaven's buried beneath a deep hill
When the Master Race meets the Chosen People!

THE IDEOLOGUES:
OR, THE TWENTIETH CENTURY REVISITED

> *Embrace the butcher, but*
> *change the world...*
> —Bertolt Brecht: The Measures Taken

Brecht

Pound

Brecht

What to say of them?

Why to say it?
Because they have given and taken importantly.
Because they have helped humankind and hurt it.

The two of you.

At what point does it become apparent,
even to genius,
that means must be golden,
that means are the only end?

Bert,
Ezra,
think of Confucius
whom you both so admired.

When you embrace the butcher
you embrace dead meat,
Brecht,

Pound.

Brecht,
never when mad murderous Uncle Joe
purged did you utter revulsion.
You knew your Hobbes, knew human nature.
You'd met the Kremlin himself.
You knew it was power not people he loved.
And later
after the rising of the 17th June
53 when the workers were shot in the Stalinallee
and the Soviet tanks rumbled again in Berlin
and you submitted,
submitting your letter supporting Ulbricht
and the censors erased every word you had written
but your statement of Socialist Party attachment
and you guiltily dreamed of fingers of workers
pointing you out,
did you wistfully wish that the State
would wither away?

And Pound,
not till Benito swung by his jackbooted
hobnailed heels
did you quit.
Not till they stopped you.

The measures taken embraced the butcher,
Brecht,
Pound,
odd duo,
Spartans,
seeking the hideous Platonic perfection,
the Toolmaker's State,

to make a machine of the human condition,
an ideology of deus ex machina.

Here are your jacks-in-the-box of Pandora:
sad angry young Schicklgruber,
failure of failures,
architect of frustration,
Der Führer, king of kitch,
more of a murderous joke
than Chaplin could make him,
Capo dei Capi
of Benito, himself no bundle of joy;
and Joe Dzugashvili,
Stalin,
self-styled "Man of Steel."
Mere murderers, the three of them.

Brecht,
didn't you notice the comic-book element?
Pound,
what of the jackboots,
the leather?
Didn't you heed the automaton goosestep?
Poets,
didn't you listen to the demagogic language?
But the ends justify
what,
dynamic duo?
The death of millions?
Hitler, hater of Jews,
Stalin, murderer of Mandelstam
for a printed reproof,
Benito, jackbooted journalist,
the three of them: murderers.

Where is the golden omelet they made?
The living became the dead,
the left wing and the right
wing are the feathery dead
and the fool's-golden bird in ashes.
To rise again?
Always,
always,
sadly, a phoenix of filth.
Whom, what, to blame?

Not the disorder of slow trains,
not the criminal economics of Versailles,
nor alas in the name of God or goodness the Jews,
but ourselves,
our soulless, soul-seeking selves,
ourselves,
the paranoids,
the schizoids,
for hearing voices,
voices of comic-book heroes,
men-of-steel,
ourselves who sanction action,
sociopathic action,
hurrying history,
hurrying heaven-on-Earth,
the on-time trains,
the golden wheat of the Five-Year Plan,
that millennium of earthly dominion,
the Thousand-Year Reich,
so we can get on with it
and in on it,
before Time takes us to our soul's Nowhere,
disapproving love,
patience with human error,

failure, weakness,
tender Bert,
generous Ez.

For a theater, Bert!
For a microphone, Ez!
For a theater,
with your Austrian passport
and your West German publisher!
for a microphone,
with your half-baked hatred of Jews
and your crazy Social Credit!

Were you naive?
Were you mad?

For a theater!
And a mike!
For a playhouse
and a megaphone!
For an audience
and a pulled-up vanity,
Bert,
Ez,
you tender and generous poetic hopes
and tyrannical human disappointments!
When poets don't know any better
what is their use on this planet?

Plato would NOT
have banned you from his perfect State,
Brecht,
Pound,
and that's your disgrace,
you lessons to be learned,

you slaves to your own slaver,
you paladins of palaver!

Where is the end of murder?

Oh for the gay days of the Hitler-Stalin Pact!

For a playhouse
and a megaphone!
For a dollhouse
and a rolled-up newspaper!
Hurry history!
Hurry the Communist heaven,
the heaven-on-earth with the workers underfoot!
Hurry the Fascist heaven!
Hurry the race white as worms!
Hurry the Platonic,
the Ideal,
the Perfect,
the Procrustean,
hurry,
hurry,
hurry,
come and get it!

PARIS RECIDIVIST

The sea-tax brought us down: my state,
after all, was operating a protection
racket, as you Chicagoans might call it.
It was a dirty game, but there you are,
it was the only game in town.
Located as we were over the mouth of
the Hellespont, we controlled all traffic
going east. For a while, everybody paid,
and we got on quite well. Troy was small,
even by the standards of the age: she had
nothing to sell—oh, nothing worth
considering—but she had the trade route,
had it by its watery throat, and everybody knew
and didn't seem to mind. Of course,
there's always something building,
but our hold was strong. No tax,
no trading with the East. It all seemed
fair enough and, somehow, to the others,
a natural thing. Then I did it,
gave the Greeks exactly what they needed:
an excuse. Helen, poor Helen, she gloried
in one thought: that it was she,
and not the sea, for whom we fought.

LIFE, A WESTERN

The dark matter of the universe
is that which filled the void
after the Big Bang, the smoke
of black powder swirling from the barrel
of Billy the Kid's six-gun.

Who exploded this dark dust?
Who squeezed the trigger on the universe?
How many must fall dead
before the Kid will holster
his garrulous gauche gun?

Si, amigo, this is the disease;
but never mind the cure;
let us learn a lesson from the cause.
The lesson is that to be born
is mighty good, but do not draw

on one so fast. But no! Draw!
And when you die with a neat
black hole in your bleeding heart,
fan the hammer as you fall
and bite the dust.

WAR COVERAGE

I THE WAR OF THE NINE AND THE SIX

Jane Goodall tells of the Nine and the Six,
the Chimps' War,
of how a tribe of fifteen male chimps
divided, Nine and Six,
and made new camps.

The Nine, she writes, because stronger
numerically, attacked
the Six, several to one,
isolating, murdering each of them,
until there were none.

These had been sons and fathers,
friends and brothers,
but had become two nations,
sniffing at borders—
foreign relations.

II THE MANWOLF

Among the wolves a tale is told
of how, when Moon is full,
some normal-seeming wolf becomes
a Manwolf, stalking, murdering all.

His fangs grow short and flat in front,
his paws grow long and fingered.
He holds a firestick in a hand,
makes fire with what is called a trigger.

The cubs who listen to the tale
howl in fear of such a fright
as wolf that looks like human horror,
naked, murdering day and night.

III Bad News

tonight (and with gleeful
   morbidity, going on
to give us a variety
of unuseable deaths
disasters mayhem murder)

But the question is
why do we need them
   "It's what you thrill to,"
wrote Lawrence, *"and if you
thrill to rape, murder . . ."*

It is inside us,
the ancient
crocodile down deep
its eyes opening, closing
its jaws aching

Ah yes, bad
news tonight
folks (and our
ears perk up,

our noses twitch,
smelling blood)

THE CULTURAL REVOLUTION
Three Poems in the Chinese Manner

I OLD CHINESE COUPLE

Their heads are touching:
one pillow in the middle of the night,
one dream from here to there
because they've been together so long.

In their dream,
they are meeting for the first time, again.
He remembers, she remembers, they remember.

Their arms are around each other.
They are warm together.
This is perfect.
But morning is near to mention
that everything is a revolution.

II A KISS OUTSIDE HER DOOR

A kiss is two rumors:
her rumor of me in her,
and my rumor of me in her.

No, a kiss is three rumors:
the third rumor is of Yin or Yang,
the child. The rumor of a child.
It is the child in each of us
who is the rumor of me in her,
her rumor and my rumor.

A kiss is one rumor.
Listen to the neighbors talk.

III Remembering You

There is always more to remember.
Memory is like a mountain forest
inside my head—trees and trees,
leaves and leaves and leaves,
and there is always more to remember.
Now there is you, and everything about you.
And now there is that you are gone
and everything that has happened since.
Memory of you is like a new high mountain
and the trees are thick with leaves
and then all the leaves fall off
and the mountain sinks.

AS GOOD AS IT GETS

I

Why does the Pope's tall rocket hat point up?
Because God's will has been removed from matter
so that we might decide what's right and wrong—
we, who are madder than the maddest hatter,
our every word a snippet of mad song;
who've served the heads of people on a platter,
or blood in a tureen for Sunday soup!

II

Karl Barth said we were no damned good. Yes, he
shared Jeffers' view of humankind. Karl Barth
was probably correct, if we agree
to measure by his standard. But what hearth
was ever won or kept by kindness? What we do,
if measured by that which we could do, seems
somehow to suit all but the elitist few.

AN EVENING WITH "BLOOD"

Art, being bartender, is never drunk;
And magic that believes itself, must die...
            —Peter Viereck

Just call when you hit town, the great poet wrote.
I like your work, and we must talk about it.
He lived one red state down, an hour's drive,
and I had business there. I called him up,
and he invited us to "Come right out,"
to hurry to his house, "and help me drink
a quart of Southern Comfort that a student
of mine has given me—I need some help.
Today above all days I need some help—
a falling down, and then a falling out!
How soon?" he asked. "As soon as we can get there."
The bard swayed hugely at his door to greet us.
"I've got *your* names locked in. You call me Blood.
It was my nickname when I was a kid.
I like your husband's work," he told my wife.
"It's very individual—which I,
and Emerson, and Wallace Stevens, think
is most important. Possum doesn't, though,
but he is wrong." The lakeside house was empty
but for the three of us, a huge TV—
the N.F.L. in combat filled the screen—
and roaring fans and players, who loomed large.
"It's an old game. I like to run the plays
and second guess with twenty-twenty hindsight.
I tore your poems apart like that and found
I couldn't take much out—that's good!
Don't write, re-write! I drop them and go back.
This took five years—to make a wall of words

stand up like that. I worked spasmodically.
The novel took ten years, but it was worth it.
It brought a lot of money, and the movie,
and the chance for me to play a part myself.
That's Blood up on the screen, that character.
He'd scare the shit out of you, wouldn't he?
That wasn't acting, that was really me.
You see this arrow? Penetrate skull-bone.
Know how to use a crossbow? Here, I'll show you.
Up—like that—that's right. Now you aim and fire.
Bring down a rhino, that thing would. But Blood
says that you need another drink, and then
I'll play the banjo for you. Read me this one—
the one about the mad marine. I *love* it,"
he told my wife. "I love the really mad ones.
Did you see how I got myself arrested?
Drunk driving. What I do is brownbag out
into the woods and turn my highbeams on
and try to see above them, not the helmet
of ordinary life down here. You too?
We yearn for levitation, flights of fancy.
I flew a lot of missions in the war.
Yes, Blood has done a major share of burning,
incendiaried towns and populations,
and no one ever understands you right
again when you've done that. My explanation
is in my poetry for those with guts to know.
As for the rest, I cannot help the world.
Above the high beams is the zodiac.
Let fools ask there about this fire-bombed world.
Blood's in the dark—like him—like you, sweet lady."

THE BOSNIAN CHERRY

> *. . . the explosion appears to have*
> *shocked the tree into blossom.*
> *—Reuters*

Friends, look with faithless unbelieving eyes
upon this miracle the bomb has wrought,
as now, in shocked conversion, I tell you
of spring against the devastated skies
of winter war, the hopelessness war brought,
and how, enveloped in explosive blue
of acrid smoke, this tree could still devise
beyond predictability. It caught
the shell's enormous heat, and grew
fluid with sap, miraculous with surprise
of spring, for all combatants to be taught
anew a faith unlearned by deathly cries,
a blossoming the human heart has sought
with every hopeful spring—a sweet-peace prize.

THE VIET VET

Christmas, the Old Bowery

> WHISKEY   70¢
> BIG BOY SHOT $1.10
> EYE-OPENERS 8 – 9 AM   80¢
> COVER YOUR COUGH!

Paper chains across the ceiling
and above the dark, desilvered mirrors,
and that snow that sprays out of aerosol cans
puffing out of the oddest places.
Sprigs of red and green here and there.
He'd been in worse places—
Da Nang, where he lost his dangler,
and he was just out
of a VA hospital that was
almost as bad. They said
he was fixed,
a no-sexed gimp.
He limped across the slimy tile floor,
his hip on fire,
careful to avoid the pot-holes,
and dragged himself on to a rickety barstool.
Ready, now, to celebrate Christmas.
    At three in the morning
    he staggered into the street.
    He drag-stepped
    through the new fallen snow
    leaving a slow Morse code of
    dots and dashes behind—
    Crippled, it said. Crippled.

Red, white, and blue neon blinked
through blinding flakes.
Freedom Flop it said.
"*Flea*-dom Flop," he answered.
"Got an empty dorm."
He dumped his change on the counter.
The clerk slid him a key,
a wooden stick attached
—88 painted on it.
He followed the red arrows
into an enormous gloomy room.
Rows of metal army cots.
Next to every cot
stood a wall locker
with a number painted on it.
It was the corps again.
Parris Island, Pendleton, Da Nang,
familiar—
home for Christmas.
He found 88,
dumped himself on it.
The room was cool,
but not cold.
On one side of him
a man lay
half-naked, coughing.
From other distances,
coughing fits echoed cavernously,
seeming to answer.
What were they trying to say
in their troubled sleep?
He had a bottle of red
bought at the bar—
glug, glug, glug.
He lay there and listened

to the stirrings and shiftings,
coughs, an occasional moan,
the gibberish of sleep.
Time ticked by. He dozed.
Then he heard a low,
trance-like voice,
somehow familiar.
Crucify him, crucify him!
What evil hath he done?
He sat up, threw his legs
over the side of the cot,
reached over and tapped
where a shoulder should be.
"Burden, that you?"
"Yes, yes; my name is Burden."
"Remember me? I know you. Da Nang."
"Da Nang?"
"Yeah. You saved my damn life
when they blew off my dick."
"Not I! Not I!"
    "Hey, fella," the clerk called,
    "I gotta clean this place up."
    Where was he going?
    His shrouded mind
    remembered his . . . nightmare?
    He found in the deep doorway
    of an empty store
    a newspaper bed
    that had been spread
    by some homeless
    soul such as himself
    and eased down
    upon it as the news came
    flying up to him from
    between his legs.

There was Christmas holly
at the top of the front page—
green leaves and red dots, berries—
but then the bold black date
told him that it was
Christmas—Nineteen-Sixty—what?
No! He shuddered with realization.
It was an anniversary.
He'd been on the Bowery
for . . how long? A year! No!
For an instant, he understood.
From the cave of his doorway refuge
he watched snow gently falling,
building up out on the street.
He tried to think.
These were not his clothes.
These laceless, scuffed,
old boondockers were not
his spit-shined shoes.
When had he come here?
How old was he now?
"Merry Christmas!"
he yelled, and fell back,
into a stupor of dreams,
some good, some bad.

FAMILY TRAGEDY

> *Show me a hero and I will*
> *write you a tragedy.*
>   —F. Scott Fitzgerald

Sweetheart of somebody else? It was Joy, she
cried, and your children were listening. Joy, she cried
       out, and again, Joy, she

  screamed, as you strangled her there, as the children
watched you in horror. It must be erased!
       They must never remember!

  Killing my cousins was hard, you said, hard. They
broke your crazed heart, because they'd never
       feared you. They went with you then, and

  breathed in the gas. Was it fear, or was trust there?
Children my age! Then you poured gasoline
       in the house and set it on

  fire. I was back from the service myself, when,
urged by my father, I visited you
       in your bedlamite world, a

  deathless and tortured thing, uncle. I winced at
sight of your burnt-paper face, and your
       fingerless hands, and your hair, so

  strange in its pattern. I'd seen you before, but
then, to a child, you seemed silver and gold,
       home from hell, and a hero.

NO

The world says No.
It has a genius for No.
Everything is No.
In the beginning was Yes
but the world says No.
By the world I mean the people.
The people No.
The people say No.
Authority says No.
Power says Yes to itself
but No to everyone else: it says No.
The police say No.
Sometimes, assuredly,
it is necessary to say No.
But I say No,
it is not always necessary to say No.
When the new child wishes
someone always says No.
When the dog barks
at his own wagging tail,
someone says No.
When the cat runs sideways,
his back up, playing,
someone says No,
you'll break the lamp.
The world says No.
When someone has a new idea,
the world says No.
The world likes to say No.
No means I know better.
No means I am stronger.
No means I am Yes and No.
The world says No.

The people say No.
Authority says No.
Power says No.
The police say No.
The teacher says No.
Love might even say No.
No is the genius of the world.

SOCIAL STUDIES

I AN EXPERIMENT IN GOVERNANCE

For some very important, and top-secret, reasons of State, the people who decided policy desired a change in the thought processes of the people they ruled, so they brought back the rusty old rack and began to stretch anyone who could not change his or her mind fast enough to suit them. Members of the public entered the Ministry of Thought at their natural height and came out about two inches taller. At last, we have become competitive, cried one of the people who decided policy. We shall become the capital of fashion, for we have some of the tallest models available. The Eureka-like quality of this observation caused the people who decided policy at the Ministry of Thought to completely forget what the very important, and top-secret, reasons were that caused them to bring back the rusty old rack in the first place. It was our intention from the beginning, they said with one voice, to open an international modeling agency: and things looked very promising for the new democracy until the people began to shrink back to their natural height, shrinking cartilage pulled down by gravity, as it were, and the people at the Ministry of Fashion, which the Ministry of Thought was now called, searched everywhere for their original reasons for bringing back the rusty old rack, but found that their drawers and filing cabinets, originally stuffed with strategic schemes, were now stuffed with dress patterns, Butterick having infiltrated the Ministry, which had become little more than a rag-shop. Such are the pitfalls of governance.

II THE ISLAND OF THE LEADERS

If kissing Napoleon's hemorrhoidal ass brings a little romance into the lives of historians, so be it, but he is still on the Island, along with Alexander the Great, Al Capone, Hitler, Stalin, Papa Doc, Il Duce, Tojo, Pol Pot, and you name the thugs, rogues, and rascals that have made this world a living hell for the nameless many, the rest of us. You may have guessed by now that I am not referring to Elba or St. Helena, but to the hitherto unknown Island of the Evil Ones, also known as the Island of the Thugs or the Island of the Stupid, Naughty, or Not-so-Nice, the location of which I am about to reveal. For, you see, I am a whistleblower. I know where the island is and what happens on it, and I am about to tell all. How do I know? I was sent there by the Historical Society to be a cummerbunned waiter and sworn never to reveal what I saw. Guess with whom I saw guess-who dancing—go ahead, guess! First, I will tell you who is *not* there. Elvis is not there. Elvis is in heaven. But Poppa Doc is there. Mae West is not there, but was that Caterina de Medici I saw dancing with Adolf? Il Duce dances on his hands. Now who would know that but someone who had been there? Of course, since I was only a lowly waiter on the Island, I cannot be expected to know the names of the innumerable "leaders" I saw there, with their burdens of medals and awards weighing them down, their epaulets, their badges and whistles. There were also the heads of many "great families," but the father of twelve who lived down the street from me when I was a kid, the one who worked himself to death to support his brood, was of course not there. No decent people were there, only monsters, which is why it is sometimes called the Island of Monsters, though it is of course known as the Island of the Great by its denizens. And one more thing I can say about the island, before I give away its location. It contains the worse tippers I have ever had the dissatisfaction of working for—real cheapos!

III THE FINAL TITHE

It was tax time, and the collectors had to deal with the usual greed—those who would hide what they still possessed behind tricks. A one-legged man danced up to a collector on two legs, in fear that if the collector knew that he had only one leg left he would have to surrender that. He had stuffed the false leg with bloody ground meat in an attempt at deception. The collectors laughed at this clumsy attempt at fraud and fined the man his left ear. All along the avenue the queue of cripples stretched and into the distance and on out of sight; for the State, having taken all else of value from the masses, had been reduced to taking cuts of meat from their bodies. Sometimes an eye was popped, sometimes a hand was cut off, depending entirely upon the taxpayer's indebtedness to the government. Sometimes so little was left of a taxpayer that he or she was brought forward on a stretcher, a mere skeleton with no more than a tenth of a life left, like a final tithe. In such case, the skin was stripped and the bones collected, resulting, finally, in death. The tax collectors were disgusted with the greed of these people, who showed signs of rational self-interest, rather than the altruism taught in the State schools. Without the flesh of the masses, it was wondered, how could the elite meet to eat? It was an infernal question, but above their pay scale, and they tried not to think of what would happen when no one was left but the elite themselves.

MURDERER'S DAY

Why is it always Murderer's Day?
Why can't it be different someday—tomorrow?
I wake to the sad and terrible news
and ask over coffee, "Why do I listen?
Why do I want to hear of the fire?
Why don't I turn from the morbid to music?"

Of all things on Earth I'm sure I love music
better than any—I could listen all day.
Is it fear that impels that the ghetto on fire
be the thing that I hear today and tomorrow,
though I ask over coffee why I should listen,
when I wake up, to such terrible news?

On goes the radio, blasting the news.
Why don't I tune in some beautiful music?
Why do I listen? Oh, why do I listen?
And why is it always Murderer's Day?
Why can't it be different someday—tomorrow?
Why is the ghetto always on fire?

Why is the world always on fire?
On goes the radio, blasting the news.
Why can't it be different someday—tomorrow?
Why can't the world be filled with sweet music?
Why is it always Murderer's Day?
So I ask over coffee, "Oh, why do I listen,

why, over coffee, do I sit and listen
to news of a world that's always on fire,
to the latest report of Murderer's Day?"
But on goes the radio, blasting the news
instead of some beautiful, good-morning music.
Why can't it be different someday—tomorrow?

Why can't it be different every tomorrow,
that never again over coffee we listen
to other than beautiful, good-morning music
describing how love is aflame and afire?
Why can't there be music instead of bad news
and no more reports about Murderer's Day?

Oh, don't let tomorrow be Murderer's Day!
Let there be music and no sign of fire,
and let us all listen to much better news!

A YELLOW CROSS

It's sad to write this on Memorial Day,
a sonnet on the subject of a draft
that's over now, but hasn't gone away,
like writing of a bribe, or ugly graft,
upon a day we honor something great,
like life these dead have given for our sake,
like courage in the face of awful threat,
like freedom we must make and then remake.

But being vet and patriotic codger,
I am compelled to write of one Unknown
whose grave is empty of its own draftdodger,
containing as it does no skeleton—
the green mound topped with a low yellow cross
as if ashamed to represent no loss.

COMMENTARY

I Aquarius

We dreamed the Golden Age
we wanted you to be,
our long hair hanging loose
and blowing in the wind,
our beads, our sandals,
jingling, flapping on our
feet, our feet encrusted
with good Woodstock
mud, smoking a joint,
and nodding, nodding word-
less, for it seemed we had
no words with which to
get beyond the chaos of the
conscience back in that time
of undeclared and endless war,
and back to Batman, Robin,
and the Joker's gang, where
Good was understandable,
for not at all complex,
and Evil slunk away,
its lesson learned.

III THE NEW

It has always been so,
that species were endangered,

indeed, that they died out,
but it has also always been so,

that they evolved into the life,
new animals, not birds that fly,

but burrowers but not moles, etc.,
and I wish I might be able

to wait for the one I have in mind,
the one with no body, the one

made of spirit, a nebulous
laughing creature, a music

of a thing, which I have faith
is somewhere out there, coming.

DIRGE FOR THE DEAD STUDENTS
(Kent State University, Ohio, 1970)

She'd only come to look
When bullets broke her flesh
A frosh, she held a book
  When bullets broke her flesh
  With almost wistful sighs
  Her face was round and fresh
With almost wistful sighs
The bullets raped her body
With almost wistful sighs
  They pierced her gentle body
  And her book dropped open to
  A page all torn and bloody
Her book dropped open to
A torn and bloody page
Containing nothing new
  A torn and bloody page
  Each child must learn to read
  A "History of Our Age"
Each child must learn to read
O study, students, study
This "History of Greed"
  O study, students, study
  Learn what they want from you
  Another age as bloody
Is what they want from you
Another age befouled
And nothing else will do
  Another age befouled
  By Great-Granddaddy's Greed
  (No wonder Ginsberg Howled!)
O Great-Granddaddy's Greed
Sucks, like a Vampire Bat,

The blood of his living seed
  Sucks, like a Vampire Bat
  The blood of our youth away
  Sucks, like a cornered rat,
The Pestilence of Our Day
And spits into our faces
The horrors of Our Day
  And spits into our faces
  Spreading disease and death
  That virus among the races
Spreading disease and death
Destruction throughout the world
With its maddening murderous breath
  Destruction throughout the world
  That Malthusian explanation
  Picture the bombs being hurled
That Malthusian explanation
And a baby crying for shelter
While the Senate is on vacation
  And a baby crying for shelter
  And her mother and father dead
  And the bombs dropping helter-skelter
And her mother and father dead
And the President making decisions
(Who will his daughter wed?)
  And the President making decisions
  Search and Destroy is the way
  And the President making revisions
Destroy all their crops on the way
And the baby is blown to pieces
While the President goes to pray
  And the baby is blown to pieces
  While the President speaks to God
  And the rich collect rent on their leases
While the President speaks to God

And the students are shot for complaining
And the Haves of the world think it odd
  That the students (who Have) are complaining
  (These children have so much to learn!)
  And the government's busy explaining
For these children have so much to learn
In double-talk tripled twice over
How we keep what we get when we earn
  In double-talk tripled twice over
  How Ends do all Means justify
  In News-Speak all wrapped up in clover
How Ends do all Means justify
And death to the man who denies it
So, hush up, dear students, or die!
  For death comes to him who denies it
  As many dead children could tell
  And praise to the bastard who buys it
As many dead children could tell
And four dead students provided
A proof in the sun when they fell
  These four dead students provided
  Us all with a living example
  That day in the sun when they tried it
Gave us proof and a living example
Of what the "Great" in their greed are about
And four dead students are ample
  To show what the State is about
  (Christ, any one baby who died
  Should have left us no shadow of doubt!)
Now four young students have died
Shot dead in the name of the law
(But in fact for the lies they denied)
  SHOT DEAD IN THE NAME OF THE LAW
  FOR THE TERRIBLE TRUTH THAT THEY SAW.

HOLY ORDERS

I SCENARIO

There was a young priest
who stalked the pornographic
night of the X-rated
movie houses and the
prostituting streets
outside them in what had
become a sexual compulsion.
Sometimes he felt that he had lost
all control of himself and
with that loss his very soul.
But his soul was saved through
the confession of his sins
and their forgiveness
by a fellow priest who
was not his own publicly
acknowledged confessor
but a fellow sinner,
an older priest who had had
a twenty-year quasi-marriage
and who would in turn ask
the young priest for
absolution after
confessing to him. When
the young priest made
confession to his acknowledged
confessor and spiritual guide
a little later, he had only
to confess to the evil
thoughts of the days since
he last stalked the streets,

thereby keeping his
spiritual guide in the dark.
He behaves as if in a
dream when he is in the grip
of this compulsion, as if
he himself has become a
character in the dirty
movie he is watching,
and in this state of
disassociation picks up
the first prostitute he sees,
and, with release, becomes
guilt-ridden and disgraced
until he must seek out
his secret-confessor.
He will find a telephone
within minutes of the event,
plug in the number, wait,
and say in a voice
thick with mixed emotions
of shame and anger,
"I must see you."
His secret confessor
never refuses,
no priest does,
but he will take
the confession with a
heavy heart, for
his friend and
for himself. The
confession, it seems,
has become part of
the compulsion, as both
have come to suspect.
Advice is traded,

elements of which might
have proven helpful to
either priest, but none
has been acted on,
until . . .

II THE NUN

I am looking at the bay
on the Staten Island ferry
watching the waves
crisscrossing each other
watching the wakes
of the wooden-shoe tugs
and the smoke
from their shoehorn stacks
catching Liberty
in the corner of my eye
but I notice the pretty young nun
as one notices a gull
or a cloud
I take in her youth
as I turn to the sea
of the bay
as one notes lovely things
and dismisses them
for they are not one's own
but belong to the church
or to the water or sky
or simply to life
I see nothing odd
but when I turn back
for the sun flashes
blinding me

I see the nun naked
her black habit down
at her small bare feet
her ebony hair flung wild
her blue eyes dancing
and she heaves by me
into the sea of the bay
into the afternoon harbor
like a white gull
or a cloud
against light
and then darker
blue or slate
rough slate
sharp slate
and the ferry turns
away from her
and I go to the other side
to see with others
where the nun went
and with relief see
her being pulled aboard
a police- or fire-boat
her slim beauty
lifted out of the water
wet and naked and
I feel somehow
finally itself

PEACE IN OUR TIME

> *O yet we trust that somehow good*
> *Will be the final goal of ill . . .*
> —Tennyson

The poet, ignorant philosopher,
Alpha & Omega beggar, posits
AND, in an Adamic naming, the
world that takes all others in:

"AND," he says, "includes the All.
OR is us & even war.
AND will keep including more.
OR is reductive, what we recall

—particulars, parts, & particles
—how many ways can it be said?—
all things unborn, & all things dead,
commas, grapes, seeds, articles

of various sorts, & written ones,
all things that are not All,
all memories we can recall,
all less than All, all suns,

all galaxies, germs, & viruses,
all parts of atoms & their parts,
all stops, reverses, starts,
all flowers, roses, irises—"

She frowned. "And so you say," she said,
"that you can live with ugly war

because it's what you call an OR.
ORs also are the many dead!"

"Yes. When struck by this, I wondered
what horrid meaning it must have.
The morality of love
was made to seem almost a blunder.

And yet, I thought, morality
must include the act of war.
For Fascists must be fought, are OR,
are fragments of eternity

gone wrong in AND, the All; are Fear.
A kinder & a gentler love
has got to be beyond, above,
& other than, this OR-world, where

it must be that, if we could see
the whole of things, we'd understand
how piece by piece (& hand in hand)
things add to form in synergy

a greater than is each alone,
as also are twinned Space & Time,
or life in clay & death in lime.
Thus, in the AND, all Ors atone."

PART THREE

DOCTOR BOP

LIFE AND OPINIONS OF DOCTOR BOP, THE BURNT-OUT PROF

for Esther Cameron
L'chaim!

I Veni, Vidi, Vici

My old man was a *Moishe Kapoyr* if you ever saw one.
This can be proved by the fact that, when I was a kid,
he thought I was a *mazik* and my brother wasn't,
but when we grew up and my brother joined the army
and made a career of it, then he was a *mazik*
and I wasn't, being around the time of which
I speak a college instructor, and I became a *momzer*.
How do you figure? Well, my old man respected
education, but, having very little, was jealous
of those who had it. He claimed fluency in five
languages, all of them Yiddish. "Polymath,"
I said, and he said, "I learned to count on the streets
of New York, making change from what I peddled."
Max was my full brother and, therefore, half Irish too.
Talk about multicultural, we are it. The Irish
side weren't keen on religion, shame to say,
so the old man had his way with us, and I guess
he forgave God for us every Yom Kippur. My mother,
a pliant woman, converted. My brother,
who is the eldest, was born at St. Vincent's
in Greenwich Village, but I was born at Maimonides,
which may suggest a few things I won't go into.
My brother took my mother's Irish name into the army,
where he remains, a Captain now, I think. A *mazik*?
A career man in the army? And not a professor?
My old man was a *Moishe Kapoyr* if you ever saw one.

From such an unpromising background
how do you get started as an academia
nut, and end up having tenure? In those days,
you join the army, of course,
to get the G.I. Bill.
I'm way too young yet,
not even *Bar Mistva'd*,
but eventually I take advantage
of my country's liberal
generosity, for which I thank
the truly great Harry S.,
et. al., and join up.
The Korean armistice was signed
at Panmunjom on July 27, 1953.
Have I got *mazel*! I get the
benefits without the pain.
My old man, who was drafted in the
Great War to end all wars,
sat reading "The Jewish Daily Forward,"
moving from Yiddish to English,
back and forth, back and forth,
learning. He said, "See, you did it again!"
He was pissed because Max,
my truly fabulous big brother,
came home wounded and
deciding to make a career of it,
and I got a vacation in Japan
and Hawaii and came home ready
to "take advantage of the taxpayers,"
like himself, the old *batlan*.
He dies in a conniption fit in '65,
overweight and over Lyndon Johnson's lies,
joining my mother, an angel.

When I was taking my masters at Columbia,
my old man, the meshugge maven, said:
"What do you care for a super goy like Donne?
You said he was a pirate once. I bet
he would come and pull the pale and
take the whole *shtetl* away with him.
And then you say, Dean of St. Paul's—
what would he care for the likes of us?"
"What do *we* care for the likes of us,"
I said, "you even failed in the rag
business, with eighteen relatives to help."
"I had no *mazel*. It's you who's had the luck.
The grants and scholarships you've won!"
"Hard work," I said, "not luck." "Not brains,"
he said. "Your grandfather, he had brains."
"I suppose you mean the Rabbi not the Priest."
"Wise off, wise guy! A sober fur-cutter is better
than a drunken bootlegger." "So why not
cut fur and get as rich as you?" I said.
"I didn't have the eyes for it," he said.
"You got the eyes for anything, and look at you:
John Donne Takes a Holy Crap and Writes a Poem.
Even your drunken Irish bootlegger grandpa
would be royally pissed at that!"

II GROOVES OF ACADEME

At the Modern Language Association,
the trees are bending down and going bare, the halls
are getting knee-deep in rusty leaves, and everyone
is pointing a withered finger-stump at everyone else.
The **Burnt-Out Prof** is a liberal, but God, a true one.
This is one of the reasons that the Bop is burnt-out:
He finds today an atmosphere of the Inner Circle

of the old Kremlin, where "normal" means what anyone
   desires.

It is like the old days when Political Correctness meant
the Party line of the week, sometimes posted in "Pravda,"
or telephoned to London, Paris, and New York, to
prepare for diplomatic divagations, on the weekend.
This week sexy is sexist, so I don't know how to explain
   myself.
I can tell you, it's getting tough to say much of anything.
1736: Patrick Henry was born. That was also the year
that Fahrenheit died and Hogarth produced his "Good
   Samaritan."
None of these things seem to have had much "impact,"
(now there's a word that I would ban) and,
while I wend my way through this historic traffic,
toward an historic college that no longer
recognizes history as a legitimate subject,
I notice that the leaves are down and tumbling
in the wind along the road to higher learning.

Taking by storm the bastions of conditioned reflex,
I sat down to reflect on the mystery of life,
but found myself instead considering whether to
   refinance
the old adobe of my dreams, now that the rates were
   lower.
The school had found my house for me—the school's my
   mother.
I had a real mother but the school's a better mother:
   Magna Mater.
(One keeps thinking of Magna-Matergate, but so far so
   good.)
Along the treelined drives etc., lateral thinking impinged,
and before you could say, "Peter Piper picked,"

I considered the deconstruction, not of all the texts in the
 school,
but of the school itself, slate by slate and brick by brick.
I could start at the highest point—was it the flagpole
or the tower clock? In an *augenblick* a Hamlet's con-
 fusion befell me.
The other day I asked our professor of Medieval History
 a question
only to learn that her expertness (or "tise") was restricted
to the period between when Constantine reigned alone
and St. Vladimir became prince of Kiev, with everything
 else
outside her field. *To our professor of Medieval History
the rest of life is a mystery;* no generalist, she. Life is not
 her field.
The middle-aged scribes on the staff correct the English
of the professors and fund-raisers alike, that no
 embarrassment
befalls these ivied halls. They are made of substantial
 stuff,
the staff, the grade- and high-school grads of yesteryear,
 like Hemingway and Faulkner.
1899: John Dewey, "School and Society." *Tunc pro nunc.*
Another new building is going up on the green.

I am Anarchus, King of Academe,
tenured to bring chaos to your campus.
I can say any goddam irresponsible fucking thing.
I am a regular irrepressible intellectual Wild Bull of the
 Pampas.

I'll be your peripatetic in the feeble rain.
I'll corrupt you with my Socratic questions.
When God commanded Hosea to associate with a whore,
wasn't that a command against the Decalogue?

Aquinas said No, because in so commanding,
the whore became Hosea's wife.
Everything fits, you see, Pangloss-like.
Just when we think something has gone wrong

it has come up right. How sure are you
of anything? The skeleton of Cro-Magnon man
was found in France in 1868.
Who moved it, and from where? And why?

In 1871, Adolf Nordenskjöld explored the interior
of Greenland. There was no there there, as Gert Stein put
   it,
but he did it because it was there, as Sir Edmund Hillary
   put it.
Hath the rain a father? Where is love?

Principles are never provable
in the order which they substantiate,
they are evident and intuitively given.
That should be some help with regard to love.

In 1805, Hosea Ballou wrote "A Treatise on Atonment."
Mobile perpetuum. You who are young
will soon be old and walking with the young.
The "Treatise" will await you in "La morgue littéraire."

Young Sirs, Bruno proclaimed the spatial and material
   infinity of the world.
Ladies, Descartes attributed positive infinity only to God.
Newton was cautious. Einstein certain. Planck con–
   fusing.
Maybe we should just make love and listen to the music
   of the rain.

When Chips left the Old School he wore its tie
and was carried out with his Wellingtons on.
But no way Mister Bop, the burnt-out prof.
Things definitely ain't what they used to be.
Bop gets to retire on something like a 401(k);
but not yet, as St. Augustine put it, not quite yet;
I'm not ready for retired sainthood yet!
The syllogisms from which Aristotle deduced the valid
are not complete. In American institutions
we fail upward to glory, and I expect
to be the mad head of the English Department before
I wallop my last tennis ball to cardiac arrest,
or do my last imitation of Johnny Weissmuller.
"Thanotopsis" is *not* my favorite poem.

III A SPEED OF SEMESTERS

"Coleridge did dope," she said.
"So one day, when he was socked out,
dreaming up this poem about Xanadu,
along came this person from Porlock
on some business and shook him out of it.
After about an hour he couldn't remember
anything but the first part of the poem.
Has that ever happened to you? I mean,
that poem of yours in the 'American Scholar'
seems unfinished, you know?" A very
finished young lady, and this is what
I get! I give them some *Biographia
Literaria*, in a vague hope . . .
"Fancy and imagination!" I roar,
and point to someone else.
"Fancy is only memory and produces
only a sensational product.

Imagination transcends time and
makes contact with higher reality."
Something occurs to me: "No,
I don't *do* dope, and the poem
is finished because it says
what it started out to say
in the way it started out to say it."
"I only meant, have you ever been
interrupted when you were writing
a poem, so that the unfinished part
transcends and makes contact with
a higher reality, like that one
in the 'American Scholar'?"
And suddenly I realized how very quick
she was, and nice, and pretty too.

The Greeks measured Earth by its shadow on the moon.
I measure it by travel, which always brings you home;
therefore, Thomas Wolfe was wrong. Good news,
   though–
Pascal was probably right. I'd be willing to bet on it.
I had an uncle in the numbers racket, himself a gambler.
Thoreau said, Time is a stream I go fishing in.
Ford said, History is the bunk. Sumerian writing
done on clay tablets, shows about 2000 pictographic
   signs.
The moon is a bad woman because she is very romantic.
We all know the trouble that can get you into. I
am romantic tonight. How many leaves lay scattered?
I guess millions, and I have a study that agrees with me.
When you pay for a study, you get what you pay for.
Therefore, all studies are romantic and have a dark side.
Humankind pays for everything it gets. Theodora,
the Byzantine empress, died in 548, one of a kind.
Her death was a big relief to some of her subjects.

Five years later disastrous earthquakes shook the entire
   world.
I offer no comment, but think about it.
The house I live in was built much later. I leave the
actual count to you. Do not use a calculator.
The first water-driven mechanical clock was
constructed in Peking in 1090, the wrist watch
around the turn of the twentieth century.
I've got a digital that I can read in the dark.
I can also read the chained and sailing moon from here.
Shaw said, give him a slate and a piece of chalk
and he'd give you the wrong answer in under five
   minutes.
A journey of a thousand miles begins with one step,
so I lift my gouty foot and lean forward. Good counting!

"Look at you," said Müller,
who taught psychology,
and later committed suicide
when implicated in war crimes.
A vegetarian, he picked
at his salad and eyed me
with distaste. I was drinking
a whiskey sour. "You have ashes
down the front of your shirt.
It is a dirty habit, smoking.
And I see you always drinking
in that cocktail bar by the
lake. You must take better
care of yourself, my friend."

"Worry is what kills you.
I grade papers there. It's
very pleasant—a beautiful view,
even in winter, when the lake looks

like a bowl of liquid iron. You
know, in 1496, Romano Pane,
a monk who accompanied Columbus,
became the first person to
describe the tobacco plant
to the old world. Tobacco
was brought from America
to Spain in 1555. In 1560,
the tobacco plant was imported
to Western Europe by Jean Nicot;
hence, nicotine. It brought
pleasure and pain, as all things do."

"How do you know such things
—dates like that, I mean?"
"I look them up. They're
comforting, definite.
Very little is." "You appear
detached." "Not detached.
Perhaps transcendent. Sir
John Hawkins introduced
tobacco into England
in 1565. That was the same
year that pencils began
to be manufactured there.
Also, Sir Thomas Gresham
founded the Royal Exchange
in London, same year. And
the Knights of St. John,
under Jean de La Valette,
defended Malta from the Turks.
The Turkish siege was broken with
the arrival of Spanish troops."

"What's the difference?"

"Exactly! Erskine Caldwell
published Tobacco Road in 1932.
Jack Kirkland's play version
of TR opened to a long run
in New York in '33. But
at the end of the century
I have to go outside to smoke,
and the autumn wind blows
the ashes all over me."

"I should like my ashes
to be scattered over the lake,"
Müller said. I lit another
cigarette, watched the smoke
scurry off in puffs and strands.
"I'll see to it," I said.

The true task is to trace the phenomena
back to the hidden Logos, i.e., spirit and reason.
The two ways of looking at this, though,
cause trouble. Is God in or not in Nature?
Have the monotheists got hold of the right end
of the stick, or have the Hindus and Buddhists;
are the Pantheists right or are the Christians?
But infinity does not exclude its middle.
God, however, can make an infinity.
1941: Étienne Gilson: *God and Philosophy*;
Reinhold Niebuhr: *The Nature and Destiny
of Man;* and Bergson died. I played war
at my grandmother's house in New Jersey.
On July 16th, the first atomic bomb
was detonated near Alamogordo, N.M.
On August 6th and August 9th, the U.S.
dropped atomic bombs on Hiroshima and
Nagasaki. On her back porch, my grandmother

told me that no one would be able to live
in those cities for a hundred years to come.
Nine years later I was there. The thousand-
year Reich had lasted twelve years. The Logos
is deeply hidden. Near the end of the war, bebop
came in. People would sit along a bar and move
their heads side to side, idiotically. The modern
school believes we must assert nothing
but "essence" and "meaning." I read
Kon-Tiki on the ship that took me to Japan.
Heyerdahl believed in the probable colonization
of Polynesia from South America around 1100.
I remember reading and looking at the water,
reading and looking at the water.

You know how it is when you feel sure
of something, maybe a date,
or a fact of some kind,
and then you find out that you were wrong
and you feel like your brain's
turned into camel-shit and got
spread across the Sahara, well,
I made a bet with a faculty member
that I knew the exact date,
there and then, and where and when,
of the invention of the thermometer.
The faculty member teaches pre-
med, and we were at a table
in the school cafeteria. She shoves
a five-dollar bill out, and triumphantly
I assert: Santorio Santorio
measured human temperature
with a thermometer in Italy in 1628.
"But he did not *invent* the thermometer,"
she says, and picks up her five-spot.

"Fahrenheit initiated mercury as a heat-
measuring medium. R.A.F. de Reaumur
used alcohol. And then there was
Celsius." I had got a hold of
the wrong end of the thermometer, and
out dropped my brain from one camel's ass,
stepped on by the big hoofs of the next, and
dragged across the desert by the caravan.
I should have learned a long time ago
about never being entirely certain
of anything. God may not play tricks,
as Einstein insisted, but life does,
with a little help from human
arrogance, of the kind I displayed,
and the endless capacity of the
human mind to misconceive and
misperceive, and the plain simple
strangeness of life itself, and
that must be the case. Maybe.

Is the peripatetic part of the meaningless goo
this autumn that is being trounced by the rain,
one with the fallen beaten leaves? Camus
and Sartre would insist on seizing pain
by the throat and giving it a throttle,
being that we are all alone with it
like a drunk in a rented room with a bottle
and not a 'toon in which to spit.
Up to us, they would say, to do something about it,
be a "Renegade" or find "No Exit"
or become one's own kind of Mister Fix-it,
but of its ultimate use, I doubt it,
doubt we can do it alone,
doubt it to the bone.

IV SABBATICAL

If the word of the creator is itself creation,
as in "Let there be light," and since the birth of the world
is linked to the birth of the word, isn't it so
that the essence of language is in the spirit, the Logos?
Then the rants of the mad and the speakers in tongues
are holy and creative rants and speakers and poets
of portmanteau words and nonsense rhymes are makers
of the solidly new and true, and are meant to be
   translated,
paraphrased or whatever can be done to understand them.

I have the distinct honor to know several people who are
   mad
and who do not mind sitting across from me and spewing
out their hearts and minds. 1533: First lunatic asylums
(without medical attention). Freud taught us to listen.
But we know now that schizophrenia is a kind of brain
   rot,
an actual physical condition, and is already treatable
with chemicals. Listening would not have helped the
   insane;
but it might have helped the sane, if they were able to
   interpret,
for the words were palpable. My friend shouts, "Mother
   ate me!"
and I get his drift; "Father buried me alive," and I dig.
"It isn't the dream but the words you use to describe the
   dream,"
wrote Freud in *The Interpretation of Dreams* in 1900.
   Blake:
"The lost traveller's dream under the hill."
I myself dreamed of being in a long queue behind
   Princess Di.

I suppose everything is in there—royalty, sex, and death.

Shall we become public figures,
sharing the thin metaphorical blood of fraternity?
Shall we be the Family of Man (and Woman, of course)
or shall we be a flesh and blood family
at war and peace with ourselves and the State?
We can't love what we don't know.
We are asked to stretch fraternity's blood
until we become anemic, pale pretenders
to emotion, vampires of passion.
It is paradox. If I keep my brother,
I become his keeper, and he the kept,
not free, not equal, not his own.
And if I turn in surrender to my vision,
I must master others, keep my brother,
and I must rob him of his vision
as my vision dominates his, oh Abel!
If I lead, he must follow whither.
He must wither following. He must say:
But where is my vision of home and hearth,
where wife, where blood-rich children?
If his children are my children,
where are his children?
Is my avuncular blood as rich
as that of his and his wife's?
Fraternity's blood runs thin and thinner
until it is water and we are bound by water
alone, ice water, not the sticky rich blood
of consanguinity, the stuff of passionate caring.
Would a watery world be better?
Remember how many vows have been broken.
Remember the blood oaths of children,
your blood-brothers and -sisters who are
gone with your childhood, how each

cut a finger enough for blood and
stuck them together, and how gone
is an event where you can only recall
what you did and not with whom
in a dark corner of the Kabbalah.

If you stop to think about it,
the twenty-six point-whatever miles back from Marathon
never did anyone much good. I used to believe
what Santayana said, but the generations are too far apart,
and one lost one will put us back to square one again.
I live near the second largest artificial lake in America,
and all my less sedentary colleagues are boaters and
   campers,
and they are always trying to get me into a boat or a
   camp;
but when I was young I spent a lot of time on ships and
   boats
and beaches, like Ulysses, and I tell them a cocktail bar
is the most civilized place on Earth. You go in and sit
   down
and order a Gibson, light up, and wait
for some intelligent conversation to break out.
Of course you are costing the public a fortune because
   none of this
is good for your health—it obviously killed George
   Burns, at
age 100, before his time—but I'm with the Sun King and
his "Après moi, le déluge." I'm a sort of professorial
   sociopath,
I guess, always thinking that if I have one life to live
I'll live it my way—so I go over and plug "My Way" on
   the jukebox.
I hope I'm a bad influence on my students, just like
   Sinatra and Socrates,

and I intend to spend the rest of my life as a Clairol
   blond,
asking plenty of pointless questions of the vacuous sky.

1913: The Armory Show introduced cubism to New
   York.
The Nude Descending a Staircase left us exhausted.
Her energy was obvious but we were drained by her élan.
In 1918 we lay there smoking and wondering who had
   been super.
In 1929 we lost faith in money, in '42 safety.
And now the last securities and guarantees have dis-
   appeared.
Living with the bomb has made tragedy impossible.
"Dr. Strangelove, or How I Learned to Live with the
   Bomb,"
is a comedy. No deliberate war was possible,
because leaders were targeted and are cowardly,
but accidents are inevitable. The little girl picking
   flowers
in Lyndon Johnson's ad, 1964: then his big lie.
The cup of our political faith became a sieve, too.
   Johnson had
done for American politics what Planck did for particle
   stability.
I can only understand myself in my hereness now.
I step forth in fact but my whereness is a mystery.
I wait outside the seasons for a cue.

V COMMENCE FIRE!

The question of the truly real
has metastasized in me,
like the spread ambition of a runner
whose toes are fat with it.

The central emotional tumor
of desire to know what is behind the
screen of existence is devouring me.
It has reached Faustian proportions with
increasing age. Sometimes I must dull
the ache of it with booze and music,
sometimes with what comedy I can find
in the happenings around me. Calling
life a game is a withdrawal symptom,
a relief from the wracked nerves of wonder,
by which I have been attended since I was a child:
wonder and wondering. I could get sick
with it, when young, and did. The doctors
wondered too, and my poor father paid them.
It's a kind of ontological hypochondria,
which has turned me, slowly, but ever so surely,
into an intellectual valetudinarian.

A poem is a posit, an assertion, an act,
and in action we forget fear: respite
in creation, the maker takes a stand, in making,
but is it a stand no better than gimmick-makers make?
Well, poetry possesses the virtue of being a record,
at least, and you can date a poem, if you wish,
thus giving it the merit of a worldly fact
contained in a system of time, which, admittedly,
is a system which is perhaps pseudo-fact itself,
or will become so as matter completes its withdrawal
upon itself to revisit its beginnings in a black hole in
   space;
and yet, until then, something like a fact,
a fact in the sense that Sherlock Holmes is almost real
and lives in Baker Street in a fictional series
in a real world that may exist only in a dream
that is being dreamed elsewhere, perhaps—dare I say—

by Yahweh; and so poetry becomes an actual little stab
and, poets hope, rip in the black sheet
that covers the deserted, haunted mansion.

If you expect happiness you get misery,
but just when you learn to live with misery
the cat comes back and wants to be fed,
so you feed the cat and that makes you feel better.
Expressionists always bring the problem of death
   forward,
demanding an "authentic death," an act of dying
that is peculiarly one's own (as in Rilke:
Notebooks of Malte Laurids Brigge).
What good does it do to say that you are an expressionist
or for that matter an existentialist, or any ist?
"Poetry is of graver import than history," said Aristotle.
Why? Because good poetry doesn't know what to do,
   doesn't try
to tell anyone else what to do. True, Yeats made a
   system,
and Blake before him, but they did it for scaffolding,
to shoot darts of insight from and toward, not
to believe in, not to insist upon—monkeybars
to climb in and to swing through. If you expect
happiness you get misery, but then the cat will come
   home,
expecting to be fed, and that makes you feel much better.

2300 folding chairs on the lawn,
relatives with an actuarial average
of 30 years left in them,
fathers less, mothers more,
and grandmothers more than ever
(I hasten to add, non-smokers
more than anyone), myself

hot on a warm June day:
commencement socializing:
1888: Lover's Leap and
Hold-Me-Tight buggies: today
expensive sports cars
for the kids, up to limousines for
the relatives. The campus
is crowded with vehicles, gleaming
colors abound: chauffeurs
stand in clusters of uniforms, smoking.
I envy them. Grads with an actuarial life
of 50 years ahead of them,
maybe 60, sweat with heat
and excitement, caps and gowns,
and in anticipation of booze,
dancing, prancing, and romancing
tonight: but first, ROTC
commissioning, Baccalaureate
Service, Supper with the
school President and his wife
(parents and their students are urged
to remain on campus for Supper),
Open Houses, faculty and staff
homes, a concert by the college choir,
a Jazz ensemble. There won't be a
hotel or motel room empty
for a radius of 50 miles.
I scan young faces in the hope
that some of them know
the difference between fancy
and the imagination,
between a Baccalaureate and
a Bacchanalia, between
an opposable behind and
a prehensile tail, etc.

Orator fit, poeta nascitur.
Poeta nascitur, non fit.
I'm halfway into the wrong racket.
I'm quitting school to write:
retiring from the fray,
I'll go to Innisfree.
Bon voyage, and
vaya con Dios, my darlings!

SPINE AND SPIRIT

to my cat, Vicki

All I care about is vertebrates.
I can't help it, I'm made that way.
It's true that invertebrates kept on evolving
after vertebrates arrived, but who cares.
There are slinky vertebrates, though,
but I won't mention any names—a job's a job.
In Western religious tradition
the spiritual is identified with a purposive order.
In 540 the Empress Theodora introduced long white dresses,
purple cloaks, gold embroidery, tiaras, and pointed shoes.
In 542 the plague of Constantinople,
imported by rats from Egypt and Syria,
spread all over Europe. By 547, the plague,
medically described by Gildas, reached Britain.
Cause and effect? The slinkiest person I ever saw
I saw at Minsky's burlesque in Newark when I was sixteen.
I think Senator Long may have met her there, backstage.
Well, different features of the human spirit have been
   stressed
in different idealist systems: knowing and the
attributes of thought, perceiving with retrospective memory
and creative imagination, willing and the tumults of striving,
purpose and the organization it gives to activity,
each have been taken as the essential activity or
distinguishing mark of spirit. Blaze Starr.
Marie Curie: 1911 Nobel Prize for Chemistry.
Also, British Official Secrets Act becomes law.
All of these things are connected to vertebrates,
even as the path of evolution leads us downward
toward television. Primacy of spirit

may be taken as a sense of mastery,
and mean the spirit's omnipotence in the world,
and in the individual the dominance of soul over body.
The notochord cannot replace the vertebrae,
so the shark is a soul-less hunger. The case
could be made. What about extraterrestrials, though?
Beings made of gas? Well, the backbone was made of gas,
i.e., Senator Long's backbone and Blaze Starr's slinky
spine: and imagine those two vertebrates going at it.
And what about Madame Curie's curious chemistry?
I must agree with Pascal, I must assert the primacy of spirit
and to hell with the backbone; but that would mean
that one must have some backbone in order to assert
the primacy of spirit, a backbreaking thought.

BALLAD OF THE BURNT-OUT PROF

> *... something ... eternally gained*
> *for the universe ...*
> *   --William James*

Old Duracell, old Mazda-man
you've got to keep the light—
it's growing dim inside you
but that's no time to hide you—
there's just a chance you might
say something shedding light.

Old Candle-wick, old Burnt-out Prof,
(who calls himself the Bop)
old hairy ears and snout,
Tochis afn tish!
you gouty worn-out lout—
oh, call yourself a name, old cuss—
because you weren't the best,
and yet you know it doesn't matter,
no, not in the least.

Old geeze, don't lose your grip,
don't fall and break your hip—
you've got to keep the light, baldspot,
you've got to keep the light,
because there's just a chance
if you keep the light, old souse,
if you keep the light,
there's still a chance, though mad,
that there's something left to add.

You've got to keep the light, old piles,

you've got to keep the light.
You know you've been a dog,
oh, you've acted like a *trayf* old hog,
but somehow in your life
you've had a loving wife,
so there must be something good about you,
you lousy lucky lout you—
all I ask of you, old candle,
is just to keep the Godblessed light,
and show a flash of pluck, old duck,
and with a bit of luck
you might come up with something
worthy of the world that you've surveyed.

You've been around so long now
you've got to hold some light,
whether hell or heaven
is waiting with its leaven
to galvanize you new again
for better or for worse,
old man of steel, who once pumped iron,
don't listen to that deathly siren,
you've got to keep the light a while,
you've got to keep that gap-toothed smile,
you've got to keep the light alive
inside your horrible old hide,
because you still might do a thing
that's worthy of its doing,
you've got to keep the light, old pipe,
you've got to keep the light.

You've written many a poem, old bard,
and published many too,
but I've got news for you, old prof,
I've got news for you—

you haven't any right, old cough,
not to keep the light.
You don't get off like that, old shakes
fall off the roof like that—
there's plenty time to die, old guy,
plenty time to die,
so keep on pumping light, old Bop,
pumping students light!

TO THE GUARDIAN AT THE GATE

Happiness over my shoulder is a cloud of ink.
Destroyed again by the world last Monday, I
can no longer agree that the fault is mine
and not in my stars. When the fault is yours
you can do something about it, take a course
in constancy or begin once again to build up your
   muscles.
You have to believe you can make life work on your own.
You have to believe in something, no matter how weird,
something to cure ill. Nicholas Prevost of Tours,
1098: "Antidotarum," a collection of 2650
medical prescriptions from Salerno. In the modern age,
the being and existence of things are determined
through comprehensibility, ascertained by us,
which amounts to saying that if we don't understand it,
it isn't. So the bad stuff isn't there because
I don't understand why it has to be. Happiness
over my shoulder turns back into a silken cloud,
which is either a way of saying that life
is what we make of it or that we are mad
as two unpaid fighting cocks with razor spurs
ripping ourselves apart for nothing but a bit of corn.
But if life is good, why are the feathers always flying?
To end on a high note, try hypnotizing yourself into hope.
Get that cloud of ink back down onto paper where it
   belongs,
and don't look back, for God's sake, don't look back!

THE ROAD TO NOWHERE

Winged and hovering overhead
Victory awaits my confession of defeat
snatched from itself by lost control.
Some tell us to be ourselves
but if ourselves contain
the seed of the enigma tree
that flowers black and hangs down so,
what should we do, *wee* ones before its cloud
of multitudinous, oily leaves?

It's not on that highway
but off into the field
for pastures of plenty,
our idea of virtue and beauty,
the apparitions row on row
of rich successes reaped
for services not rendered,
not endured.

BREATHLESS; OR, OVERTURE TO HYPERVENTILATION

You know how it is with daily life,
never enough time to do anything,
and especially never enough time for making love:
early rising rushing to exhaustion earning a living,
no food for thought, and especially no stimulating Ovidian oysters.
Lunch in a bag, maybe. Make the bag big enough for your head
and save it, you'll need it. This is the overture to hyper–ventilation,
which leads to the loss of carbon dioxide from the blood.
1944: Lewis Mumford: "The Condition of Man," who
is understood as being thrown out of a state of security
and into a dark night of suffering where the world is lost to him
and back upon himself and forced to reflection, self-awakening,
and finally to authentic, breathless being,
as he climbs the stairs to his bedroom at night,
where his beloved awaits him like an opening rose.
471: Aeschylus introduces a second actor.
But Arthur Miller says tragedy is impossible in our time.
Only drama. It's dramatic to lose your breath.
When you get it back, you laugh because you were so silly,
and life returns to comedy. Mostly, life is comedy with gravitas,
universal, intergalactic comedy, but the mice on the mudball
are forced to take it seriously. Ah breathless, breathless!
Kierkegaard possessed a certain sense of security,

but his way would mean church and no love on Sunday
   morning,
the only remaining opportunity. Working people need a
   chance.
The Spanish close shop and take a two-hour siesta after–
   noons
but I wager don't get much more than a catnap out of it.
And, Venus, when you rise naked before me on the half-
   shell
of our conch-colored couch, my heart goes into rapid fire,
for the time has finally come, as it will to the good and
   the patient,
and I gulp for breath at sight of you and breathe until I'm
   breathless.

APOLOGIA

I've been told that I don't take life seriously enough,
or, conversely, that I make a serious effort at skimming its
   surface,
that I'm content to be a generalist, the kind of roller-blader
who shies at summersaults, the runner who runs the
   marathon
to see the crowd, the kind of drinker who tries not to get
   drunk,
the kind of no-good clod who would call an activist an
   officious-intermeddler
or, worse, a busybody, the kind of not-engaged guy who
   won't march,
who looks out at the world through stained glass eyes
as if it were his 57th visit to the Rocky Horror Picture Show.

Well, I can't account for what others may think, but,
my apologia is, that, with the rest of the variously displaced
   modern world,
I've experienced a surfeit leading to confusion, have become
   ideophobic,
even a doubter of doubts, who wonders at times if the old
   oak tree is its phenomenology,
or its rugged trunk and russet autumn leaves that lend it its
   poetic dignity
and pictorial poetry: for I think that our gravest thoughts are
   rooted
in buried and forgotten or half-forgotten metaphor, as in "the
   sun rises,"
rather than "the Earth goes down," and that the corrupt text
   of our political language
is too obvious a deconstructivist challenge for an intelligent
   child.

Donne couldn't have imagined that his hated "New
 philosophy"
  would bring us to a world of ephemerons and quarks,
nor that, scarcely out of the dark ages, his renaissance would
  lead to the
evils of the century we have just nearly struggled through.
  No
   thanks, been there, done that, it's a lost cause.
The stately metaphorical summertime virescence of the next
  century awaits us. Sure it does.

Part Four

HERACLITUS

HERACLITUS

a sequence for Lieutenant Elbert Harkins

They told me, Heraclitus, they told me you were dead . . .
                                            William Johnson Cory

I HUSH, HUSH, NEW HOUSE IN CHARLOTTE

Our new old house climbs a hill,
backside sagging on stilts, porch chinning up
the short front lawn's long shaggy grass.
The hill drops down darkly behind the house.
Our eye-hooked back door isn't safe,
the basement a wedge of black cheese
for a great, grinning rat. Trees,
with octopus roots and upward tentacles, tap the roof.
The floors slant, decks frozen in a pitch.
As to the furnace, it groans, goes on,
and heat hisses up from floor vents. Off,
say a word in one room and you hear it in another,
pad about and it sounds from somewhere else.
The former tenant was old and mad as bees.
He shot at shadows with a Magnum,
out back, down there, in the tarpool.
He blew them out of the night, usually.
By day he walked out naked, hating neighbors.
He had the house boarded up, from inside,
and kept two sleek Dobermans. The kennel
lurked in the black cheese-wedge down there,
made out of all the inside doors in the house.
We broke it up, put the doors back on their hinges,
and now can smell them, doggy and dangerous.
That first was our initiation night:

up the back steps: pumpf, pumpf, pumpf, pumpf!
My daughter woke my mother, who woke my other
  daughter,
and they listened by the basement door. Pumpf!
six-footed, three-throated Fear flew to us,
my wife and I, and banged on our bedroom door.
"What is it? What did you hear?" "Pumpf, pumpf,
  pumpf!"
I hoped it was the heat, or our own feet,
padding about, leaping from the vents.
I went to the basement door, nevertheless,
and yelled down, "I've got a gun!" Pumpf!
I yelled down, "Get away while you can!"
Pumpf! I pushed open the basement door,
snapped the switch, and darkness disappeared.
We're home now. We've had our first fear.

II MARTIAL MUSIC AT A BAND CONCERT

Now, as we hum a rousing martial tune, a Sousa,
a "Marching to Pretoria," an "Over There,"
what we are doing is the conjuring of courage,
that necessary, difficult, quixotic friend
who'll leave us in a lurch but then return to save us,
who, like a hero, leads us on to take the hill,
to take the burning pillbox hill of day, and hold it
until the smoke is drifting off and evening falls.

We need this friend more than we do the light of reason.
So do not sing to me of love's romantic passions,
nor of fraternal fellowship, nor happiness,
but conjure with me in a rousing martial tune,
or march with me to some tin drum that brings it out,
that courage necessary to our daily lives.

III War Two Words

"There is a mounted gun on a flat-bed,
and it is firing at some splintered shed.
I hear those high-pitched screams that multiply—
a Kindergarten!—then a bullet sigh,
and something forms inside me like a node.
Life stands above me and recites the Ode
to Melancholy. I stare at the blue sky
and see it for the first time, and it's *God!*

Two purple hearts, two silver stars, and I
am home for a parade to glorify
my hero's part in that dark episode.
I understand the latest bombs *im*plode,
suck in and swallow, following my view
that monsters eat their children, *a la mode!*"

IV The Good Ones

I guess the good ones stay with everyone,
   the ones we knew who made us proud to know
them at some point somewhere beneath the sun,
   but, to the good, I think, the others go
into a fading place and so are lost,
   the others who were not so good to know.
The pain of course stays like an ugly ghost.
   But I suppose in time it too will go.
I could name names, but only of the good,
   the ones I knew that I was proud to know.
They are the heroes of my life. I would
   keep them forever fresh, not let them go.
It isn't hard to keep the two apart,
the heroes and the zeros of the heart.

V POSTCARD

You are growing old, & too sad for your own good, judging
by your last missive where you wrote that you were tired

of reading bad unrhyming *vers libre*, as you put it,
& newspaper headlines filled with murder & mayhem,

& that we humans are merely the slaves of all we survey,
meaning I take it the slaves of our impulses & not

the lords & owners of our faces as Shakespeare wrote
in one of those sonnets of his which you used to read

as others read the Bible, the Bible which you attribute to
 lesser poets
whose muse is a God in whom you do not believe.

Is it your loss of my proximity that has led you to this
 depression?
For you seem depressed & lonely, & I'm sorry I had to move
 away.

I had a family to care for & this distant spot served the
 purpose,
& now one child has a child & there are others here on the
 way.

See the photograph of the lake on the other side of this card—
it is beautiful here, but let me tell you something about it.

Out on the lake fishing the husband of the woman next door
was stung by a bee & died before he could dock.

He was a slave to the lake & the fish, I suppose,
if you are correct when you say we are slaves to all we survey.

The bee must have been a slave to the man in the boat

since he got close enough to lose his stinger to him.

But I am also writing with reference to unrhyming Kilroy
whom you deplore & who has just won the Nobel Prize.

Actually Kilroy writes both with rhyme and without
as did Shakespeare & Whitman ("O Captain! My Captain!")
   & Frost.

Even now I am writing you an unrhyming poem called "To a
   Sad Friend."
Why not come & visit me—we can go out & fish on the lake.

The fish & the bees can survey us & be our bright slaves
& I'll do my best to cheer you up about Kilroy

& meaningless unrhyming poems & mayhem & murder.
You can look at the children & see there is some good in life.

VI ROANOKE RETURN

Six-hundred miles above my southern exposure
my friend in extremis waits,
a man old enough to be my father,
and I am heading up North Carolina
in the long heartless dark,
to big, bad, only-the-dead-know Brooklyn,
headlights blazing on high beams,
being blinked at, warned and horned
—for I am faring to where one half
of my split spirit dies, in my war hero
drinking buddy, Elbert, two silver stars,
two purple hearts, smiling up ahead of me,
wan smile of age: Normandy's gone.

Tarheeled, tarwheeled, I wend my way,
blinking lights streaming into my brain,
to Brooklyn, that Elbert calls God's,
over hills of North Carolina night,
knowing the running greens and pines along the road,
how they set themselves against the running moon,
in my camouflaged combat jumpsuit
big enough for Santa jumping Claus,
soaked through with unholdable brew,
while the moon swings. . . the two moons
. . . and Elbert swings. . . in and out. . .
of the Fort Hamilton Veteran's Hospital
with his lungs smoked away, brave as ever—
Elbert, I give you a new medal,
the moon, the two moons, one for each
black lung—we will jag together once again
in your unbelieved-in-God's country,
where you might be looking at the moon, too.

It is a mad quest of hope and love
up 77 to Roanoke, link up with 85,
smooth overdrive to Harrisburg,
up the night to Jersey, climbing up,
up the great flying sky-harp cathedral Verrazano
and dumped at your Fort Hamilton feet—
Elbert, I salute you!

My olive-drab seabag bounces in back
like a wild love pregnant with burning vodka
and cheap-at-the-source Carolina cigs, deadly
gifts Elbert begged me to bring, only sooner,
in time for us to enjoy them together,
a lifetime of death brought now
and become magic to stop him from dying,
burning and unburnt offerings!

. . . in and out of smoking clouds,
lightnings, with the moon in and out,
escaping, seeking, avoiding love, age,
death, my wife, children, responsibilities
that begin in dreams. . . waves of water,
wind pressing me across lane lines,
and I am in the fast lane, pulling
around a slow-climbing eighteen-wheeler
honking like a tug, beaming me down,
wet speed and mild madness streaming away behind me.
It is a hot shower in a Roanoke motel room
and a nightmaring, dream-drunken sleep.
It is black coffee and a long-distance call,
and it is all too late, for me, for Elbert,
Officialdom now in charge of his skinny bones
—I hoped the metastasizing crab broke its teeth
on the embedded shrapnel that for fifty years
stabbed out through his skin in bloody stigmata
—and it is the long sad hungover journey home
in a day dark as night and relentless rain
falling down Virginia, North Carolina,
it is "Pardon me, boy. . ."
on the static-stuttering radio,
blanking, blanking out in the low country,
and it is the wrong rainy road, ascending. . .
looking out at water-colored what?
A Wailing Wall of water—
and I am high and outside, low and inside,
denim-backed white-duck fog and no lights, no cars,
no world but rain, alone, blood-shot eyes cotton-blind,
gearing up and down, burning brakes, clutch,
going round the side of something big
—the wet rockface of a Great Smoky,
with the steaming abyss of eternity below.
Elbert the Brave, be here as I quake,

strengthen me, breathless, on high,
going down, down down down too fast,
I dip, I spin, I slide, I am sideways,
backwards, tottering at a precipice
facing the past, rocking, rocking, stopped.
I am in heaven with nothing but down on one side,
hungover, scared—ALIVE—with the land down under
wet blue and green between layers of stranding smoke,
money in fog banks, and I pull off, away
from one possible end, sidestepping death.
All praise to Elbert, I am steady.
Love, I will be home tonight!

VII LOOKING DOWN AT A FRIEND

Always, now, truth is the tight suit that you wear.
You twirl your diamonded cane as you dance in stillness.
Forever takes you no time at all, so you can't
be expected to wait for those who loved you, slow
alive and grieving unlike your fast asleep self
playing on the moon, transported everywhere at once.
Friend, you seem not to miss your old friends, you
seem to be busy elsewhere, unfaithful seeker.

Dare you not remember those who loved you? Dare you?
Whom you have caused such suffering? What do you seek,
now, in the no-wind wind, in the no-place place
where nothing is most powerfully itself?
Lying there, where are you going with your stolen self?
You were always one on a journey somewhere, even when
  still.

Part Five

ASPECTS OF LOVE
(Charis, Eros, and Agape, etc.)

POETRY IN MOTION

It was disheartening when physics told us
the universe was alien, indifferent.
I'm glad it's changed its doubting tune back to
the music of the spheres, of sorts;
especially now that I again see you
walking in the garden as you used to do
long, long ago. You haven't changed a bit—
gripping your brocade with one small hand
and with the other feinting flowers at the bees.
I'd have thought that I'd gone mad before,
but no more since the famous physicist has said,
upon accepting his Nobel, "It's poetry,
out there, and deep in here," pointing at his head.
"The microscope and telescope look in and out
but not across the warp and woof of time."
And that's where you go walking in the garden
(the garden of the old house that is gone,
the garden that's a parking lot downtown),
feinting at the bees with your hand of flowers
and lifting your brocaded summer gown.

AN ACROSTIC

for my wife, Patricia Schorb

Poe wrote a riddling good acrostic once.
  DAvies turned trick into a feeling tribute
Be**Th** could take pride in. Well, I'm not a dunce.
  You**R** servant, you will find, is a glib brute,
ma'am. *I* am able, any time I choose,
  to do a**C**rostics cleverer than theirs,
Presto! **I**t is the nature of my muse,
  Patrici**A**—money as to millionaires.

Now here i**S** what to look for: scan the page—
  then, if you **C**an't see anything, try counting
inward, from **H**igh to low. Soon a presage
  of what is to c**O**me, love, will form, this mounting
as you proceed. **R**emember, it's a name.
Patricia Schor**B**? You *got* it! Here's to fame!

WANT OF TIME

*Two months after a
two week honeymoon*

Two weeks were plenty in those days
before we met for words of praise,
but now two months are not enough
to express to you my degree of love.
For in those days I knew no one
who could undo words as they were done
by gaining beauty and new light
much faster, love, than I could write.
But now, my dear, while charged with love,
I have this failing, seen above:
I can't design around your hair
accomplished words, express and fair,
for it improves at such a rate
it leaves me in a wordless state.
Nor can I write a faint disguise
with speed enough to cloak your eyes.
Ah, no, my love, it's of no use
to match my words, to their abuse,
against improving loveliness
and leave the words to mean the less!
I'll not do harm to poetry
trying to say what I can see.
Instead, I'll simply say that I
will follow through Eternity
until your beauty's all around
and I am left within, quite sound,
to sing that anniversary—
Millenium of You and Me!

A TUMBLE FOR SKELTON

Wherein Margaret Patricia Hill is Championed

Well done,
sweet John!
But I'd make a bet
that my Margaret
could contest against
that *midsummer flower*
that *hawk of the tower*
whom you have advanced,
in summer assaulting,
in tumbling in down,
who would be vaulting
but never be faulting
but always be salting
sweet red tomatoes
and spreading her toes
and sticking her breasty
where Philip was roosting
and cooing for fair
out of that lair
into the air
where her heart would be pounding
and pulses resounding
to the tapping of toes
in little high heels
of glittering shoes,
not spinning her wheels,
charming John,
you old Don Juan.

Yes, I'd take the bet

that my Margaret
ungauded, ungirdled,
in a contest had hurtled
beyond your yon Hussey
like a beautiful horsey
or a flying flamingo
and be all ago
so joyously
so womanly
her demeaning
in everything
far far passing
that I can indite
or suffice to write
how superiorly
my lady would be
to Margaret Hussey
to make her seem fussy
and in the end dusty
and yet even musty
and leave her behind
never to find
while my winning lady
would take prize
at flashing her eyes
on that gay day
and laurel for her head
and goose feathers in bed,
but your lady, dear John,
you sweet old Don Juan,
your lady'd be lead
compared with my Margaret,
and I'd make that bet!

THE VANTAGE POINT

If you allow your thoughts to run, gray man,
utrammelled grist, along the belt of mind,
do you discover there one grain of truth,

or one remembered woman not mundane?
Was every step ill-chosen or ill-timed?
Your passion in abeyance, or patience rushed?

I stand at noon, and wonder at the night.
From where I stand the morning was of dun.
The afternoon ahead could be still worse.

I hope somehow to see it light and bright;
I hope somehow to share it with someone,—
a woman in my arms, both warm and wise.

CÉLESTINE

Louis Bertrand sought his Célestine to no avail. She was older than Louis, and possessed a past not entirely to be admired; but this handsome romantic, if tubercular, poet roused her not in the least, for he lacked wealth, which brought her passion to the boil. An ugly untalented burgher with a bag of gold was beautiful and desirable in her eyes; a poor, sick poet, not so. She combed the prose poems from Louis' *Gaspard de la Nuit* from her heavy, dark hair each night. What fizzes and sparkles as she raked the comb down! What lapidary art fell to the floor! So poor Louis, being ashamed of his down-at-heels shoes, his tattered cape, his crumpled cap, went into hiding, where he wasted away; but his bones were so fine that he only became more touchingly beautiful to behold. In his sick bed, he brought such weeping to strong men that they became desiccated. For he was the whole of romance, a wild horse leaping in a canyon. He was the embodiment of leaping romance, yet his poor body was still, for he was dying. *Gaspard de la Nuit* was the first of its kind: a book of prose poems. No matter how minor, first is first, and bears its own golden crown. Louis thinks of this as he sinks and searches for breath, one more breath, one last breath, for the air to float the heavens, to utter *Célestine!*

FOR PATRICIA

A fleece of fine doves
is too crude,
Patricia.

A fleece of fine doves,
murdered for love,
is not enough.

THE REQUEST

In her grave smile, I saw
myself reflected, too,
in a likeness not too near,
not as some unified law,
but as one whom I knew
before her face was there,
one from inside of me,
so whom I could not see.

And I reached out to her
across a deepening flood,
and asked if she could see
in my bleak-featured stare
and dark, unrisible blood,
her own grave self in me,
and if she could, advise
death be not recognized.

TRANSFORMATIONS

If in place of my lady's eyes
there were other eyes as beautiful,
if this woman had other eyes;

if my lady's eyes were emerald
like the Irish Isles and this woman's eyes
were violet like the flower;

if in place of my lady's hair
there was other hair as long and
wonderful to see and touch;

if this woman had different hair;
if my lady's hair was shot with gold and silver,
or gunmetal gray, and this woman's hair

was of that Oriental black, flashing green,
or rainbowed; if in place of my lady's ears,
other ears perched upon this woman's head;

if my lady's ears were curly, tiny cakes
with pink and white icing, cherried perhaps,
and this women's ears were brown and pendant,

with lobes like long strong loops, hung with spiral shells;
if in place of my lady's upswept nose
there was the aquiline, or bulbous, or flat and flared;

if instead of my lady's pink aureoles
there were two burnished copper coins,
and if they made complete my lady's

perky breasts and the others did the same
for the pendulous breasts of the woman
by whom my lady was being replaced;

if my lady's slender waist vanished and became another's,
girdled with lacy jeweled chains instead of Shantung Pongee silk,
pale as Caucasian chalk or the limestone cliffs of Dover,

with belly button out instead of belly button in;
if my lady's pale round thighs, untouched by sun,
were found to be the lithe, athletic thighs

of a bronzed goddess who bathed all day in sun,
or thighs of Oriental gold or Melanotic mocha;
if my lady's ballerina's calves had been replaced

by hunger's calves in stockings made in diamond net;
if my lady's ankleted, once-bound feet, impossibly small,
should be replaced by webbed paddle-feet, ruby-toed,

and dusted with reflective sand; and if my lady's
smiling mouth, containing pearly cubes in a row,
should be replaced by the bitter, appealing mouth

of someone else, another woman, with buff dentures
that had chewed raw meat, like a leopard's;
if, in short, my lady were replaced in her entirety,

and I beheld her there, upon that high pedestal
where I had placed her, should I approve?
If her soul could be the same, despite

the physical transformation; if she could say
the same words, the words that I had almost
come to understand, after ages of agonizing struggle,

I think that I should not know that she was a different lady,
another woman, nor would it be true, in essence,
any more than I would be a different lover

without my beret, my bouquet of dew-damp,
fresh-cut, long-stemmed roses,
and my cornucopia of poetry.

FOR UNITY

Forster cried *Connect*.
Is there no way to correct
this unbearable condition
of lack of inter-recognition,
to commune, to sympathize,
even then to empathize,
to be on a path together
in the same weather
with a beloved other,
wife, child, mother,
or must miscalculation
of depression or elation
cause constant misconnection,
and be the sad projection
until the very end,
and all joys unfriend?
Hope, be harbinger,
not pretender, not stranger.
Love, let us be gifted,
by communion granted.

SUBJECTS IN MIRROR
ARE CLOSER THAN THEY APPEAR

Not on its reflecting surface, but in the depths of the mirror, the "scenes" appeared. I turned away, then back, incredulous, aware of the tricks the mind can play. Friends, relatives, lovers, even barely-met workmen, the electrician who came to do some wiring, the plumber who came to fix the pipes, the cable man, the woman from the next apartment who had lost her keys, and some I did not remember or recognize, all stared into their own eyes, into their nostrils and mouths, picking and probing—even the baby-sitter with her young lover behind her, watching her own young lust, whom I thought to have been so innocent. And then there was somewhere else, a gilded room not recognizable, a previous place, the antique mirror apparently having travelled, and a strange, beautiful woman, her long, fair, platinum-streaked hair unravelled to her narrow waist, over her bare bronzed shoulders and breasts; and oh that scene was worse than the earlier scenes, with those unabashed, secret performers, some of whom I thought I knew, for nothing moved but the woman's jade eyes, up and down, back and forth, even more lustful for herself than any man might show himself to be, had he been watching her. And I realized now how sickeningly full the mirror was, a mirror of disturbing Narcissism and animalistic impulses; and, as I watched the self-lust burning in the beautiful woman's eyes in the mirror that had given up its secrets, my throat ached and I began to choke with tears for the human race; and that was when the mirror broke, and I withdrew my bleeding hand, which had been reaching in to touch what was in the terrible, honest mirror.

NO ANGEL

Because you are you

& because they do not suffer
because their weather is never harsh
& they share nothing of the storms
that drive us in and burn us out
& because they are never in trouble
because they do not dance but on a pin
because they have no heat for anger
because they have no blood because
they do not eat drink nor defecate
& because they have no sense of humor
& because their lips are not discernable
but for a wide thin crease from ear to ear
& because their eyes are empty
but for the expansive light of heaven
& because they have not heard of sex
because they are never lonely
& because they do not judge
because they are not human
because they are abstract
& because their bodies are illusion
& because their wings beat nothing
& because they have no will but God's

you are higher than the angels

THIS MAN INSISTING UPON LIVING

How can I leave you with only one?
If I give you nothing but that which I give
what will protect you? Is this, do you think,
only a rationalization, because I want to live?
Is my heart as black as this typing ink?
But I cannot leave you with only one!

No, no, no! Nor can I leave you
with only these, stamped and stamped, only these two:
nor could I leave you with more if I had any more;
no, not with three, if it were that three
were here for me to leave, or
even if I were lucky and had . . .
but I cannot leave you with only two.

Nor could I dream of
leaving you with only these three.
How would you survive;
how could you ever get along?
I must leave you with at least four.
Do you think that four will be enough?

No, I don't either; I'm sure you'll need more:
five at the very least, yes, at least five.
Oh, I am going to worry, worry so!
I had better re-think this.
Yes, I had better think more about this,
for how could I live with myself

if you didn't have enough to get by on?
Yes, it had better be six, or seven, ten perhaps,
and if I stay until tomorrow, I can, if I try,
make it twenty or thirty, a thousand—yes!
It must be a million: I must keep up my strength:
perhaps I had better not go: I'm so busy.

GRAY'S ANATOMY

I Bada-Bing Bones

A stripper stripped down to her skin, then began to remove her skin by means of a zipper up the back and two more down the backs of the legs. Then she began to remove the muscles, unhooking them from the joints, like springs, and laying them out on the stage. What throbbing music! An old man in the front row fainted. A doctor in the back row called Stop! But the stripper proceeded to strip down to the bone, so that all that was left on the stage was a dancing skeleton. Somebody said it was a trick. But her skull-face called back, Dig it, boys—this is the real thing! Then the stripper snapped some bones out, one of her thighbones, one of her arm bones. A collar bone flew into the air to the sound of a drumroll. She picked up the collar bone, broke it, and shook some marrow from it. Then she called, That's it for tonight, boys. And as the curtains swooped down and closed, she was heard by the audience to order the attendants backstage to gather up her things. Hurry, she was overheard to say, I've got a heavy date.

II The Makeover

Sheets in pink and blue and wearing shadows and polkadots of red surrounded him. Come down from the ceiling! called the Board Certified plastic surgeons. Come back from the tunnel! cried the nurses. They were ironing his chest. If he had not been shaved, he'd have smelled the scorching hair. Zap! And he gave them that shiteaten expression he always wore when he was in trouble. I've got a pulse! cried a nurse. And then he remembered his fabulous visit to the other side. It was "a clean, well-lighted place," and the nurses were there, naked. No doctors allowed. The nurses sat at his feet, begging his attention. He's our fat Buddha, one said. Oh, my, but his now thirty-inch waistline hurt! They must have sucked fifty pounds of fat out of him. He saw a tube full of thick yellow syrup, a tube full of cheeseburgers, actually, and chocolate bars, and French fries, probably. His blood pressure is stabilizing! Look at that waistline, said a nurse. And the jowls are flat, now. Shall we start tucking that skin? Look at that butt! Good enough to eat! He's going to be beautiful! Too bad his heart had to stop. This is not an exact science, said a doctor. It's an art. Speaking of art, said the chubby nurse, I liked him when he was a character actor on that soap opera "The Sadder Day." I like him now, said a nurse who looked like a model. He was gone for over five minutes, said a doctor. We'll probably be sued. Brain damage, you know. I don't care if he *is* stupid, said the nurse who looked like a model, I'm taking him home with me. Everybody laughed. His wife, mother, and five daughters are waiting to hear how he is. Well, tell them he's lost fifty pounds and a lot of I.Q. and will probably get a divorce as soon as he can find his way to a lawyer, said the head doctor. That's what I would do, if I had his looks and no brains left. And a beautiful new profile. And an enlarged penis. And a flat gut. And a tight ass. And a plastic chin. I told you, said the nurse who looked like a model, I'm taking him home with me—dumb schmuck, but what a beautiful creation!

VANITY FAIR

I THE FASHION SHOW

The slim young women float their subtle curves
   before a fashion-conscious audience.
Diaphanous enough to tickle nerves,
   their gowns lift off them in a breezy dance
as left leg forward forces right hip out,
   and small breasts, bra-less, bounce beneath a gauze
of punctuated pink. Their red lips pout.
   Their veteran eyes, dark shadowed, seek applause.

Young women and some not so truly young,
   whose art it is to show another's art,
can you be sirens of whom Homer sung,
   can so much softness be so hard at heart,
that you would make this hard-pressed buyer sin,
forget the gowns, and buy the mannequin?

II THE STEROID LADY

The steroid lady stands, flashing her smile,
   upon a pedestal at Muscle Beach.
She's come a long way, baby; the last mile
   was not beyond her iron-willed, wiry reach.
Delts, pecs, abs, obliques, gluts, hamstrings, triceps,
   erectus spinus: she walks in beauty like
a knight in well-oiled armor, flexing biceps,
   and spreading lats and giving traps a hike.

What hope for man is left? She's made of iron!
   She looks like Mike, my hirsute little friend,
but that she's hairless. Is she also barren?
   For mothers must have fat or hormones end.
The softness of a woman has been taken.
I feel as if my manhood's been forsaken.

ODE ON SEX

I

Come, let me champion your cause, mind-altering Sex,
disintegrator of great family names and fortunes,
despoiler of priests, wild joker in each Jack and Jill's
young life, who eggs their egos on aggressively;
delightful Sex, who makes us foolish to ourselves
in alleys or in cars or in motel rooms rented
in titillated glee and paid for all our lives.

II

Come, let me champion your cause, mind-altering Sex,
for Mother Nature gives no whit for social problems,
nor loves the individual more than the whole;
cares little for the personal life, or not at all,
but is a painted slut, big-bellied and prolific,
drugged drunk on hormones, sprawled with open legs and
    mouth,
and ignorant of consequence—"couldn't care less!"

III

Come, let me champion your cause, mind-altering Sex,
for whom in Tijuana town I paid two dollars cash
and two weeks on the isolation stool when I was young;
who bows and bends the gay and kills them for their
    trouble;
who loves no one but lusts for every orifice—
O Sex, mind-altering Sex, sad Sex, are you all bad?
O Sex, then what is Cupid's so sweet Psyche for?

IV

The juggling of the genes—the double-helix shuffle,
survival's muted laughing need to mix us up—
causes the countless changes in two families
in lines that branch back into great antiquity.
See them as weaving an enormous web shaped like
a geodesic dome, our primal mother-creature
at bottom and at top two families conjoining.

V

When Jack and Jill, the twins, the scared and hungry
   ones,
the little red, white, brown, or golden berries, come,
give them a shower, sharing wealth and love alike,
for Sex brings Love into the world with motherhood,
and even orphans know the heart above their head
that shook the womb they grew in, know another there,
and know most certainly the need, mind-altering Sex.

THE SEX OF WATER

Water is naked but for its diaphanous gown, which can best be detected when the water falls over an escarpment. Then the gown shimmers like silk in the sun or at night with the glow of the moon. She who is underneath the gown is Water, who is always a dancer, and is then a hula dancer, or a belly dancer, but can be at other times a ballerina, an adagio dancer, or whatever, but always a dancer, at least always ready to dance. The Water in your glass, if it is not a glass made opaque by color, seems to be sleeping (in a black glass it seems dead). But Water does not sleep for very long. It cat-naps, but is as ready to swing into action as is a cat who has detected the slightest creeping of a mouse. Water appears to be feminine, but a great, broad-shouldered wave, one of those that come from the sea and flow over land, destroying whole cities, Water in that form would give us the sense of powerful masculinity, like a football player. Everyone knows that Water is graceful--a fountain spray, for instance—but it can also seem clumsy, as in a stagnant flood of several weeks duration, when dead animals float on it, and its lovely perfume dissipates and is replaced by a sulphurous stench, the odor of the dead. This is when Water seems to be connected to the warriors of the wasteland, and distinctly masculine, the destruction men make, which is so unlike the fecundity of the sparkling, egg-rich stream full of fish, which seems feminine. So Water is both Yin and Yang, the Lingam and the Yoni, or appears in such aspects, apparently at will. Of course how it is contained tells the story, in a tall clear glass or falling between two jutting rocks. Water, then, tends to conform to its surroundings and is coy in its pretenses. So, if we think of Water at all, it is as an hermaphrodite, as he-she or she-he Water, a sideshow trickster, like that star one can point to, that glittering dew drop in the night sky, which has been gone for a billion or more years.

TODAY, NOON TRAFFIC CROWDING

Today, noon traffic crowding, heat appalling,
I saw the double of someone I knew.
A face from long ago, I heard it calling
as plain as I might now be hearing you.

Thank God I'm not a king, or Canon Law
would have me married to the woman yet!
Pathetic creature! Not the one I saw.
That woman looked like one I would forget.

I mustn't be unkind! Resentment speaks.
So many years to hold a useless grudge!
Life's like a faulty sink from which love leaks.
Would you believe I stopped and couldn't budge?

    Forgive my grief, then, when I turn aside.
    I have at heart what I had thought had died.

ABOVE THE HIGH BEAMS

Parked
in the dark,
the motor running for
the heat against the winter,
with its packed and dirty snow
sinking in the soil beneath
the car, our divorce survived
by my loss of you, my youth,
by feelings that are hard,
and I've kicked out, hitting
the high beams, brightening
the bare trees, and spreading
a ghostly glow above them;
noticing how even that faint light
obscured the blinking stars,
the dulling and deformed
configurations of myth
punctuating storied night
with asterisks and commas,
exclamation points
and, o my lost one,
those damning, twisted
question marks. How
they decline, fade,
the longer I look
above the high beams,
the music of the battery-
charging motor making
an accompaniment
and a strangely endless
diminuendo to the late-
come light of the possibly,
but surely not surely, dead stars.

LOVER'S QUARREL

I live alone with my wife
who lives by herself with me.

Late sleeper, early riser,
big talker, shut-my-mouth,

our life together is apart;
apart, our life together.

We have no intimacy, we
have quality time together,

have quality time together.
Sure, no clue to each other,

and we've got to sleep apart,
in separate rooms, dreaming

not of each other, but no other,
of halls and doorways and walls.

Thirty years, how well
we know each other, how well

could be called not well at all,
thirty years not well at all.

Why do we stay together?
Because we have been together,

and no one knows us better,
no one knows us better.

THE LAY OF THE LORN MARINE

Pearl Harbor, Hawaii

ADMIRAL JONES was posted on the lawn,
but from an upper window Joe was called to,
"Come!" He saw her then again the second
time, on that wondrous, windy day. He looked
about. It seemed that no one saw him, so
he ventured to the house and stood in front
and she repeated, "Come! The door's unlocked."
He looked about again and then went in.
"Up here," she called, from somewhere up above.
He found and climbed the stairs. She called,
"In here!" And there she was. She wore
a flowing white and frilly thing he had no name
for, but was very pretty, and, underneath,
for he could see right through it, she was naked.
"Take off your clothes," she said, and so he did,
and stood embarrassed as she inspected him.
"Oh my!" Downstairs somewhere a door began
to bang, bang, bang, and suddenly loss
came over him. This was against the Code,
and could result in life in Leavenworth. She said,
"It's just the old screen door that's banging.
I never heard of a scaredy-cat Marine." It was
a sultry day, and what they might have shared,
a hot, tropical love, all that afternoon,
grew less probable with every bang, bang, bang,
of that damned frightening door and, finally,
he grabbed his clothes and scrambled out the window.
She called after him, "Joe, You scaredy-cat!"
His memory of that sad day has never left him,
a day of the most shameful of retreats, called hereafter
"The Day of the Lost Lay of the Lorn Marine."

LIPSTICK SKIES

She is Sunrise and Sunset, two women,
one who, in the morning, making up,
smears lipstick on her mouth, then sips
her tea or coffee, so that her smile,
while bright, is not quite tamed,
but somewhat wild against the morning sky
as if blossoming all over like a rose;
and another who has seen it all and lived
and still possesses quietly her passion,
which anyone can see, as she sinks down,
beyond her prime, beyond her day,
her sad mouth smiling knowingly
(for she has done some things she knows
that she should not have done,
has lived, has *lived!*) and now is near
the end. Behind the ridge her smile
breaks, with the lips of age,
crimson, plum, scarlet, not rose red,
for with the dusk she cannot see
to pick it out and put it right.
And she is thinking of a thing to say,
of some last word, as the great globe
raises its darkening horizon, but she
can only smile and kiss goodbye.

GOOD WORKS ARE LOVE

Today I noticed, randomly,
on my shelf of poetry
Bill Empson and Bill Williams
sitting side by side,
the scholar and the doctor,
Seven Types of Ambiguity
and "No ideas but in things"
the intellectual and the
know-nothing natural man.

The war between what each
was representative of
is still alive, but why?
Each wrote poems one can—
admire? Each did his thing.

To think that in an art
requiring tolerance, at least,
a war abides between two ways
of working words for what they're worth
—it troubles, reminding us—
does it not?—of all intolerance,
of the religious wars, and of
the white-sheeted racist and
the hanging black-skinned man.

WINTER WAKING

Toward dawn
the ululation of an early dog,
amorous with the moon,
echoes hollowly from the hill,

and I turn over in my half sleep,
away from the new light,
away from the window,
into my pillow.

But the dog howls,
sounding lugubrious in his desire,
and sleep falls away
as I remember myself.

BECAUSE OF YOU

I bear a burden, difficult,
 of guilt and my despair
for things I know that are my fault
 and only my affair.

And yet I speak of them to you,
 who seem so innocent,
and wonder if it can be true,
 at last, that I repent.

FLASHBACKS

You are doing something thoroughly mundane one day,
say, peeling carrots, and you are suddenly where
you once were while your hands go on with their work
and you are staring into the sun from under a shed
roof, where you and your other are arguing over
what you have done and now you remember that part,
the part of it that was about what you had done:
then you are wondering why you did it, what
ever possessed you to do such a stupid thing,
and it occurs to you as it has in a past you've
almost forgotten that you might have been arrested
for doing such a thing and no wonder that you and
your other argued over it, how could it have been
otherwise?
              Of course it was a terrible mistake
to have made: it was a wonder that your other stayed
with you, who had done such a thing, but in the shed
in the last light of evening you finally made up and
even now you experience the sweetness of the kiss
of forgiveness as if it were warming your lips as you
peel the last of the carrots and you remember what
you are supposed to be doing though it is difficult
to draw away from that moment in the sunset shed
that seems somehow to be happening as you stand
where you are: but then you realize that you have cut
yourself and are bleeding. You must bandage your finger.
You must wash the carrots and cook them. You must not
forget this event, you think, as you have so many others.

READY TO WALK

Lipstick and mascara are the bright spots of the room. She reflects in the mirror, one of her is there, then the other. What is that blue shadow in the mirror, lack of silver? That cloudiness is a secret. Paints her face to the point of erotic innocence, hiding the plain true innocence. Paints over her brown eyes with green paint, paints over her white lips with red paint, paints a red bull's-eye on her stretch-marked belly, paints her other lips, powders her other cheeks. Sprays a garden down her front, lifts it up and sprays some more. Studies the heart-tattoo on her thigh. Studies the crooked tattoos on her arms, palms up, in the mirror, then applies creamy foundation to them. A new beauty mark has appeared, several. She says, "I want to see my baby again." Then she slips into her soiled golden pumps, ready to walk.

TIPPY'S RAINY DAY BLUES

Once Madam told, sipping champagne,
how poverty built her disgrace.
What is the loss? What is the gain?
Poor Madam wears silk hose and lace
while her smug family reside
in Potter's Field's lowly embrace—
all things will level with the tide.

My Johnny feared the ball-and-chain
and left me flat, a welfare case.
What is the loss? What is the gain?
These days I love at a faster pace
than any ordinary bride!
Though Johnny's gone and left no trace,
all things will level with the tide.

When I was good, they called me plain.
The simple farmboys would grimace.
What is the loss? What is the gain?
Now men come to this sultry place
and, smiling, up to me they stride.
It seems that sin improves my face.
All things will level with the tide.

On rainy days I watch the rain
that falls straight down like tears outside.
What is the loss? What is the gain?
All things will level with the tide.

TIPPY REMEMBERS REVEREND SMYTHE

"The men I fancy most,
they have erectile heads
like the cobra-di-capello.
You remember what they tell O
of the preacher, now a ghost,
how the veins of his neck would swell O
and his face in different reds
would flush until the flesh
stretched like a taut balloon?
Expansion of his meaning,
like an increasing wish,
was forced by the poor fellow
to the point of apoplexy.
We girls could only swoon.
For oh, his paroxysms,
how eloquent they were,
as if he were unspleening
himself of his hauteur
(we called him Mister Sexy,
but just among ourselves:
it was one of our witticisms,
or better, barbarisms;
because he wasn't like that at all).
I smile to think about him,
and yet it casts a pall
(it's sad when memory delves
like a baited hook on a line
and suddenly has a weight).
What shall we do without him,
we who loved him well O?
What shall we do without him,
that bulbous-headed fellow?"

BEREFT

By artificial time, full of dates,
the pygmy time of people, not
the giant genuine time of stars,
she is late, the alarm rings out desire.
Artificial time is murdering his lust.
And the all-night lover of years ago
(his sleepy-eyed but vivacious wife
hurriedly hitching stockings to
garterbelt, slipping into heels)
looks on, bereft.   A hard life
has left him exhausted by night,
but a dream's sensual levitation
engages his tumescent morning lust.
Faithfully, this indiscipline of oversleep
by one who understands his plight,
he tries to see as healthy nerves;
although old men of the gold watch,
being doubtful of prowess, suspect
always a planned escape, yet
feign indifference.   The clock's
silent now, the old man blows smoke,
the coffee in his cup cold as his heart.
The choice was made between himself
and sleep. His wife had lust for sleep
and not himself. She has escaped
when she might have wakened early,
like a morning-glory, for his tested love.

DESCANT

> *O Meister, liebster Meister mein!*
> —Goethe

His American granddaughter, the nurse, called him Pops.
When she came home from work, she needed *Schnapps*.
*Ich weiss nicht, weiss nicht... Aber der Herr
Tod lebt. Vielleicht ist er an der Tür.*

Away in his own room she could hear Pops sing
a broken, depressing *Lied*—his own thing.
*Herein, Herr Tod! Ich bin allein,
"O Meister, liebster Meister mein!"*

Her grandmother gave her chocolate for her tears.
She knew Pops missed his *Liebchen*—married fifty years!
*Ich weiss nicht, weiss nicht... Obgleich
diese Schwärze ist irgendwie lehrreich.*

Why did her hard old Pops sit alone in the dark?
She nursed old people now—took Pops to the park.
*Mein Haar ist grau, meine Backen sind blau.
Nun ich muss schlafen, mit meinem Blut lau.*

She was middle-aged herself, a white-smocked Valkyrie,
but still a little girl underneath a tree.
*Bis morgen, Herr Tod! Ich bin müde und alt.
Wie die Bäume im Winter, ich bin sehr kalt!*

She'd be off to the old in the nursing home tomorrow,
to face again the selfsame sadness, the selfsame sorrow.
Man kann, was man will, wenn man nur will, was man kann.
We can do what we will, if we *will* to do what we can.

DREAM GIRL

The woman who lives in me, wet with desire,
can never give me up, no matter what I do.
For a fortnight I ignore her, but she's there
waiting pantyless and panting near my heart
that pumps for her and fills my member up.
She is my muse of sex, my succubus,
my sensuality so I can paint a nude.
When I look at winter her warmth flows into me,
and when I march, she is my vivandière.
She gets the outer ones to bear the children of my loins
so she can keep her figure that my mouth may water.
When I harass her with my sex, I hear her laughter.
Oh she needs no foreplay and she never sues.
She keeps my age so she can die with me.

TORCH SONG

Lucky that you love me!
Lucky that you care!
Thought you'd treat me roughly
if I were to try
to attract your eye,
so I didn't dare.

Then one day you saw me
sulking in the corner.
No one came to paw me.
No one even tried!
Guess they thought I'd died!
Only you, a mourner,

staring at me there
with a solemn look
on a face so fair
I near fell apart
pounding with my heart.
Half the ballroom shook!

You came over then,
smiling, saying Hello,
different from other men,
smarter, I thought, somehow,
making your slight bow,
voice so soft and mellow.

Later, asking you
how it was you married
—I was feeling blue—
plain and simple me,
music ceased, and we
talked the while we tarried

on the muffled floor
waiting for the band to
play our song once more.
This is what you said:
"Dearest, your sweet head,
filled with bunk they hand you

—utterly unreal
books and films and such—
having the ideal
constantly in mind,
searching, will not find
answers overmuch.

Love has many reasons,
being what it is:
many different seasons
drifting in and out,
flowering in doubt,
freezing in a kiss. . ."

You fell silent then,
but the music rolled!
I felt gay again,
happy with alarm
dancing against the storm
which your words foretold!

SMOKE

A poem in dialogue as if performed by Bogie and Bacall

She paused, gazing without expression at the smoldering, unfiltered cigarette she held between her fingers, then said, "You know, the thing about love is . . ."

"Like your cigarette," he said. "It has to be unfiltered and leave stains on your fingers."

"When you say the word love," she said, "smoke should come from your tongue."

"You mean that it's dangerous."

"I mean don't say it unless you mean it. It's a sacred word."

"And who uses it should be willing to die for its subject."

"Die for me. I'd die for you."

"You mean you'd die for love."

"Look at my beautiful fingers."

"Stained."

"Look at my beautiful eyes."

"Red."

"Here, take a deep drag," she said, and turned the wet end toward his wet mouth.

"It's hot and wet," he said.

"Like my best kiss."

"Your smokey kiss."

"Like a street in L.A., where you have to run inside at every corner to catch a breath of air-conditioned air, or your eyes will burn and tear until you can't see where you're going. Take a long drag."

"It's dangerous."

"Yes."

"I can taste your chewing gum in in. Juicy Fruit."

"And now I can taste your breakfast. Coffee. Coffee and more coffee."

"Our habits become identity."

"Love is more than I can bear," she said, snuffing the butt out in an ashtray full of similar, lipsticked butts, ashes on her crimson nails. "Almost," she added, shaking another unfiltered cig from a pack. "I'm a chain smoker," she said, then laughed. "I'm also a chain-lover."

"You've got the habit," he said. "Both habits. Both bad."

"But I'm starting on a brand-new pack of Luckies," she said, lighting up.

THE WIDOWER

    The clock of the cock at morningrise,
   or machine of the city sweeper,
rips the tape of the night from the wound of the day,
   painful to the sleeper

    who, hurled from his world of dreaming, hugs
   the airy shape of his wife
who left him most malignantly
   alone with his widower's life.

    Then, as his arms pass through the space
   that his wife has left in passing
and collapse within the O of prayer
   as if the man were massing,

    his eyes in surprise are opened to see
   that his prayer is sensual,
or that his prayer is a wife of air
   as the moon is menstrual.

    Thus, winning beginning again and again,
   though something each morning is lost,
he's gifted with pain to go on again
   by the wrinkled sheet of a ghost.

RX: THE FLOWER CURE

Cerato for self-doubt, a cause of sexual dysfunction. Mix with Aspen. Make a tea. Gentian leaves relieve depression. Make a broth with a dash of Sweet Chestnut. Also, for gloom and melancholia, Mustard Flowers. Impatiens for impatience. Make a soup of gold, add black olives to allay mental fatigue, and Hornbeam for decrepitude. Then go to the Hollybush for vigor. If your love remains indifferent, offer a few sips of Clematis. But heed this, lover, heed this: Take your love into the country and pick these flowers together!

INSECT LOVE SONG

Sing, downfalling measure!
Dog-day cicada, sing!

Oh, don't let up,
stout fellows, Falstaffs,
fat, winged knights!
I was losing myself
in your music. Sing on!
Give us the belly laugh,
the long vibrating call!

Sing on, grasshopper!
Harvest fly, sing on!

There's a harvest moon,
and many a star.

Night wind shucks the corn.

Webs are weaving.

Rain is coming.

Sing on! Sing on!
You harvest flies!
You katydids!
Sing for your ladyloves!
Sing for the sad world!

Leap to the bar, cricket!
The crescendo! The mad song!

LAST EXIT TO EAST HAMPTON

I will get off the 4:19 in Easthampton at 7:15.
                                    —*Frank O'Hara*

"Entre nous, Roger and I visited some friends out on East Hampton, and there was a wealthy and beautiful chatelaine there, sans man, whose name I have conveniently forgotten, and Roger took up with her, because, *I* think, she looked like Truman Capote, blond and a little plump, and the next thing I know I'm soloing it with my Martini very dry and feeling like a dipstick in the sand. Roger and I are always together and I could not understand such isolation as had befallen me. After all, I was being dumped for a female—well, maybe. But just as I was reaching the blue dog black funk basement on the down elevator, a woman wearing an amazing diamond choker passed on some interesting and distracting gossip. Apparently, Bergdorf's had appropriated Augustus John's portrait of Talullah, to whom adieu, which cheered me I can't tell you how much; and, after swallowing the last of my Martini very dry, I sighed happily, and said, Oh well, we still have beaucoup de music classique et moderne. There was a band all in gold. The diamond-choker lady elbowed my ribs, indicating the door, and so I saw Roger leaving with the beautiful lady (maybe). Absolutely horrid of him, of course. Still, I tittered anyway. Later I took a dive in the pool to cool off. You know how it is. These people are harder than they look, like a roll of Krugerrands you put in your fist to make your hand strong when you punch somebody's lights out. Oh hell, life is beautiful, don't you think?"

INSPIRATION AT THE ART GALLERY

A beautiful little love seat,
   with nails pounded through
from in back and underneath,
   was an exhibit at the gallery.
The symbolism was clear,
   I thought, until the artist
came in and sat down on it.
   He wore coveralls which were
full of tiny holes, as if shot
   with a shotgun, and blood-
drenched. He stretched out
   on the love seat and fell
promptly asleep, as if drugged,
   and then began tossing and
turning. Now I realized
   that he was not a sculptor
but a performance artist,
   and this was not symbolism
but life itself. This man knew
   what a love seat was, and he
inspired me at long last
   to take action. I went home
to my suburban house and began
   putting nails through anything
I could penetrate—a nail-gun
   helped. "Have you gone mad?"
my wife of thirty years asked me.
   "You're ruining everything."
"I am making it all make sense,"
   I said, "because, as you know,
I am about to retire, and
   I want what I have worked for
to be an honest record

    of my patience and labor,
something to be proud of."
    She threw up her hands, but
seemed, at last, to understand,
    and began to help me with a hammer.
When there was no place left
    to sit or stand or to lie down on,
we left by the front door,
    stepping gingerly over the sharp
spikes at the threshold, the
    neighbors speechless, gaping,
and went off in different
    directions in search of another,
perhaps last and happy, life.

WHAT'S THE MATTER?

Love, as our particles impact,
and bounce, as they needs must,
it should be clear, my dear, we are
but dust disturbing dust.

CHANCE

For whatever reason,
we have found our lives
joined this morning,
as the sun roars up
beyond the patio and
its green vista.
You will have to go
beyond the chance
to find the purpose
of our being here,
like this, together,
beyond the purpose
once again to find
the chance. Rilke's
angels are the
potential others
of Planck's quanta.
Some seeds of time
will germinate,
some disintegrate,
and some, like us,
discover faces
in the mirror and
across the table.
I only know my eyes
see you (my neurons
say my eyes see you),
and seeing you I see
this moment as a
fragment of all love.

THE RED SHIFT

When I angered you, you grew red in the face, and that red shift meant that you were leaving me, growing more distant, so I took your delicate hand and kissed it, uttering into it that I was sorry for any pain I had caused you, and the red faded from your cheeks, and gradually you turned pale with pink places, like an impressionist's dabs, here and there, neck and forehead, and I could see that the red shift was reversing and you were moving toward me again, the gravity of my larger body pulling you in like an angelfish on a fine silver line, like a seaward moon, like a meteor, and I thought what damage a meteor could do: a meteor could tilt me on my axis, could cause me to become engulfed in smoke, and blinded, and possibly extinct, so I pushed you back away from me. I held you at arm's length, and you began to turn red again, another red-shift, and that was not what I desired, so I pulled you to me and held you as tightly as I could, and, when I looked again, you had turned blue and your open mouth and eyes were dark, like holes in space.

THE BROKEN CROW

Along the cliffs she wandered,
   a song sublimely sung,
along the cliffs, and pondered
   the sea they overhung—

"The sea is vast and deep,
   the cliffs are high and wide.
Now let me plunge in sleep,
   and in black water hide

my body that is dying
   away from loving friends,
away from any crying
   and have the best of ends."

It was a swan who dove
   into the sea below:
next day at Fisher's Cove
   they found a broken crow.

Her friends were there and crying.
   It was the worst of ends.
Oh, she who had been dying
   could never make amends.

THE NORTH OF LOVE

I.

Winter, that great doomed ermine,
challenges the serpent and the mouse,
buries each in his crude house,
silences the summer din
of birds: and bells ring across white silence
—where thickets are ungainly ghosts,
leaning together, gossiping in wind
—to herald a distant sleigh,
their chiming voices thinned
by the crystal distances of air
and the vast inertia of the trackless snow.

Through lacework windows
I see the bare white birch,
frail virgin of the timberline,
new bride of snow, the Eskimo;
I watch as he caresses
her modest, proffered limbs
and pale, gripping feet—
this mating of tree and snow
reminds me of all love . . .

II.

When the phantasmagorial leafless trees blossom anew
    with blue, frozen tears,
and the wind-whipped snow at evening and the creeping
    mist make an indivisible ectoplasmic figure
that hovers above the lake and lurks near its frigid
    banks,
and the ominous cold evening sky describes the vale

    of lost things, with its gray upon gray of cloud
        upon sky,
and the moon is a pale disk in the pale, tall light
        of evening,
and the wind halloos down from the mountain like the
        voice of the Cyclops demanding more wine,

  and blindly it tumbles the house to one side;

when the dull, small stars go shivering about in the
        heavens,
and the serpent and mouse and the beaver and mole lay
        locked in their crude, white houses, afraid,

then we suffer from reminiscences of all the folly of
        the misspent years;
for winter is an end; above all a time of summing up:
      to take in hand and stop the spinning whirligig,
      your
life, to examine in the cold light how love fools,
        outflanks
you, takes you and makes you and breaks you again, no
        matter what sweet cynicism you think you have
        achieved. Do not try
to riddle this phenomenon any more than the heavening
hawk riddles his hunger. But remember the bare
        white birch, frail virgin of the timberline,

  the firnificated kisses of her bride-

groom gathering in cold, pallid clumps along her limbs,
        covens
of wind weighing against her, mountain-bred, bitter,
        flaying, as all love's too often made . . . .

III.

I strengthen in this northern solitude:

When constellations wrangle overhead
and wind roars, the sudden shiftings cancel
the sound I listen for, the sound of bells,
and I fall into winter stupor, dreaming—
I dream of trekking up the mountainside,
the moon ahead, old-woman faced; behind,
the frail white birch, deflowered bride of snow.
I dream myself withstanding wind and cold;
and, breathing hard against the altitude,
of climbing up Love's Everest, to breathe
the cold significant wind of mountaintops.

CAESAR AND CLEOPATRA

When Cleopatra rolled out from the rug—
that was the end of the Republic. Caesar,
involved in mid-life crisis, felt the tug
of pagan godhood, plus the need to squeeze her.

She took him on a tour of Egypt, showed
him secrets, like the tunnels used by priests
in their predictions of the Nile, and rowed
him on her barge. She showed him that her breasts

were fully formed, those of a goddess waiting
for him to join her in the Royal Way.
"A balding man should wear a crown." Her baiting,
her teasing, proved Great Caesar's feet were clay.

She laughed to see democracy go down
and Caesar turn from great man into clown.

SILVAMOONLAKE

Resplendent tonight, the moon spreads silver. Moonlight drops from the trees like silver leaves on the far side of the lake. It ripples across the lake like floating silver petals. It washes up on the glittering banks, and some of it angles across our evening picnic table in long tappping fingers. Our white wine glistens golden, our stemmed glasses reflect. My love reaches out to me and her hand slides under silver. The silver climbs her arm as she reaches toward me. She becomes a silver lover. Oh, she begins to tarnish! I reach over to her, out of my shadow, and dab her forehead with soft white linen. The napkin comes away with a dark, glistering smear. She darkens and hardens. She becomes a statue. I reach out and touch a cold shoulder. Aghast, I lift her stiff form and carry her inside the cabin. Where is the silver polish? Thank heaven, I find some under the sink. Time and oxygen are destroying her. I must work fast or love will escape me. Mad for her riches, I polish her like a thief.

RIVAL SLEEP

I have a rival for my darling's heart,
that dog called Sleep. She cannot let him lie.
It is the same now as it was to start:
she loves Sleep better than she loves my sigh,
my upright passion—which will never quit—
my tenderness of touch—all naked me!
She loves Sleep more than thunder's lightning wit
or downpour's sonorous profundity.

She loves Sleep better even than my kisses,
and cuddles him, not me, the long night through.
When I sat next to them and heard his hisses,
snake-tongued, in her sweet breath, I sadly knew
  that deepest Sleep would keep her in the end—
  my loving never could make her attend.

TRACT

The human race is richly blessed,
for it's at liberty to choose
the path above the dark forest

where it evolved from small tree shrews.
When we were young, in those dark ages
when trees were gods, we could refuse

our few objective pilgrimages
their bright discoveries forthwith.
We'd stronger gods and images

of potency surpassing truth.
It wasn't innocence we had
but ignorance, like any youth.

And ignorance of good and bad
we can't equate with innocence,
for ignorance is something sad

and innocence is happy; hence,
that Eden Garden written of
to show our disobedience

could not have been a place of love.
Nor did the ignorant within
(whose bodies fitted hand-in-glove)

deserve God's angriest chagrin
for plucking knowledge from the tree.
How was their action any sin
in seeking knowledge, lovingly?

CARNIVAL SESTINA

Within the underbrush, beneath the leaves,
they sought the blinding sun for one quick flash.
The carny was in town, the crowd was quick,
merry-go-rounds were going round, and music
lent them its pace, though talk was near at hand
and certain someones wandered in the crowd.

When, later, they rejoined the noisy crowd,
she brushing from her skirt the golden leaves
that all that autumn fell, and he, his hand
above his eyes, avoiding the last flash
of evening sun, they noticed that the music
seemed in some doubt if they were dead or quick.

They separated then, and George was quick
to find the other two among the crowd,
who, when they saw him, laughed above the music,
crying, "You two were there, and then like leaves
in autumn, gone! We lost you in a flash!"
"From this point on," said George, "I'll hold your hand."

"But where's my wife?" asked Keith. "I want *her* hand."
I haven't seen her, Keith," George lied, too quick
to answer, sounding false, and, in a flash,
it came to Keith that they had used the crowd,
his best friend and his wife, to lie in leaves,
betraying him and George's wife, while music

played, lulling them to think that love was music
like an unending song, and with a hand
drew George's wife to him, and into leaves
they vanished from the crowd, the others quick
to note that they were gone now from the crowd.
In leafy shadows, Keith told her in a flash

of his suspicions, also in a flash
what she had always hoped, and it was music
to George's wife, who hated that false crowd,
but truly loved dark Keith, who held her hand
in his and kissed it, slow, and not too quick-
ly drew her down with him into the leaves.

"We've lost them in a flash," Keith said, his hand
lifting her breast. "Quick now," she cried, "while music
drives on the crowd, and I wear only leaves . . ."

BUCOLIC SONG

When dead dreams are dreamt anew
  As my once dead ones are,
Homage must be paid to you,
Fargone time's renewer, who
  Can renew a goneby summer,
Winter, or a wind that blew
      Long, long ago.

Ah love, return my heart from dead
  And gone to wondrous hours,
Give me golden times ahead,
Let my heart and hope re-wed
  Here among new-verdant bowers,
Let their lovely vows be said
      As breezes blow.

THE COUPLE IN THE GARDEN

Forgive him, he
walked wickedly
toward his loss and capture.

Forgive her, she
stepped stunningly,
entrapped, within her rapture.

FIVE MILE MOVIE DANCE

You wore flowers,
something flowery,
and my arm around
your waist lifted
you, two, three,
maybe five miles,
dancing, never stopping
for the breath we
did not need, being
young, over all
obstacles, cars,
steps, up and down
porches, around fire
-hydrants and light
-poles, using them
like movie props,
swinging on them,
like a pair of
movie dancers,
Fred and Ginger, so
that we could remind
each other, all
these years later,
how we danced
through Brooklyn and
all the way home.

Part Six

AMERICAN MOBILE

AT HEART, SPEED

At heart, speed is about being where you are going sooner than you can get there, and putting it all behind you. As you race forward to get where you are going, much is dropping behind, falling away from your frontal interest, as it were. If you were as fast as an atom, say, you could probably spin back and pick up some of what you have left behind and so take it with you as you propel forward, wherever that is now—for we have thoroughly muddled the issue in having gone back to pick up what was left behind because in having gone back we have made back forward, forward back. At heart, speed is an attempt to avoid as much as possible until we get to something we may or may not have in mind and stop there, but of course as we arrive there we find that we have just left and are now on our way to something that resembles in its lack of interest to us all that we have attempted to leave behind, so, in a sense, we are going backward, or, we should be going backward, toward what we wanted to get to in the first place. At heart, speed is our heart beating and speeding its beat until it has run out of beats. At heart, then, speed is our heart excitedly beating a trail to its end.

AMERICAN MOBILE

The pure products of America go crazy...
—William Carlos Williams

Miss Smith, she dead.

...my blind left eye don't stop me
I swivel quick around then get ahead
back at the panorama
striped down and then back up the hill
to any future peak greened brown black cut through
white striped like up the leg on a uniform
the wind don't wall me
my aerodynamics
they'd lift my license for my eye full of sugar
but I still drink
that VA doctor's lower'n fish shit
no beer no way
but I drink Lite test my blood take my insulin
I eat right mostly but my Drake's cakes
I'm thirty-three feet back
sixty-six long times to here
always dreamed of motorhoming
free to be you and me
Maxine's you
she sips at that beer
stares through the wraparound
like she's watching home movies
and shoots bytes at me like look there
did you see that
she's frightened at being sixty next week
I told her look at me—you plus six
and I'm still steering

still truckin' but I never was a trucker
was a kid a soldier a vet a cop and
a guard at Disney's that was my whole damned life
that back there behind me on the road
but it comes along with me in my sugar-eye
my shotup shoulder from War Two
my skin cancer from standing all those years in the sun
reflecting off tarmac and parked cars at Disney World

Max says look Jersey plates
she says Joisey we started out in Jersey
we fell in love haven't slept together in years
Max thinks I'm not well interested
but it's the sugar
I don't tell nobody not even her not especially her
suppose she knew I couldn't
what kind of man would she think
look she says back in back her mother sees it too
I don't know what it is must be on my blind side
but I don't say no way I let them know
I'm blind as a blackboard over there
not hurtling along at eighty
they'd piss their beer
you got to hold to your lane
the old lady's nearly ninety but full of it
not only beer either if you know
look Max says
shut up Max but I don't say it
I don't listen about Alabama moons
Georgia peaches glorious Asheville leaves
I talk to myself my only friend
they suck me in like black holes
the old lady and Max everything goes
into them nothing out toward me
did I believe in love

I've stopped laughing even
I've been driving too long

I see us off the edge of a cliff if I don't keep him awake
old man hunched up at the wheel was he my hero
I think there's something wrong with his eyes now
the way he jerks around to see   I've noticed
I ride not swiveled in a bucket by a tilted instrument pod
but sometimes behind him astraddle his first Harley
his long blond hair snapping in my eyes no helmets
my fingers feeling in the deep holes
through his shoulder and his ribs
where the sniper's bullet drilled through
he died he said and came alive again on a table in England
I still wore his white dress shirt
hanging out over my rolled-up blue jeans
shiny pennies in my loafers
Frank Sinatra made me scream Elvis my one daughter
Buddy's blonde princess the Dead my grandson
nobody sings anymore all back there somewhere
with my mother boozed up at ninety
a Depression-made cheapskate
sipping cheap port
and a hundred thousand in the bank
how did we get here

where are we going   why must I come
Harry could save me
clever with life how left-handed he
mangled his right hand in the leather machine
made them think he was right-handed
more compensation
at last a little house and money in the bank
and I got us out of Jersey
like war in the project then

the Sixties the long hot summers
bullets through the windows
down to Max and Buddy in Orlando to my little house
Harry why must I travel with them
the youngsters even are old but Harry's gone
crazy at the end
fighting in the trenches again
Argonne Belleau Wood
gone on the road behind us
dead and buried in Orlando
buried and lost his grave lost
we are going to sue
I have no place to put flowers
no place to talk to him anymore
they lost my Harry
tough leather guy from Brooklyn
tough guy so sweet once
poor old crazy man
gone back to the trenches back to Pershing
mustardgas and Belleau Wood
another world so far away
to his grave at ninety-five
I don't want cable
only my one soap-opera station
only my wine
don't even want life to come back
what is the wind
Star stories say some of us are aliens
supermarket tabloids Maxine calls them
and tries to make me think they print lies
sometimes I think Buddy and maybe even Maxine too
I bore her but maybe pod people have taken over her body
like that old movie
maybe she isn't Maxine at all she doesn't act like Maxine
I could have a baby too

like the hundred year old woman in Australia
it would kill me at ninety they must eat something
yogurt like those Russians who live forever aliens too
and the little girl no older than smaller than
who had quadruplets by a tom cat
all of them born with whiskers
the pictures were right there I saw them
whiskers and pointed ears and long tails I saw them
what is that going by where are they taking me

"Good Housekeeping" said
the kitchen was the warm womb
of the colonial home and early-American women
would stand at the hearth watching the turkey turn
as they pumped up the flames
packing sandwiches for an airline ain't exactly
the big time but we made it
Buddy and I paid off the American dream
for his bedroom and my bedroom
and the alligators down on the lawn
to the rock seawall wanting sun
what's life
put the rocks back put
back build up fall put back
two slices Wonder Bread
one slice waterpumped ham mayo mustard
my long thin fingers all little silver scars
I'm nobody what did I deserve
not Buddy and my mother anyway
sixty ain't the end yet
not even with all my loose belly skin and
stupid strokefoot dragging when I'm tired
like Buddy on Omaha Beach
but I got it right through the head
like being brain-shot and nine weeks in the hospital

stealing our money
there she is sipping her wine at ninety
defying nature and three out of five of us kids with strokes
always demanding maybe she gave us the strokes
but nobody's dead yet they say we are all lucky
so that's what luck is not being dead
a case could be made

driving into the dusk is like driving into a dream
better hit the lights
that big cluster of stars down there
I aim my good eye on ahead
now in the dusk it gets tricky
but I don't let Max know
extreme macular degeneration
sugar-induced doc says
then he says you got varicose veins in your eye
laser beams he says burn 'em out
so I see blue for a week from the dye
and the blue fades to gray and that's it
my credit's good
social security veteran's pension Disney retirement
I'm a triple dipper
plus equity in the house poor boy makes good
I'm driving fifty thousand dollars across America
like I started out with anything but
a piano-teaching widowed mother
like I had a chance in life
I play my own tapes me at the organ
singing Willy Nelson songs
"On the Road Again" Max hates my music
she's jealous but says I could of made a living
at it could of but couldn't take the joints
composed some myself guitar piano organ
my tape plays "King of the Road"

my plates say NO MORTGAGE NO BOSS
NO JOB NO WORRIES I'M RETIRED
twenty years standing in the sun eating Twinkies skin cancer
Harry thought Max could do better
he never had a home like ours right on the gators' water
he'd say he never had alligators on his lawn either
only stinkbugs in his old palm tree
sometimes I miss fighting with him
him on the Kaiser me on Hitler
who was worse all ancient history
even the Commies are dead
nothing left for Freedom to fight
and the world moves moves into the next century
away from us what we did and needed
it'll all be computers and new people
no more like us we're dinosaurs
old people but we move
and we take our houses with us like hermit crabs
we circle Asheville in leaves we land at Normandy
not ten minutes in and all my bones break
until I wake up on the table in England
purple heart silver star
I remember the sea swashing puffs of smoke
our flag it still stands   yesterday's news who cares
Max is sarcastic once she was proud
I can't help it Max
it's the sugar sugar

. . . who betrayed me so many times with his Harley
with somebody else's legs around him
fingers in his wounds
hot stuff and joins the police
to wear his beautiful blue uniform
and ride his police cycle with his blond hair
fluffed all around his blue visored hat

and me pregnant alone with his blonde love in my stomach
stud making a fool of his wife making a fool of his life
with nogood burgling cops only Orlando left for us
thank the chief who saved us and that was when I began
when I began I began began to be old

Maxine looks like me at sixty
you could compare her to a picture of me then
O Harry do you remember
where are we
North Carolina
why are we here climbing this mountain
full of beautiful leaves
is that heaven up there what is that up there
a jetstream
a flying saucer
why don't we just stay home
where I know where things are
they don't think about me how I can't see
how I wish Harry were here
how he was when he was young
so neat courtly so kind and sweet
not like at the end afraid of the Hun
hiding under the table gone crazy old man
with old-timers disease
it was all there again for him
no time had happened
no me no all that life all wiped out
and he was there again and it made me wonder
if we aren't all just here or there or where are we

Asheville we pack it in at Nashville
Max and the old lady won't go to the Grand Ole Opry
so I'll leave them to themselves
I'll go like I always said I would

could hear it in Jersey when I was a kid
could hear it all over the country
Hank Williams Minnie Pearl Tex Ritter Hillbilly Heaven
a southern yankee I *never get enough of that wonderful stuff*
Max says we should of gone the other route
to Memphis first Graceland Elvis can wait I say
but it turns out to be Hank Williams Junior and Rockabilly
not like I dreamed of it glitz and bang
even a vet can yearn for the old sweetstuff
Junior's daddy the original Hank the real thing
the lyrics were in a language I could understand
we fought the wars and longed for love
they march for peace and seem to hate
like I'm still waiting for the fat lady to sing
President Truman even introduced Kate
Smith to the Queen
as "America" *Oh beautiful for spacious skies*
but the Opry's like the rest of it now
maybe we should try Dollyland at Pigeon Forge
no Max wouldn't like it because

angels come to our door but Buddy won't let them in
do you know these are the last days
not if you have something spiritual
it's on Earth
he was sent by the God of Love
that's why Graceland is a church
even if it's like they say
that his body ate twenty Big Macs a day
his soul had to live on Earth didn't it had to eat
so Buddy's blonde daughter tells me
my daughter too but more his blonde like him
now nearly bald not her him not dark like me
well gray but if Elvis could bring happiness
then he is a god

he's one of those aliens Max
he was sent here to sing and bring love
they say Graceland is more beautiful than Heaven
that it's all blue like the sky with no clouds
no thunderbooms and tin-roof rain clatter
where are we

like when Buddy grinds his choppers
he is eating us up in his sleep
our night war like our day war cannibal
shoved our beds apart into separate rooms
trumpets saxophones trombones
Buddy names my snoring while he grinds on
and her crazy on the convertible back there
all night coughs and chatters in her sleep
about chicken wing prices
it's like a gone-nuts orchestra
OOMPA OOMPA CLICKETY-CLICK BLAH BLAH
his teeth telling how much he hates his life
at different times broken uppers and lowers
life that never did what he wanted it to do
we rocked that motorpark in Nashville
hooked up Winnebago nearly laughed itself free
electric lines tore out as it rolled over on its side
and later shaking with screaming
Mama and I had sucked the city of any last drop
of Southern Comfort
Buddy never came back from the Opry till it was dying out
drunk himself from shit-kicking with urban cowboys
I told him his sugar'll kill him he sleeps grinding his life
like steak into hamburger I'm his life
what's life
Mama refuses to die until we do
gray and stroked and sugared and beer'd under
but how could we leave her at home who'd watch her

nobody'll take her in if we go she has to go
won't go to nursing home no way you know no how
and I don't mean not to go go go before I die
thank GOD for Winnebagos
next stopover next postcard
P.S. life's a war and you can't give up
love Max at sixty

heaven is a place like Graceland
they say Elvis's daughter owns it now
she's the spitting image spitting image
listen Max at least the foreigners don't own Graceland
like they do everything else
it ain't true that we don't work as hard as the Japs
but the unions Max I never did trust the unions
you think like a scab-cop
my father was a union man Buddy
her father was a union man
Harry was always a good union man
and a good Democrat
if they're good for anything the aliens'll be UNION
if I didn't belong to a union
do you think they'd of paid me so much
for making lousy sandwiches
did you get enough sleep
we should of gone to Graceland first
read a "Reader's Digest" article once
first it was the farmlife held us to place
then industry mills and trading and
later the big factories up north
made cities centers now no more
anyone anywhere now the computers
no more fixed life no more unions no more
democrats no more stay put go go go
like the damned beatniks hippies used to do

on the road in the sky
a whole corporation inside your portable
computer workforce anywhere
regions don't mean nothing cities countries
my country 'tis of thee
I'm caught between the old lady back there
and my grandson
he'll be part of it the brave new world he said
college boy and his kids won't even know
what we were
can't you just see it grandpa
no boundaries no borders
even space the moon Mars
business everywhere signals flying through the air
caught between times becoming part of it
losing it at the same time
with my sugar walking down the street
I never noticed how sweet beer is
injections they'll be able to fix that too grandpa
and the whole world and even space
will become AMERICA

you look at your mother and you think
how could I have come out of that sixty years ago
HAPPY BIRTHDAY Max
it's a chorus of whiskey-cracked voices
a duo of dead and gone ghosts
calling back over their shoulders
it's bye-bye Maxine you're as good as dead
with your mastectomied pumped-up plastic tits
what'd you need them for for *him*
could of caused the stroke I'm told
but then why my brother and sister stroked out too
my face I had burned with acid and scraped
for him forty years ago

acne pits from her tea and cheap day-old cake
to stuff us just before supper all of us
faces like burned-red moons
from her brother-can-you-spare-a-dime
cheap Depression soul
the old man back from Belleau Wood
mustard gas and the formaldehyde stink of the tannery
the whole goddamned century's been a war
I could live to see the end of it
no more goddamned Twentieth Century
now we fight each other we can't stop fighting
we're like three hairy-assed Marines
landing on each other's beaches
HAPPY BIRTHDAY Maxine
Christ he kissed me breath like death blow out my candle
if I could I'd blow them out of the Winnebago
and get my wish a little time on earth alone a little life
before I die

Max was always tough even as a little girl
she always fought
her father'd have to drag her off
from a fight but he was proud
my Max don't take no shit he said
we had to be tough Jersey we all glow in the dark
better than hard cold and cheap
we had nothin' but trouble like the plague
Nineteen-Nineteen she says
the doughboys brought the influenza back from Europe
all those displaced persons
my best girlfriend died of it everybody
was dying you're too young to know
good to be too young for some things
why do you think God does it
screw that

God helps them who help themselves Buddy
he likes that one   damned Republican
but he's right it's like Elvis
a success a blond guy with black hair and a cape
God loves us all Max He's sending them to help us
well He's got a damned funny way of showing it
your granddaughter says He sent Elvis
or is it Elvis sent her
I told her he came in on a saucer
they'll all be here soon
Buddy singing playing the organ he installed
coming in on a wing and a prayer
his feet pumping he loves to show off
he says Harry was just a leather worker
says my mother taught piano   class will tell
your people don't have no class no way
then it's a Donnybrook
in the musical world

in heaven this couldn't of happened
if Max would spell me
I'd go back and get drunk with the old lady
sit in my *Seat w/Telescoping Pedestal*
and stare at her until I could see inside her BRAIN
but Max won't spell me won't drive no way no how
just sucks in sixpacks and farts at speed bumps
I'm mustard gassed like Harry at Belleau Wood
turn on the BTU's she says watch out
open the vents here comes Max
but she admits it was damned embarrassing
we got the Arizona state troopers all over us
here's the old lady telling the pump jockey
at our time of life we want full service telling him
I'M BEING KIDNAPPED BY ALIENS
I have a lovely home in Orlando

they're forcing me to go with them
they want my money a hundred thousand dollars
it belongs to Harry he earned it with the wrong hand
call the police help help
it takes some explaining but I tell them me I'm an ex-cop
look I say but they got me and Max over a car hood
if I had one of those BIG FOOT trucks
I'd drive right over top of this traffic jam
crushing cars like an angry giant
that's why everybody loves Big Foot
I look at the cops and twirl
my finger in a circle at my temple
nuts the both of them I say
they feel sorry for me and because I'm an ex-cop

get real Buddy do you think God's in California
or in the Painted Desert or the Petrified Forest
I want to see the first Disney place is all
Max is *mad* like Mel great roadman
people say it's the end of America
from the coast there on it's out forever
and the sea climbs into the sky
Buddy it's your music
sometimes you sound like some godawful poet
song of the open road Max
there's good trucker songs Max
trucker poets cowboy poets
you're ignorant Max
don't start Buddy don't start
I tell you what Buddy
Vegas is God
you get a bucketful of change and pull handles
until something good happens
gangsters built Vegas Max
gangsters built everything Buddy

Bugsy Siegel is God and Vegas is heaven
for shame Maxine
what do you know Mama
it's all a chance and to hell with your aliens
can't you see saucers Maxine
clouds Mama we're in the mountains
Sierra Nevadas Mama
I'm not *your* mother I'm hers maybe
and the white bombs of love
like the Star says it's Elvis in his saucer
lots of Elvises because this is the end of time
they have big dark eyes and sideburns down to here
real smooth cheeks and they wear wonderful jumpsuits
with colors like Las Vegas that night
the first or second so it was stacks of colors
and everything blinking they wear clothes like that
with glittery things hanging down from their sleeves
I was a little girl when Dreamland burned down
my mother your grandmother Maxine
said you could see Dreamland burning from Jersey
I had been to Coney Island I had been to Dreamland
I'm sure I saw Vesuvius erupt and a great naval battle
where New York was bombarded by foreign ships
and then an American admiral went out
and defeated all of them
you see children it is all a dream
and you keep waking up to something new
we aren't really here at all we are here
and somewhere else at the same time in Dreamland
Meet me tonight in Dreamland under the silvery moon
my mother used to play that one Mama
I am not your mother don't call me Mama
you're alone in the world Harry never liked you
motorcycle-head he called you
Maxine's got me if she *is* Maxine

of course I'm Maxine
Christ of course white bombs
SNOW
where are we Maxine
if I smashed this pedal down down hill
I saw a movie once about a wagon train full of people
heading west on Donner tha's it the Donner party
they were going over these very mountains they were up
here
high like this and there was a blizzard and they got caught
and they couldn't get down out of it
blizzard starved and they began to eat each other
don't look at me Buddy
the saucers will save us
they'll snatch us up into Graceland
they can do anything they can make us fly
can they take us back to where they came from
is it a musical place
of course it's a musical place
Elvis is King
yeah Graceland is the real true blue heaven
beyond the cheap chicken wings of the world Mama
beyond the world Maxine
or whoever you are
Buddy my ears just popped
we're climbing Max
it's getting dark Buddy
you better stop
can't stop on the highway
some articulated eighteenwheeler
some BIG FOOT
come behind us
no visibility
now I nail my one good eye
to the white-dark wraparound

like one big cataract
faint red lights
turning off ahead
now nothing
down there's a turn
somewhere down there
I hit the gas down hard to the floor
it's dark and white like being wrapped in ermine
if we weren't doing eighty ninety a hundred
it's like a toboggan like the OLYMPICS
SWOOSH SWOOSH and we're out off in SPACE
the cold moon and stars ahead
I push my *WING-EXTENDER* BUTTON
and now it's STAR TREK
THE PANORAMA OF SPACE
I can see through the thick clusters of stars
ahead there deep
GOD'S BRIGHT MUSICAL CASTLE
but the saucers hold us floating in air
HIGH OVER GRACELAND
you can see the lights
I told them I told them
and THOUSANDS and THOUSANDS
of GOLDEN COINS COME GLITTERING
CRASHING OUT

CODA: THE GHOSTS GO HOME

> O lost and by the wind grieved,
> ghost, come back again.
> —Thomas Wolfe

. . . so this is luck says Maxine
you can take your freaking luck and shove it

*Mama says it was the aliens who helped us
hundreds of flying saucers piloted by
Elvises in sequined pod suits
they lifted us off the cliff
I told you they would I told you
she's nuts Buddy we're dead right now
dead and floating away Max dispersing smoke
and just when I thought I was going to heaven
to God's bright musical castle
where I could play the organ
play* Meet Me Tonight in Dreamland
*for all the heavenly days of my death
O.K. Buddy but what in hell do you think
I'm travelling for
we left the other goddamned Disney place
three thousand miles back
I want to get away from it all
that's my heaven
every place is the same Max
every place is Disneyland
now don't you start sniveling Mama
but home is where the heart is
my heart is with Harry in Orlando
poor old Alzheimer man
I loved him so much
for God's sake we got all freaking bummed out
I sent a card back home to tell
how you've acted you son-of-a-bitch you killed us
and I think you did it on purpose
you think you can drive through space now Buddy
still steering Max
Maxine
what Mama
you children are enough to drive me out of my mind
but the National Star*

and the Pod People keep me sane
look at all that space
can you fly this thing Buddy
an American G.I. can do anything he has to do Mama
Buddy sometimes you remind me of Harry
why thanks Mama
doughboys is what we called G.I.s in my day
like you he came back full of holes
but gassed in Belleau Wood
beautiful name to be so horrible
I know I don't tell you very much
but now that I know we are all going to
heaven together or somewhere
well wherever the pod people take us
I love you both
we love you too Mama
don't we Max
O.K. so all us suckers love each other
just keep this smoke floating
Mama I think Maxine is blubbering up
crocodile tears Buddy she's hard as a rock
no Mama you should see her up here
shut up Buddy
she's had too much beer
no I think the crash is just now sinking in on me
but I'm not going to stop drinking my Lite
I don't care if I'm dead
you are dead Max we're all dead
Buddy are you sure you can fly are you
does smoke rise up from a fire
and finally vanish in the sky
I keep on truckin' like I always done Max
through war and peace Mama
our flag must still wave
through hell and high water Max

*I could go on flying this big beautiful
Winnebago with the eagle wing span of an
Enola Gay forever across America
back and forth across this great big
God bless America country
FROM SEA TO SHINING SEA*

URANIUM BLUES

Driveshaft

      distributing eighty, ninety, a hundred

CLANG clank clank clank
outside Moab Utah
                        falling dusk
long white snake line
                     blacktop
shimmering off

             shimmer dimming out
mountains far

         low ahead
smoke a cigarette   wait   smoke

wait   sky bleeding up
down behind mountains   wait

sun's hiss   sidewinder's sandshuffle rattle
first long low leap of hare

car walls away last hot sticks of sun
cigarette's smoke-signal saves you
palm it & let it go   toot
toot
         a hum   something
down the road   crosseyed lights

stand up   wave   cowboy
like the cavalry   out & under
driveshaft down   pickup's got a tow

haul you in   patch you up   come daylight
get drunk tonight

                    heigho Silver
gaining on   shadowed   etched
mountains   hauling ass   through pyramids
huge wide-based sinister cones   hundreds

through falling night   under stars
uranium
              inside mega-tons of pyramids
house up high there's Mister Big Bucks
made him a hill built him a house
them from Washington   big wigs
& queen bees
                        down here's enlisted workers'
mobiles   hauled in   you ever
seen such a one?   long as a railway car
star-glitter's ore   hot stuff's in there
just awaitin' ta burn down hell   hot damn
we going to blow up the whole
freaking world
                        break out the booze
we got us a writer here   going to Gollywood
play you a tune   strum strum strum
sing along   sing a song of uranium
uranium blues   glitter glitter
stars all over   up & down
same whole hotdamn universe
blowin' itself up   bee–you-tiffle
all night outside on the nailedtogether
radio active porch   strumming, swigging beer
on a tilting planet   singing the Big One
BIG ONE   everything doing a slow
burn   slow burn

                              Heraclitean
rise up   up   Mister Sun
sleeping   until dark again   lit up

drive off singing   the atomic world
in the dark starbright early morning night
headlights glaring
                        singing Uranium Blues

HOT TEEN HOGS

They rub the blue out of their bluejeaned crotches.
  They rip the teeth out of their red-hot zippers.
  They fan the flames, and then curl up like kippers.
At last they check their charioteering watches.

They tell each other where to meet next week.
  They shake their leather jackets free of gunk,
  and she with red nails combs her ducktailed hunk,
as he wipes damp mascara from her cheek.

From this day forth their dream becomes to make love
  naked in bed, not fake it in a park
  behind some bushes in the evening dark.

They swear that not again will they forsake love
  in greasy leather garments, harshly studded,
  to go home dirty, lying, and guilt-flooded.

THE ISLANDS OF LANGERHANS

*Islands of Langerhans--
scattered cell groups in the
pancreas which produce insulin*

*Stream of consciousness, WWII Veteran,
Hospitalized, diabetic, dying . . .*

           Woke once to   Islands of Langerhans
    white-smocked aliens   emerald islands
        their poetic rap   in a crystalline sea
          the crystalline   in Oceanside in
      active principle of   Golden Land
  the Islands of Langerhans   Silver Hollows
                insulin   in Golden Land
      palm trees swaying   near the sea
           ukulele music   where you can see
                sarongs   the Islands of Langerhans
  Hollywood presents the   in an echo
     Islands of Langerhans   of crystalline footsteps
      with Boris Karloff   down a hollow hall
        as Langerhans   where white-smocked
  mad scientist who invites   aliens
  alien pod people to land   rap poetically
and institutional footsteps   where you forgot to take
      down the hollow hall   your insulin
    hollow footsteps down   you know you can go
        hollow footsteps   into sugar shock or
      in an echo chamber   insulin shock
Silver Hollows near the sea   if you don't take care of
          ukulele music   your only friend
        on the crystalline   and you like a kid

        have to spend all day
               at Disneyland
       eating cake and candy
         and swilling beer
                unbalanced
Disneyland in Golden Land
                  Hollywood
                     sarongs
              ukulele music
         palm trees swaying
the Islands of Langerhans
             their crystalline
              active principle
            poetic rap of the
       white-smocked aliens
          who took samples
               of your blood
       on a raised white table

The beach at Langerhans
           is heavily fortified
     and there's a rough surf
                many died
  before they hit the beach
   awarded the Purple Elvis
    and the Flying Saucer
   for the bullet plugged in
                at the neck
          and drove down

and out through the ribs
under the right arm
rapping he'll be out of it
in a day or two
rebalance of sugar-insulin
treat as shock
then nothing but the
white-smocked aliens
who landed at Langerhans
I was afraid
when I saw them
they echo'd and echo'd
down the long hallways
a Silver Hollows sound
but they will transfer me
to a VA hospital
heard their crystalline
poetic rap
footsteps
echoing down
wasn't afraid of God's
musical castle
wasn't afraid at all
because old was young
when we hit the beach
at Langerhans at
not Langerhans
at Normandy

SINGLEWIDE

If they thought of us,
how all of us lived in the singlewide, fourteen feet
deep and forty long,
on no money but the wealth of God
sending us on our mission,
bringing seven children, his, mine, and ours,
with the early death he bore in him, to leave
me, after five hard, bleeding years,
rooms spattered with blood, aplastic
anemia hemorrhages, him, my love, gone,
and me left with the beloved brats,
the marina rich would know
it was their Christian duty to buy us out
at a decent price.

I tell the buyers how God told us
this was where to stop,
how I planted the redtips to shade the
thin back from the sun, the fig from the Bible;
how I lost my faith in sorrow at his death
and drank my way
into Alcoholics
Anonymous and found
my new man there, who pumps iron,
sweats tea, but wants beer,
a tattoo'd boy not older, not
less wild, than my son,
and needing a mother-wife,
why we drink iced tea in winter in this cold
singlewide, how he hauls red-necked dynamite to
mines on eight fat wheels;
and the well-dressed buyers look at me
like I'm crazy as I tell them
I'll sell real cheap,

but not as cheap as the
marina rich will pay
for a sad eyesore;
and they don't think I know investors
when I see them, who'll put some other
poor souls in here, or tear it down for
the lake land; crazy because I will take
the money to Texas on the border to start my dream,
my homeless and battered women's mission.

My big lug's trucker's license goes far. Only
a relapse to fear, to drugs or drink,
can stop my heart's compassionate work,
or the mission is mine, to bring them the
visions of Isaiah and the trials of Job,
which I know in my used woman's body,
burnt-up with sex and sin, my pretty nose
and cheeks fried with small veins
from the days of bleeding and empty death.

The buyers smile in kindness at my dream,
my mission, my need for direction—
they think they are too smart and can
live without God. Well, let them, if they can.
How much will they give me for my life? His anger
is not turned away and his hand is stretched out still.

I loved these woods that drop down to the rich man's lake,
condominiums, marinas, and the trees I planted to shade
my only wealth beside the Lord, my Savior.
But I bargain, with my stretch marks,
my unpainted, veined nose,
for my singlewide,
which no one wants, not even
these patient souls!

CARPOOLING IT IN THE CARAVAN

a *New York Transit Strike*

Such amazement at reality
as to make it seem unreal,
and the knowledge of the
confluence of disparate events,
where impulsiveness and
inventiveness meet, such
amazement and such knowledge
have sometimes thrilled me
out of thought so that I
must seem a victim of logorrhea
in the library of life,
gleaning a joke out of the
quiet morning business commute,
the one the serious morning
newspaper readers want ejected
from the carpool.
Facts become treasures
in an uncertain world.
They are cheese to mice
on a flying mudball.
Since the past is deepest dark,
and no binding statement concerning
the future is possible, my fellow
travellers engross themselves
with the headlines and sports pages,
ignorant of ultimate purpose, and,
unlike me, content with now.

DRY-GULCHED

The mother-of-pearl
    desert dawn
reddened. Grit-eyed,
    I stared through
the Chuck Wagon's window
    at an almost ghost
      town of
    haunted hotel,
  false-fronted saloon,
hermitic mechanic's shop,
    my Mercury lame,
      waiting for
    a new engine
    with its block
      not split
    by Mojave heat,
and saw the celluloid
     posse of
my matinee boyhood
ride in with the dawn.

BAD TRIP

I noticed what beautiful teeth the young man had. Mine are missing or turned to coffee, red wine, and smoke. The hitchhiker had a seabag stencilled with my name. I have an unusual name and it could not have been sheer coincidence. I was going west—he said west was fine with him. The Mojave highway was empty for as far as I could see. I stopped the car. He tried to open the door, but I had them all locked. I shot him, then unlocked the doors and pushed his body out into the roadside sand. I got out and rolled him out of view, down a sand dune, and buried him, dust to dust. Well, I might as well have done so, even if I didn't. What I did to him was nearly as bad, maybe worse. I let him live and become me. So most of my life I have been living inside a much younger man. It was quite an adventure, being young. He ran a lot, ran long distances and very quickly short, marathons and dashes. He got embarrassing erections on buses, hanging on to the strap, and would have to face away in a twisted posture, but the rest of him, being loose, not stiff, he could contort and hide his secret lust. In middle age, he was big-voiced and positive, sure of everything, in a way I find impossible; I, who doubt all. I have many photographs of him. Lifting barbells. Boxing. He is always glad to pose. Myself, I hate having my picture taken. It is certain to come back to me as an old fart, grinning stupidly at the camera, as if to say, "I am still like him, like that hitchhiker." But I am not just like him, not at all like him, inside or out. I miss him but I don't want him back. I would rather crawl forward and under; for, now that I think about it, he never was so hot, never the number he thought he was.

AN AMERICAN POET ON TOUR

I suppose it was somewhat
like this in the Hellenistic
age, when you could go in every direction
from Athens and still be a Greek
and I suppose it was somewhat
like this in the Roman
when all roads led away
and back to Rome and
I suppose it was somewhat
like this when the sun never set
on the old British Empire,
so this is what we Americans get
for being the so-called superpower.
I have been thinking these thoughts
on a plane for an hour—
how every place I land
seems like the place I just left—
and now I think I understand
just what Gert Stein meant
when she said what she said
in her odd and idiosyncratic bent
about the place she had come from
where there was no there there.
Anyway this morning wherever I am
the weather seems fair
and I'm sure to like it there.
I'm good for anywhere.

LIKE THE TITANIC

Earth was to warm, the icecaps melt, and the land disappear
in a large low sea where the continents would rise like
 tropical islands
beckoning the water-stranded, the arked, the rafted and the
 routed,
but instead Earth cracked in two, making commuters work
 harder,
and instead of a Nuclear Winter there was the Radiant
 Summer
and instead of the Third World War there was the Time of
 the Thousand Fracases
and the last pair of African elephants was saved by the
 Cartel of Poachers
to be bred for their ivory which at long last was discovered
 to actually have medicinal value and aphrodisiacal effect,
and everyone learned Turkish, making the Common Market
 an unanticipated success,
and there really was a Man in the Moon, which turned out to
 be a well-disguised alien listening post
and the point of origin for flying saucers, which the KGB
 and the CIA, who had been working together for years,
  had known all along.

No, the meek never did inherit Earth; instead they grew
 cruel and
powerful and took control from the rich who had grown
 kind
and Halley's Comet returned twice in one year,
confounding astronomers, who now project that it does this
 every millionth turn,
but where it goes when it does this nobody knows
even though many are prepared to stake the world on their
 theories,

speaking of which, Einstein and Planck never could be reconciled
and instead of the poet dying like a young swan an old one honked on monotonously
into the night, only saving his audience with much cheese and wine,
once again proving himself in error, according to human certitude,
which any fool can prophesy, is not to be trusted.

INCOGNITO

Le monde est le livre des femmes.
          —Rousseau

Imagine arriving, ermine-clad,
thinking yourself forgotten there,
in a village in a valley, nearly a col,
ringed by alps, in one of those mysterious little
border countries in the Balkans, having chugged
uphill and tobogganed down until
you have left the other world behind,
where it is real and true, and have come finally
to your Ultima Thule, a guttural in a tongue
nobody outside knows; where,
stepping down from the powerful, steaming
train, containing the last of the known world,
you become again part of the place where you began,
unknown and young and beautiful and frightened,
decades and decades ago, before the shame and scorn.

Thanks to the enormous wealth you have amassed
as a world-famous courtesan, you have kept
your health and strength—money for monkey
glands, spas, etc.—and with them
some of the qualities you had
as a youth, particularly your fierce,
imperious temperament. And everyone moves at
the tilt of your wide-brimmed hat, everyone bows
—for even here there has been news of you—everyone
looks up at you in awe—your great height an
illusion created by power—and you say, finally,
after a lifetime of waiting: Bring them to me,
those who so hurt me that I had no choice but to succeed.

Your beautiful rival of youth waddles up.
She is just your age, but looks a thousand,
horrible, hairy. You sicken at the sight,
this porcine hirsute sight. She stole your man.
He stands beside her. What, not him! You give them
  alms.
But what of the dreadful mayor? Dead, long dead.
And what of your former employer, that hateful woman?
In a nursing home, gone daft with age. She sometimes
calls for you. They sweep you off to see her.
And she calls for you. You bring the bedpan in
yourself. You pat her hair. Where have you been,
you dreadful girl? You've been around the world
in company with kings. The *Almanach de Gotha*
mentions you. When your mistress falls into a comatose
dementia, a talking, tossing sleep, you watch the moon
sail across her curving window, and make a mental list.
Surely somewhere there is someone worthy of your
  wrath.

THE GETAWAY

There was a rosy dawn in the mountains,
but it was the city he needed;
there were morning stars; but he needed the rain-wet
ashcans and the morning Danish.
He needed the containered coffee and the dank puddled
 streets
and the steam up like a seeping vapor out of hell
from the drains and the hellbent crowds
walking right over the tops of taxis
in the impossible pace; he needed
the banana-peeled gutters and the knife in the back
and the long low slow limos with ominous dark windows.

There was a rosy dawn in the mountains
and there were early morning stars and a scimitar moon
and the cabin hung over the cliff and groaned
and the rainbow trout would jump right into your net
and you could breakfast on trout every morning
and while you ate the sun would run along the cliff
and turn everything into gold.
You could write all morning to the warbling
in an ornithologist's dream; but he needed
the poem of the city in order to write of his hero,
the gumshoe, the poor sucker the city folks loved.

SPRING RIDES

It is like this now at the end of winter.
The poor trees have survived, like
the poor blacks and the poor whites
along the highway, who wave as you fly by.
They have survived another long winter.

Now suppose someone in a passing car,
someone very rich, were to heave from the car
a suitcase filled with money,
then in spring the trees would spend it
on new clothes and the little girls
would be wearing fresh leaves and flowers
on a breezy church day and would look "like a million"—
Well, there you have the waiting trees with their tight buds.

It is like that now at the beginning of warmth.
I have been waiting, like a willow for the wind,
hanging loose but useless, for the busy world outside,
though I have run my leagues and burned my wheels
waiting for winter to haul out—for here is not Aspen
down the slopes but a pickup stuck in a bog—
and now my drive is full of Flowering Judas,
and older today I feel younger than yesterday
and for no real reason am convinced of tomorrow.

ON WHEELS

Once, in a mind, and many times again, a wheel
rolled overland toward a far horizon, a wheel
twinned with another on a wooden pole, then
four wheels turned overland toward some always
West, grinding eternal ruts in time. A wheel
attired, a formal wheel, became four tires
in white-walled best, spinning overland toward
the setting sun, a white-hot wheel, a round thing
in the mind. Some wheels fall flat and spin, and
some stand up. Wheels chipped and put together
make up gears. A gear is just a chipped wheel in
a mind free for a moment from the threats of time.
A wheel is a round rock turned on its edge.
A wheel is just a round thing in a mind.

Part Seven

CATECHISM

AFTER THE STORM

The Tragic Sense of Life in Men and Peoples
—Unamuno and I look out in tragic joy
as congregations see their floating steeples—
each steeple tossing like a leaping buoy—
and make a joyful noise unto the Lord,
and we, bereft of faith, still join the song—
it is the Word we doubt, we doubt the Word,
and we have doubted it for very long—

but if the people, tragic people, want it,
we join their joy, another name for hope,
a name that comes for tragic time to blunt it,
but let it help the tragic people cope!
They stand and look at wreckage, then recapture
—eventually—their tragic sense of rapture.

WALLACE STEVENS CONTEMPLATES SUNDAY SERVICE IN HADDAM

The day was nooning toward its bells,
and all were late, and yet he lingered there
enjoying summer and gold-nugget bees
divorced from gravity. He felt, at last,
that he was master of his mind, one of
the few who've made a satisfying picture
of the world and of the world's world,
the inclusive all, the one containing
all the perfect particles, the one
he was among the ones of, watching as
his hand scooped air as if it were
ice cream, a clean fresh strawberry,
an air so clean it glittered to his eyes
and melted on his tongue, an air
of summer on a Sunday. He wouldn't go,
and finally the others left him there.

SUNDAY QUESTION

Now Sabbath bells are ringing happiness
for saints without the need. But what of us,
the still unrisen sinners of the sun
who run through grassy woods towards our ruin?
We, the innocents to wisdom; the birds, the beasts;
we who, famished, kill, and then who feast;
we the deaf the dumb the blind the hurt and hunted;
for us the tale of Sabbath bells is blunted.
Come and explain, O understanding saint;
we wish to worship, even in complaint.

SYMBOLS

Pro Deo, contra ecclesia   Fidei Corticula Crux

1. THE CROSS

These Crosses are quite various in kind:
the ones the Romans punished with were wood,
but others have been precious metals, shined
by priests with polish, symbolizing good.
There's one which, on its side, looks like an X,
and symbolizes Scotland's Saint Andrew.
Another stays the vampire with its hex,
though many think that simply can't be true.

The Cross Impotens, with its crutch-like ends,
stands for St. Philip and St. Anthony—
yes, both, disabled, share a single Cross,
but, being saints, I doubt if either minds.
The Greek is lengthened, centered equally.
I think it mostly symbolizes loss.

2. THE FISH

What symbolizes baptizing in water?
An anagram in Greek, ichthus, or fish,
for Jesous Christos, Theou Uios Soter,
or Jesus Christ, the son of God, our Saviour.
When seen in Christian settings, make a wish
to have a happy life in which to live
(which Torquemadas never can forgive,
so don't let church spies notice your behaviour).

St. Peter was a fisherman, they say,
and one day caught a sole and then another
and soon his bobbing boat was full of fish.
All soles, he said, are one another's brother
(most women were excluded in his day),
and, rinsing it with wine, he cleaned his dish.

3. THE LION

The Lion's an emblem of Jerome, the hermit,
used to denote his death, and deaths of others
as martyrs in the Roman amphitheatre.
Nero did not have any need of permit
to throw these Christians to the lions. Mothers
would wail while watching in loud keening plaints,
but some would not let drop one little tear
for certain knowledge that their sons were saints.

It was a joyful day for them, to see
the lion's tooth transfix transfiguration.
Caligula and Nero were not gods
but did His work without their knowledge. He
made instruments of them, against all odds.
Death is God's mode of reinvigoration.

4. THE PEACOCK

The Peacock stands for immortality.
"The spirit passes from this life to more
and better life to come," supposedly.
The impress of the moment on the mind
may be as much as one will ever find
of depth and length in life and space and time,

and so much then for all fatality.
We may have seen the best life has in store.

The Peahen waits the Peacock's grand display
(she nearly always finds that it's enough
his immortality has come her way).
Perhaps the reason's in the thousand eyes
that like a strange horizon hypnotize
and egg her always on to call his bluff.

5. The Dove

The Dove denotes the purity of woman,
whatever that can mean beyond her love.
Well, I suppose it's something far above
what I can think of when I think as human,
and not as someone supernatural,
my mind an impure thing, half-animal,
incapable of knowing purity,
but not, I hasten, without sympathy.

The Dove is symbol of the Holy Spirit
and also of all females saintly dead.
I wonder how it is that we inherit
through Patriarchs unmerciful, rock-hard,
this image of unwomanly white love,
seeing instead of woman, bird—a Dove!

6. The Dragon

The Dragon stands for evil, sin, or Satan,
denoting how we fell before we stood
on our hind legs inside that scarey wood

that we remember now as Garden Eden,
a paradise and snakepit all at once;
and conquest over paganism, too,
as when "St. George the dreadful dragon slew,"
as when he proved that dragon was a dunce.

(St. Michael, too, was made extremely tense
by legless serpents and their fiery kin.)
Once, snakes were at the water for a drink,
thinking the mild oasis was their sink
and not the desert paradise of men,
when stones of primates taught them better sense.

7. THE LAMB

Begin with sacrifice: an offering
made by all races, usually in youth;
made by the pagans as they groped for truth;
made by the primitive; a proffering
of something that we have for what we want;
almost of Isaac by good Abraham,
whose homeopathic magic was quite blunt;
also by Aztecs till the Spanish came.

Would Christ approve of such insanity
more than he would approve the rack or rod?
But publicists must make their stories tall,
and Saul it was, who, turning into Paul,
made sacrifice of Christ, the "Lamb of God,"
the centerpiece of Christianity.

"BATTER MY HEART . . ."

I, John Donne, poet, priest, and sinner,
upon seeing two things which emanated
into creation by human misuse and by the mis-
conception of the body's termination as death,
by bearing the one, learned that the other
could then painfully invade even virtue's heritage
of unsullied and everlasting life. First,
I grew ruinous and out of harmony, having
had imperfect faith, and, secondly, suffered
melancholia and dejection, proving my heart
to be mere clay and divested of the spirit.
For I understand myself as being mere walls of clay,
condensed, then scattered, dust, and, being so,
so also am I sacrilegiously already half wasted,
in that I half wasted my body in youth, and
in that now my gray-shrouded time is almost gone.
But, nonetheless, increase Your flame within me,
Your flame which produces tears of repentance,
and let that flame so rush out through my flesh,
even if it causes agony, that it goes everywhere,
and that I may see it in everything.
Help me to approximate integration of power,
love, and knowledge, so that with these three
forces functioning in harmony, I may better know
and love You. And may the martyrs come to me
to beg that I continue to live my life, and not die
by my own hand, my own Dioclesian and persecutor,
so that I become a wholly living martyr deprived
of my death and final belonging. And if the Experts
do their best to interpret the Register of the Elect,
and to unravel my confusions, keep me mindful of the
flaw invested in them, and necessary to them, and
let me forgive them their love of knowing, and mine.

When this is heard, my ears are shut, for listener
and answerer are one in one. And while all are
joined in a universal choir, which is also a
meditation on on three things, viz., "hope, bear, and do,"
help me to seek renewal even in a short, gray space.

DARK AGES

> *More light!*
> *—Goethe, on his deathbed*

O there was never any actually powerful light
by which to comprehend the common day,
merely the milktoast light of we benight-
ed, who cannot understand what we see.
But whose fault is that if we sadly try,
standing clumsily up to our full height
like doomed, dim-minded begging bears
that with sad hungry hearts are so unbright?

Is it any wonder that all we do is fight?
Is it any wonder that all we do is lie?
Is it any wonder that what we do is trite?
Is it any wonder that we stand and sigh,
   who are graced with only such a little sun
   by which to try to be someone, anyone?

I HEAR YOU KNOCKING

When all the matter of the universe finally finds a wall or floor or ceiling, the knocking will be enormous, and it will have to be heard, because, if there is a wall there is logically something on the other side of it, something that can hear it, wouldn't you say? I suppose you can't take this seriously, but it is in my peculiar chemistry to find it plausible. What could be on the other side of the wall? The dead? Well—the souls of the dead? It's hopeful. In such case, they would be sitting at God's feet and learning wisdom like a flock of hippies on a mountain learning from a guru. The wall would be dancing, of course, scientifically speaking, and the matter of the universe, made of mere ephemerons and faked to look like a façade, would not be half as solid as the wall of God's projective garden. Pascal would know how to penetrate it, though, thinking reed that he was, his thought would go through like wind-music; and that would be his great gambler's soul. *Oh, but God!* When all the matter of the universe finally finds a wall, the knocking will be truly mighty, like the beginning of B's Fifth!

ECLOGUE

Non nostrum inter vos tantas componere lites.
                —Vergil, Eclogues

FIRST SHEPHERD:

We meet again upon this hill
but now we climb it with a will,
when only last time, when we met,
our breath was easier to get.

I see your flock has grown greatly
over what you had just lately.
Oh, you'll die rich, but what's it matter?
Will wings of faith make your mound flatter?

SECOND SHEPHERD:

My soul is tended by a priest
whose duty it is to see to the least
among his flock as it is ours
to see to our sheep during their short hours.

FS: Much as you'd see to your fine flock
piece by piece on the butcher's block.
SS: We have had this argument before.
FS: Ho! Then, my friend, I'll say no more.
SS: Why do you plague me with dark thoughts?
You ought to think—
FS: Ought me no oughts
because you're a serious man who hurries
from hill to hill, enjoying worries
that do not matter, and I'm a herder
who knows how to laugh in the face of murder,

for what would the murderer be taking
and what would the victim be foresaking?
SS: You were a foolish fellow when
we last met, and are again.
FS: As indeed are you, who think you see
your way out in a fantasy,
in buying a pass to the eternal
from a priest whose heart's an infernal
machine of greed and mumbo-jumbo.
Did he have you drink his magic gumbo?
SS: Of dragon-bones. How did you know?
FS: I know many shepherds who go
to these purveyors of clipped toenails
and what you will. The game never fails
to take them in more than they do meat.
SS: I'm sensible.
FS: But they defeat
good sense because they offer what
good sense just simply hasn't got—
essence of Self, the thing we love,
outside, beyond the body, and above
that body's gross and greedy needs
which cause so many dirty deeds.
Your health is good. You need not worry.
SS: I do not worry.
FS: You heave and hurry,
and with your staff you vault the hill
as if to leap to heaven. Will
nor wealth can keep you whole.
SS: And when they tug and pull and toll
the bell for you, where will you go?
FS: What can we see? What can we know?
Go nowhere and become the sand,
a stuff run through the little hand
of an infant on a wide wide shore.

Like you, my friend, I'll be no more.
SS: Unbeliever!
FS: Self-deceiver!
SS: Your little flock is moving on.
FS: And I shall follow and be gone.
SS: Farewell, poor doubting soul!
FS: Farewell, and keep you whole!
SS: Next year, perhaps—upon this hill.
FS: If flesh is quick and has a will.

THE MARTYR

a Televangelist

The heart of the true God would break
for such fools. Christ would cry
for them in their stupidity—
husbands and wives signing away
their homes; the old, the hard-
handed scrawny, betraying their
children for such as these
plastic saints, with their radio
and television towers rising
all over the world, towers
of their power, and time-
shares for these poor-fool
souls, to visit a plastic heaven
and be regarded as its angels,
like the angels of a Broadway Show,
to shine in their pride before
that great production—God's
Follies. The impresario smiling
out at them from his great stage
knows they will not turn against him,
for to do so would make heaven fall,
would make him the devil of their days
and them the devil's dupes.
So, when he's exposed,
when he has his *Dies Irae*,
they march against the courts
declaiming his innocence, proclaiming
his martyrdom, while he hides under
a bed and cries, and must be dragged
out, and off to prison, the final

soul-less product of materialism,
eventually to return to the public
stage, bringing a best-seller of
his efforts at reform in a white-
collar prison and, perversely, of
his innocence and terrible martyrdom.

MISSIONARIES

Wending our way, we wonder where
the Guys and the Gals went who seem to be gone.
Are we to wander inside of this weather
until we are lost as the others were?

Why were they lost, we wonder moreover,
the brave Moravian men with their women,
the ones in canoes and the cannibals too?
Some seemed to drown in the ever-new river,

some went along for the ride because lonely,
and some never got to the gates made of horn;
but some sought to come back to where they were born,
the ones who cried only, if only, if only.

THE PRAYER

I

Today, the hurricane is coming.
Many are already dead, floods
rise like megalomaniacal hopes,
birds have been stolen by wind,
broken, or beaten off into peace.

II

My umbrella broke off, spinning away
in the wind like a whirling mushroom.
I was left with the hook in my hand
and a face like a Keystone comic.
I boarded the bus to applause.

III

The hanging signs flapped wildly
and one, like an ace of spades,
was dealt to a wagging dog.
A shopkeeper recovered the corpse
while the bus hummed in horror to go.

IV

"It could have been me," an old lady said.
"The government does us no good!
Oh Lord, stop the wind in its
irreverent rush, stop the rain,
stop all that we cannot control!"

THE PERUVIAN APPARITION

Thousands of people saw this occur, saw
the Madonna come down and go back into the sun.
I myself took a photo which came out pure gold.
I sent it to the National Geographic. Back

it came with a rejection letter, the substance
of which was that the photo editor could see
nothing in a Kodachrome of gold. The Madonna,
I wrote back, was herself pure gold, and I

myself saw her come down from the sky, and ducked,
like thousands of Peruvians who ducked that day,
at sight of this wonderful apparition.
But my letter was to no avail.

I keep my square of gold pinned on the wall.

THE LEAP

Faith says to leap, forget the brain;
  Brain, I am Without-which-not.
Many a night I have lain
  in my bed and, cold and hot
by turns, have tossed,
and known the cost

of ambiguity about
  which way to go: if I should throw
away the brain, be like some lout
  bulldozing what I do not know,
without clear sense
or evidence;

or, on the other hand, should pray
  that I can make the leap of faith
and throw the troubled brain away,
  and so acquire at my due death,
through sacrifice,
a paradise.

WALKIE-TALKIE

I admit my presentation isn't tops,
but I have been assured that You ignore
that kind of thing and go right to the spirit,
that You're interested in the heart of the matter,
as well as the matter of the heart—flesh,
but what dances it too.   So, if I ask,
do I offend? But before I ask, You know,
so do I offend even before I ask, am I
offensive by nature? My nature is nature's,
what am I to do? You know me to be turning
a corner before I go out for a walk.
Maybe You have a brick waiting for me there.
Maybe a divine breath has wobbled it, just
a little, and now, as I go by, down it falls.
Maybe it misses. Then it was just a warning,
right? But if it hits, I'm home free—no?
Please tell me the right way to go!

Now, please, pay attention to my list.
I don't need to read it out loud to You.
I don't need to say it inside my head.
If You deign to know, You already know.

Is the list too long? It's all about life.
Well, You know that. Why do I say it?
You know what we all want. But we want
the wrong things, don't we? And we get
what we really need—yes? So I don't
have to ask, I don't really have to pray.
I'll get what's coming to me, won't I?

Part Eight

Dream Spa Journal

DREAM SPA JOURNAL

> *In dreams begin responsibilities.*
> *—Old Irish Play*

I would rejoin myself, deserted long ago,
that wandering shade somewhere in its separate time.
They say that the spirit hovers above the body while we sleep
and if we awaken suddenly we are dazed until it returns.
I would rejoin my earliest remembrance and start anew.
Travelling warily all roads,
I would be a dangerous companion for the unwary,
a disturbance in the calm weather of thought.
But that shade, transparent as an angel fish,
luminous at night as the moon on a mote of dust,
O, the lost bodiless distant song of that shade!
What wilderness of calm does it wander
bravely seeking the way home to chaos?

The Association for the Study of Lucid Dreams
summoned me from mad Hollywood,
drugs, writer's block, and a sick affair,
to the Hotel Paradiso in Puerto Vallarta
to participate in a study in which I was to sleep
and be awakened while I was dreaming
and was to maintain my dream
and then to convert it
into whatever dream I wished it to become.

Lucid dreams are more vivid
than common dreams.
Inscape is energized,
so that the world of the dream
is like that of Hopkins or Van Gogh,

pulsating, dynamic, vital.
Such imagery is said to be
the manifestation of cosmic holograms,
and if I can convert them,
I can convert my life, like a wizard,
turn it into what I want it to be,
or wished it were or had become,
bring time back
with what and whom I loved, set a new
course for myself, and embark.

I saw white gulls arise, upon arrival,
from the emerald maze in the huge garden
surrounding the Hotel Paradiso. White gulls.
And that night I dreamed I saw an instant,
which was a dewdrop in my dream,
yes, a dewdrop and a stellar instant,
like that of the wild gulls, pulling
the air with their wide wings,
an image, a vision of heavenly flight—
an ascent, a transcendence—
a nano-second and a shimmering drop,
or, shifting, a shimmering shield,
hovering in space, and what looked like
a moonbeam crossed the dark,
the silver dark of a swirling dust mote,
a hazed, illumined, impossible dark,
fingered, like a laser, touched the instant,
the drop, the Lilliputian planet,
with the most tender touch imaginable,
angling this way and that, so that
with each angle an entire eternal history was
displayed,
        with all of the mass and multiplicity of life.

It seemed in my dream that there was no death,
but a cottage-coziness everywhere, and of us
and of the mountains and the waters, seemed
that all these are projections of personality,
(what I see I see because I am I)
spiritual manifestations, tilts at the dewdrop,
incarnations and aspects of the All-in-all,
the anomalon itself, yes, and even that sheen,
that spark, on the oriflamme of time; seemed
that we are the one hologram of life,
and that the family portrait
is the portrait of all who ever lived,
with mountains and waters and creatures
wild and domesticated; seemed that
the holographic plate is angled
for this simulacrum, this three-dimensional portrait
of a universe-apparent, which portrait
is not a memento mori but a glory
in a turning in time, a journey around a star.

My dream suggested that behind my waking back
a deeper reality existed;
not the reality I saw before me,
amazing pattern that it is,
a life-long complicated quilt,
tangible, deep in its seams,
full in its bosomy pads; but another,
finer, more ethereal, fabric, a cloth-of-gold,
glorious, gorgeous, radiant beyond imagination
with a light unknown here, waves
in an intensity beyond experience,
yet that do no damage to the eye,
light that seems to love the eye—
and that is the Word, I thought,
with new insight: Love—which is

expressed in its star-stuff, its human
potential, but never for good and all,
for there is more, we feel certain, we who
are the stars singing, the vibratory expression
of matter, tuning fork to tuning fork,
the template of interference-patterns making
concentric intersecting rings until
with perfect pitch achieved
the magical-appearing universe
leaps into view—and the great music
is made tangible and a table and chairs
and a world and a universe, full of stars
to look at, from a cottage
in an enchanted wood,
where I sit, appear.
That pill I took before bed
contained that dream.

L.S.D. Now
I watch the wilted wonders of my past
parade in phalanx. I dream
that I can change my present state
by intervening there,
where those wonders are and now parade,
multiplicities of self, time-separated,
rude and naked strutting fools,
but soon, with a maturing vision,
refreshed with vivid hope,
their formation ordered,
their banners held high,
becoming what they might have been,
myself in time where time must be
to make a memory,
and invested with new direction,
can have them at command fall out

or turn about or right or left,
know they are free in paradox,
not locked forever there, in constant error—
yet go on, the same, as if my will
required my life—perhaps
some missing faith, perhaps some expiation.
Again perhaps the wonders are mirage
and I was born this very instant,
tilted to a history and told a fate.

These reality fields are open for inspection,
like model homes, and, in an augenblick,
we are visiting an infinity of them.
They are where you are,
you need not go to see them:
no agent is necessary. Intersecting
concentric rings are vibrating
everything into view. The reality fields
present glories and horrors to behold:
they are moral reflections, purifying
the spirit, cleansing the dewdrop,
keeping it clear and clean, all
that I love borne with me
through time and back out of it,
the lovelight never out, always tilting,
becoming a new vision!

But a Bodhisattva,
or even a Beverly Hills guru,
might say, might well say, did say:
"Dead flesh is mad with flies.
The world is mad with lies!"

Memory, or lucid dream?
The therapy continues.

This hologram-like universe
seems solid, appears to have parts, can be
taken apart—(I, too, am like a child and
love a stack of gears)—so we take it apart,
emotionally, mechanically, mathematically,
take it apart as children will a watch,
begin to conceive of it as a watch, as Voltaire
did (and generously gave it a Watchmaker),
and become convinced that it is a kind of watch.
We lift out structures, sequences, relationships,
and rearrange them, and they become to us
what we come to believe they are—
ballbearings unto infinity.

Answers generate questions in the mechanical sphere:
the universe expands, more complicates itself.
We are made to ask and so increase
dimension, to multiply dimensions to the point
of dementia, to make the picture greater,
more inclusive of the non-existent,
to take back the ghosts and reinvest them,
to live again in the mirage, to beat the golden soul
so fine it floats and flutters like a translucent gauze.
The impulsion to think is part of the expansion itself,
and we must think like messenger-angels,
in a completeness of service, or we confuse ourselves
and take the wrong turn, and miss the point—
shall we say the dewdrop—in which
courage and intelligence and praise
meet, and await us.

Poetry possesses the virtue of being a record,
and you can date a poem, if you wish,
thus giving it the merit of a worldly fact
contained in a system of time, which, admittedly,

is a system which is perhaps pseudo-fact itself,
or will become so as matter completes its withdrawal
upon itself to revisit its origins in a hole in space;
and yet, until then, something like a fact,
a fact in the sense that Sherlock Holmes is almost real
and lives at 221-B Baker Street in a fictional series
in a real world that may exist only in a dream
that is being dreamed elsewhere,
perhaps by the clever Its of Else in Otherwhere;
and so poetry becomes an actual little stab
and, poets hope, rip in the black sheet
that covers the deserted, haunted mansion.
> *In many moods,*
> *the poet broods,*
> *on dice and swans*
> *or old bygones,*

the hurts of a lifetime piling at the poet's knees,
the joys stacking under the poet's chin,
and should the poet be deceived, what of it?
The created icons of the poet's labor remain, untrue
perhaps to truth but true enough to themselves,
like Doctor Watson waiting for Holmes
   at 221-B Baker Street,
the poems piling like paintings or statuary, marking
the poet's being there, the idiosyncratic spelling
   the poet's own,
the music the sweet strain of the poet's soul
asking the rhetorical questions of the poet's life,
the unanswerables called eternal questions, the poet
insisting upon the attempt, one more human attempt,
which the poet was made for, wondering about
> *new turns of fate*
> *in love and hate,*
> *or what wild words*
> *are sung by birds.*

There was a time when no season prevailed,
when whatever season it presumed itself to be
held no distinction: day and night fell too
into the inconsequential: all units failed,
for they failed in the beholder, the keeper of time:
and all distinctions faded, for the beholder
could not distinguish one thing from another.
The curious will ask how this occurred.
This much we know: that there was love
gone wrong, and there was death, death
of one most beloved—all share the news—
and there was inability produced, nurtured,
by the particular way of the life itself:
but even before these triggers, fast and slow,
were pulled, the life had been filled with walls
within which lurked the known fear
and beyond which lurked the unknown fear.
And the child's head had been early cloaked
in a liripipe, shut about the eyes
as dark as blindness: and the mind,
in its strange bonehouse, dwelt,
trying to see into and through the dark.
That is the state in which we feel little,
avoid sensations of pain or joy
through the medium of an inner mechanism
not fully understood. In this state
we seem to be neither living nor dead,
but existing without sensation,
seemingly dead, while still experiencing
some state of being approximating to life,
like the dream-state of the butterfly soul
that we experience in sleep, or, say,
the vague state of life of the slug or worm,

and we are sometimes found to be
existing in this manner as the result
of our inability to cope with the life
we have been living. It is as if
the transmigratory process had been
frustrated, leaving the victim in limbo,
neither able to progress nor to regress
to a previous state, like death but not death,
like life but not life as the living know it,
merely a camelopard likeness of it,
cataleptic, painless and joyless. Patience
is called for in such cases. Kindness helps
to undo harm, but the victim
will awaken only when ready.

In trying to discover the source of pain,
the poet, strange researcher into reality,
dipso-dreamer, lover of passion fruit,
unhappy hedonist of heterodoxy,
explores the familiar territory of the heart—
nothing but red caves and periodic floods.
He then travels up his plaque-clogged carotid
to the brain and comes upon a land of gray clouds
capped by a bone-pale dome. Under those
electrically-charged gray clouds, he listens
as the dome reverberates with the tom-tom beat of
"Worship me," and "Worship me."
I think I am getting close to the source of pain,
he tells himself. But it is only a false start,
a Lake Tanganyika. This cannot be the source
of the Nile of Pain. Here he is attacked by Synapses,
who pitch fiery assagais upon him without regard
for his gifts; he has no gifts; he is long pig;
he surrenders and they make him their slave.
What to do? He must escape if he is ever to find

the source of pain—which is now active in his heart.
He gives the gift of full worship to the King of the
    Synapses,
who drinks blood and eats oxygen, and,
for the gift of his blood, his oxygen, is set free
to go on looking for the source of pain.
He travels over rough, cortical country,
dead cells adrift in offshoot rivers and rivulets
of his previous life's best cognac, until, at last,
he comes to what appears to be a veritable
Victoria of a lake, an inland sea, too large to measure
with his meager instruments of sound and sense.
It is paradisal, even Heavenly,
for brightness shows down now
from the dome of Sunday. This is indeed
the source of Pain, for it is the citadel of sad desire;
and it is then and there that he makes
his most astounding discovery: to wit,
that in leaving this place, pain begins to flow
and flows on until it reaches the fell Falls of Destiny,
and, undeterred, goes over the falls in a barrel,
the inside of which is stained and caked
with the lees of the grapes of wrath.
He awakens on a Bowery-of-the-mind,
in a lake of golden pee, none-the-worse,
nor better, for his adventure,
but his mouth dry as a marrowless bone.

This makeshift shadowy world is metaphor,
        which is our chariot of choice,
    our light-inducting dark-proof vehicle
ready to ride the road and river of space and time,
            to deliver us from evil,
        which is all that isn't in the vision
        of the cloud-bodied hungry soul

   when it goes through the gate to the mystery
      of unanswering love,
  and we see from there how all things flow
     outward toward wisdom
and back upon themselves toward joy
 and that love is always answering,
    is the cloud formed into self,
  which is others and all, at once.

The dying Greek Egyptologist,
my fellow guest and subject of study,
spoke in his hypnotized sleep.
The group, bat-eared, heard
his inner voice, a *cri de coeur*,
from the garden with its green
labyrinth, like a sea-wind.
The group, empathizing, were there to understand.
We were there to change our fate.

   Where did the parting begin?
   Why did the soul of the boy go away?
   How has the man made his father and mother?
   Why is his flesh like androgynous clothing?
   What is the meaning of being oneself?

That voice,
I, too, have heard that voice.
It spoke to me once in lake water among the lilies,
as I drowned. Or was I dreaming?
It is the strangest voice in the world,
the voice of one's self,
heard only at moments,
only at night,
perhaps only in lucid dreams.

The dying Greek says that he cannot tell
the horn from the ivory, the true from the false.
"The world is mad with lies.
I do not think that I shall die."
Nonetheless, an inner voice said,
and I think all of us heard that haunting voice—

> *I embarked from the black lava beaches of Thira*
> *for deadly sun-jewelled Egypt.*
>
> *Yes, Egypt is the only place to die.*
> *There they know how to treat a soul.*
> *There, when you go down,*
> *you go down to go on,*
> *if in another way.*
>
> *Ask at Alexandria.*

The Greek has a terminal virus of some kind,
a growing vegetation of the brain.
A virus has more organized life than a star,
though a star has an order of appearance,
star in the sky and star on stage.
We have a famous film star with us—
è bell' attrice—addicted, suicidal.
Parmenides mentored Zeno to believe
in the unchanging universe
behind the changing one.
In Rome, the film star could only find
a scrolling phantom life, too unsubstantial
for her rippling flesh. She sought *la dolce vita*
in men and now, three times removed
from her dream of life, she tries again
in the labyrinth of the Minotaur, unaware
that she is filming Beauty and the Beast.

But I am speaking of organic life,
though a star on the stage
or a movie star has organic life,
more, in fact, than the Greek's virus.
Laurie opened a cardtable
at Hollywood and Vine,
broke except the heroin
still coursing through his veins
and a few small artifacts
of his film career.
He, too, is here for the duel.
But humans are gaudy coelenterates:
my liver heaves, my bowels twist,
squirm with excitement
and lead their own lives inside me.
I need a new part. It flowers, pulsates.
It is not my friend, it is itself.
But perhaps we can get along, after a time.
At first, other parts reject it,
but eventually they are tamed.
You are all working for me, I cry.
We are our own liver, kidney, heart.
I am not your heart. You have no heart.
Your better half told you that.
You have no other half.
It is all a golden fiction, inspired by sex.
Your sex organs aren't even your own—
they do as they please.
As the real estate agent told the homeowner
who questioned him about an easement,
you don't own property, you control it.
You don't own yourself, and you barely,
for social reasons, control yourself.
One anti-social day, a day my tenure
and my poems almost couldn't save me,

one mad and drunken day, I stripped
and ran around the studio,
down from the stuffy offices,
breaking up the sets,
terrifying the great pretenders,
a proud if pallid paladin.

I've heard the calls again, through the long night,
material manifestations of the ghostly immaterial.
Or, if you are not of a fanciful turn of mind,
if you prefer the psychological explanation
for every sort of phenomenon,
it must have been the wind I heard,
and the hotel settling
(an ancient building creaks),
the water pipes gurgling,
the radiators knocking, the cats
in the garden, skulking,
and transformed these in my mind
into the calls I thought I heard
that sounded to me like the crying out
of the earth's multitudinous dead.
And what I felt they told me
of my life's unmeaning,
my time's misuse,
my soul's fear,
out of the vastness,
the great underdarkness,
caused me to writhe in my wet white sheets
and sweat, glistening, like a great, limbed worm.
I awakened, startled, and, finally, I slept again,
a victim of circadian rhythm,
and dreamed of the drab furnished rooms
of my infancy, the dismal corners
occasionally shot with sunlight,

the fascinating dust swirls
that were my first view of the universe.

Déjà vu is the constant companion
of every twice-thinking poet.
One minute I was sitting on a dull linoleum rose,
watching the swirling dust motes with my toys,
and the next they were utterly lost to me,
travelling down the street in a brown paper bag
in a grinding garbage truck.
My musical sweet-potato was crushed and wheezing
in my mouth, and tears were spraying silver on gold
in the windowlight for my melted Mickey doll,
my only friend.
                    Yes, I am there—here—there!
But now I sit in a porcelain tub that smells
of chlorine and soap,
pouring from a fifth, hearing the Fifth—
da-da-da-dum— da-da-da-dum—
frowning, frowning, for the bird's song,
or Death knocking—in a tiled room full of steam,
with no childhood left, a tired man with a gray beard
and no toys but a cheap, green cigar.

When first I arrived at the Hotel Paradiso
and was elevated many levels and taken back down
and led through long halls of many mysterious doors
to the suite of the Association, I felt oppressed,
and the notion of an open labyrinth came to me,
I was so desirous of freedom, of escape,
and found myself wandering through such a labyrinth,
or maze changeable as a tour puzzle, in the garden,
one made of many walls of either hard matter,
compressed particles to stop the Minotaur,
or something else and softer, miraculously

drawn into the continuum, perhaps hedgerows,
greens of light and dark hues in hearted leaves
and dimensionalized by back-shadows
of sunstruck and ever-variable mauve.
Beneath my feet were gravity's flagstones,
embedded in endless grains of sand,
and above my head mindless undisciplined
cloud formations backed by a dream of blue.

The open labyrinth my mind had conjured
was not a place in which to get completely lost,
nor in which a quarantine prevailed.
There others step out of nowhere, or seem to,
because the labyrinth has spaces for crossing
from one side of its elusive walls to the other,
with many signs pointing the way out. And yet
we remain lost, we remain lost even as we are given
exact directions. Why? Why is this the case?
Because we do not want to leave the open labyrinth,
even though we are becoming famished
for what is outside it, which well might be
a void. Politely, we listen to directions
we are given, then go another way,
hoping that wherever we go will lead us
deeper than ever into the heart of the maze.
And even so, we advise others on how to escape.
And our advice is exact, for we know how to escape.
We know that we need do nothing at all but wait,
with an immense show of patience, here or there,
this side or that.
                    But truly we have no desire to leave,
for all our hopes and fears are here where we wander,
aimlessly, aimlessly but full of purpose.

For breakfast at the Hotel Paradiso

a wrinkled yellow passion fruit is served.
Judging from the taste of it, there's paradise inside,
and juice of it must be the rivers, lakes, and seas
of such a place that could produce a native
whose perfume turns the head of each new traveller there
and makes of him a siren's hind, a slave
of persons of the place, one who is so compelled,
entrapped, that that awed visitor would never leave,
would think it madness to travel after smelling
compelling sweetness on a vivid gust;
judging from the taste of it,
paradise could be described as what we all
most dream of goodness wished for in that safest place
the heart can find, where, unafraid of anything,
we ask for what we truly want—
that which we dare not hint before—
and then are more than satisfied,
and soonest, and most easily.
O judging from the taste of such sweet fruit,
there truly is a paradise and all we wish is deep inside it—
the life, the love, the death.

It is this heavenly tale,
that the child in one could wish for,
that keeps me awake tonight,
on the eve of my departure,
fearing death and wishing for grace,
not knowing what either is,
or even if either is,
though the unbreathing stillness of bodies
has me fairly convinced of the former,
and of the latter I have seen so little
as to doubt what I have seen as aberrant,
some twist in the air and light that,
so full of desire for the magic of exemption,

I have deluded myself, half knowing I lied,
half believing my own white lie.
But by now I've come to believe
that the only grace
is the goodness of the rational mind,
and the only evil
the old instinctive animal brain,
the knob of the cerebellum,
seeking its own satisfactions
of food and sex and selfhood,
the ultimate isolate one,
that yet does not understand
that we are together
in this flowing, amazing hologram,
with or without a creator
that may or may not care;
that, come to consciousness,
we have every right to judge
the nature of existence, for,
however arrived at, our brains
are analytic, not made to hunker down
in obeisance to riddling gods,
nor to any phantom
that hides in a cloud of unknowing.
For we have one another and
have courage and the hope of courage and
the practice of courage, to help us,
and, when the wind is calm,
and the waters lean down for the moon,
we have lonely senses to share
till at last our time has run out.

Now, as I think in the night,
somewhat afraid of the day
that will see me another day older

and that much closer to death,
I mark the speed of time
that has seen me, a moment ago,
a child walking home from school,
or a man going off to harm's way,
or this or that or the other,
and think of these things that we have,
of others and courage and love,
and I think that I'll sleep and awaken
less anxious than I was considering
a heavenly tale,
          for in the realist's reality,
the closest thing to the truth,
there is finally a peace of mind
that is a grace in a sweet surrender.
It is the heavenly tale
that the child in one should wish for.
It will allow me to sleep
on the eve of my departure.

But there is no way to sleep off the memory
of what is forgotten. Only the lemon morning,
bringing eggs and coffee, can rewind the clock.
Only the pink, shaved face. Only the white suit,
the Panama. Memory's gulls are gone.
That great wild rising!
My lap-top, my Saratoga, are waiting.
Something should have been done.
Once upon a time, something that was not done
still waits in disappointment. *Amor fati!*
Ah, sleep, ah, dreams! *Farewell!*

# PART NINE

MUDDLING THROUGH

CIRCADIAN RHYTHM

SPINDRIFT

Upon receiving a Fellowship

I saw the ghost of the old Provincetown Playhouse
perched on the end of a pier that wasn't there anymore
and hovering in the wet wind above the bucking water
that is forever eroding the sands and stones of old Cape Cod.
I had walked a long way on Commercial Street in heavy rain,
close by the beach, peeking between the old, weathered
  buildings,
and down beyond them, glimpsing fogbound boats,
until I found the megalith with the bronze plaque on it.
Once out there on the water stood the fish house shack
that had been converted into a theater, and there
in the mist and spindrift walked Eugene O'Neill
to the opening of the first of his *Seven Plays of the Sea*.
Now I saw Edna Millay dance out to the ghostly playhouse,
laughing, with her crushed umbrella, her wet red hair,
and the pages of a script flying off like paper hats—
Oh, and there go Clifford Odets, and the young John Garfield!
I puffed on a damp and smokeless cigarette and stared out
at the invisible converted shack. I could see and hear them
out there, their histrionics and high laughter commingling
in a crescendo with the watery, spindrift symphony.
Maybe I'll join them out there someday, for a time may come,
as magical as circular, when someone else may come and see
  me
in that enthusiastic crowd of poets and playwrights and
  players,
perhaps a little audience of curious locals, doubtfully
  applauding.

FORTY ACRES AND A MULE

Thoughts while sowing

Just when your hope is highest for the vow
  of Time to be your friend and earn the deed,
it droughts your spring and breaks your brand-new plow.

Is this the way that Time will do us now?
  Time most betrays you when you're most in need.
Just when your hope is highest for the vow

of Time to golden calve your finest cow,
  she and her calf both die of poison weed.
Time droughts your spring and breaks your brand-new plow.

The weather always wins, no matter how—
  too hot, too cold, too wet, too dry; indeed,
just when your hope is highest for Time's vow.

Does Time protect you from the butting prow
  of sun-dried wind that skims topsoil and seed?
It droughts your spring and breaks your brand-new plow!

Foreclosure looms ahead, the hanging bough
  of an old lynching tree. Should you concede,
just when your hope is highest for Time's vow?
Time droughts your spring and breaks your brand-new
  plow!

ENDINGS

I KNIGHT'S END

The lily-chalk
within me broke
and scattered like sharp, shattered glass.
My bones were here,
my bones were there;
I saw the splinters everywhere:
my flesh's fall,
the Golden Rule,
my armor hammered into plate.

II NOVEMBER WIND

The beginning beyond the end
is what November brings;
the sense of leaving home,
the odd thing round the bend:
and the leaves fall like birds,
and the birds like leaves are gone;
and nothing anymore sings
but the wind toward the end.

ON AN INLAND ISLAND

off Pamlico Sound

On this calm coast the small iambic waves
  remind me of Shakespearean blank verse
  that some apprentice actor must rehearse
repeatedly, as echoes speak in caves.

It almost makes one fancy life behaves—
  because it's hard to think of something worse
  than this salt zephyr, unequipped to curse,
while watching here, where palms are calm as graves.

  And yet they tell me that the hurricane
sent tentacles of wind and water here,
while wreaking havoc off on far Cape Fear,
  and that a storm-surge drowned the chatelaine
whose hideaway stood near this very beach,
which one would think was simply out of reach.

KYRIE ELEISON

Tonight the house across the street is sunny
with flames. It crackles with a solar static.
It brightens night as if a star had landed.
Hardworking people like ourselves, we think,
but thank our lucky stars it isn't us.
Yet, What a world, we sigh but do not say,
and to propitiate the gods, like Greeks,
invite the poor souls in to spend the night.
Then stand and watch the final sparks fly upward.

The fire trucks take their slowly-clanging leave,
their tolled bells sounding in an exequy,
while my poor counterpart consoles himself
with certain clauses in his policy,
a standard H.O.P., but without flood;
for we are on high ground and need not brood
about the water-levels hereabouts
becoming a dramatic factor. Nor earthquakes.
This rock's been stable now for centuries.

THOUGHTS FOR LATER

No matter how clean we are, or how neat,
we always have dirt on the soles of our feet.

There's always the stuff in the cup of the tooth
giving to infancy, childhood, and youth

the pain and the poignancy which we forget
when we look back in time as if at the set

of a play which then seems paradisal and pure,
from the vantage of age and the pain that is sure.

OUTSIDE THE HOSPITAL

The sentence of night, the comma-moon,
the asterisks and periods of light,
tell a tale of a great dark space.

And who is the writer of the night
tale, who is the author of hours
during which one waits for relief,

as the jangled nervous system mutely
screams, as the heavens revolve, as
your world waits to face the dawn?

AMBITIONS

I would like to write a prologue to all that is noble.
I would like to ratify and validate the good.
I would like to express a few cogent thoughts
with regard to love.
I would like to express myself in terms of flowers.
I would like to tell you all about squareness
and a little at least, about weight.
I would like to remind you
that the blood of wood
can look like
the disintegrating
arrangements of roses
when observed from the corner of
a shadowy room.
I would like to address myself to
parti-colored parrots
dead in tropical heat.
I would like to stroke the hood
of a speeding car.
I would very much like to gather up
an explosion.

THE SECRET AGENT

I am an agent for the stone
and the dust, I am an agent for the quanta
who have sent me here to buy them answers.
They want to know what they are
and why they have the jumping disease,
they want to know why they cannot rest;
when they fill the flowers, the flowers speak,
they shout in the full spectrum of colors,
they want to know what they are doing,
they want to know why, when they are comfortable
and blowing in a fine breeze, they are assaulted,
they want to know why they wither and die.

I am an agent for the water
and the ice and the steam, tell me
what they need to know, tell the Earth
why it hurtles, tell the moon why it follows,
tell the sun why it burns,
tell the universe why it is black
and full of fiery suns,
tell the suns what they are.

I have come here to buy answers.
I will pay with the flowers' colors,
with the birds' feathers, with Hope's breath.
Give me the price for my answers.
Name it, and the day will give you its light.
Name it, and the atoms will charge it.

I am an agent for a principal
that can afford to spend a million stars.

A PILE OF LEAVES

They lose their scent,
that freshness of
beginning, but
something replaces it,
some odor on the air
out of the eternal
olla podrida of
decay, a gift,
folded in dimensions
not yet understood,
tied with the
string theory,
bowed and ribboned
with a Monarch's
living wings. They
tap the earth,
dissolve into pure
spirit—of leaves,
of cells, of atoms
—and return,
bodiless angels,
to the place from which
all is projected,
where intelligent
spirits prepare
for new flight,
the old injuries
understood,
assimilated,
forgiven.

THE WEEPING BUTCHER

for Jack Parker

The butcher weeps for onions, not for steak,
and yet he is capable of heartache.

One day he came out smiling
from the refrigerator—"You *are* beguiling."

The lady tittered—"A sweet man, Smith."
He ground her up some chuck forthwith.

But why do you drink, butcher, hiding in back?
When you have wife, children, home, what do you lack?

Smiling, pig's head in hand, he shrugs.
Blood's on his apron. The pig's head winks and mugs.

Poet, butchers aren't so different from us,
only they don't make such a fuss.

GRAFFITI

A Busybody

a busy
body be
comes an ac
tivist be
comes a ter
rorist be
comes my
way or high
way or
die

Pretty

as a black
rose
the sleek
little black
snake
rode the
broom handle
to the grass
& vanished
in it
quickly

NEIGHBORS

I To a Rat

Greenwich Village

Rat, you frighten me,
though I understand perfectly well
that I as well frighten,
indeed frightened you,
coming around the corner
from the garbage bag,
your whiskers winking
on your corrugated snout
and your two little
beads of eyes glinting,
black beads
with some little mind
behind them
and a soul.

Ah yes, you have a soul:
I saw it with my own two
frightened eyes,
little rat.

I was alone
when you waddled
around the corner,
saw me and, for an instant,
flattened everything about yourself,
sniffing snout,
bead eyes,

long gray tail,
then scampered off,
terrified,
like the rat that you are,
you rat,
you dirty rat,
you poor little devil,
you sad little pilferer,
you filth, you pest,
you spreader of plague,
you biter of babies,
you rodent,
you cousin
of the bright-eyed squirrel,
you poor
relation, you scum,
you inelegant bum!

Now there's a trap
in the corner
with a cheese slice in it.
Don't make it snap.
Things are tough
enough
as they are.

II MY WAR WITH ROACHES

Pitt Street, Lower East Side

I looked into a half-filled beer bottle
left opened and standing out,

saw six dead roaches floating atop the stale, flat beer.
I was disappointed.
I could have drunk the stuff.
I had no aversion to warm, stale, flat beer,
and had learned to put a head on it
by dropping an Alka-Seltzer tablet into it.
But I wasn't about to drink beer that had
six dead roaches floating in it,
bodies like boats and legs like oars raised up,
so aimlessly.
The place was filthy.
I needed order!

I went out, bought roach spray,
sprayed the walls, up and down,
back and forth, until billowing clouds
of poison were closing on me from every corner.
It was bitter cold out, but I knocked the
cardboard out of the windows
and let the fresh frosty air suck the poison
out from under my nose.
I blocked the windows again.
I surveyed the carnage.
Roaches of all sizes and shapes were swarming
over the walls, dropping from the cracked ceiling
with small, ticking sounds and
rocking on their curled, chitinous backs,
flicking, flailing, their feelers drooping.

The kitchen gas range was a stronghold,
a fortress of greasy grooves and baked-in crevices.
I lit the oven and watched until the top
of the stove glowed red.
Out they came by the swarming hundreds,
feet burned away, feelers melting

into kinky hairs. They ran over the stove
in desperation, panic, trying to find places
where they could put their feet.
Expectant mothers, their eggs in chitinous cases
at their rear ends, struggled with their hindmost legs,
as with an instinct to save their offspring,
to force or kick the cases loose.
Some had their cases dangling
by only one side when they leaped
from the top of the stove.
As they landed on the floor and tried to crawl,
with their burnt feet, their dragging, kinked feelers,
with their wings askew, and their dangling,
thread-hanging egg cases, I sprayed them madly
then trampled, kicked, jumped up and down on them,
only wanting them dead.
I saw a fat, hideous albino roach,
already like the pale ghost of its dead self,
leap from the stove.
I squashed it underfoot and swore
I could hear its white shell crack and
spray the pale muck of its insides out: squish!
When I lifted my shoe it dragged itself,
like animated pus, into a heap of glittering
brownish bodies. Thousands of crooked legs
moved sluggishly—then, here and there,
with sudden convulsive speed—
over the place where the ghost had gone.

On the wall was a wooden plaque
that held sets of false teeth, an exhibit,
sold by a dental supply firm to dentists.
It belonged to an artist friend who was to use it
for some arcane artistic purpose
but who had forgetfully left it here.

I grabbed the plaque from the wall
and mashed it down atop this horrible mass
of half life. Then I jumped on it, up and down,
not distinguishing the sound of the breaking teeth
from the sound of roaches snapping on the stove
like popcorn. When I looked down
there were rolling and bouncing human teeth
among the slimy dead and still crawling.
Sakyamuni says they will live again.
Needed: Sneaky Pete, pot, peyote.

III NOW, THE FOX!

Country Living

A thousand times I've had this urban dream and
asked a doctor what it meant
   to no avail. "It was the city's grip on
an impressionable child,"
   one doctor told me. I was dropped once down a
hellish, pitch-black pit, a deep
   dumbwaiter shaft, and fell a floor before I
landed, more or less intact.
   I bear a scar above my eye. Could that be
it, dropped by a drunken man,
   a family friend, when I was still an infant?
Meaning harmlessly to play,
   he swore off drink, I'm told. In any case I
have these nightmares constantly,
   and doubt if they will ever go away. Waking,
after one, I'm shaken to
   the bone. I live now in the country, where I

   hoped to find diminishment
     of terror, over time. But here's the strange part:
rabies is a major threat
     here in the country in the summer—dogs and
cats can get it from the wild-
     life teeming in the woods—and just the other
night I dreamed a foaming fox
     that chased me back into the cityscape I
hoped so much to free myself
     from, years before, by coming to the country.
Waking horror brought me new
      concern for peace of mind and where to find it.

ON MUDDLING THROUGH

I like the English saying "muddle through."
It's always better than perfecting things,
although the human race keeps trying to,
keeps carving for stone Victory stone wings.

SHADOW OVER AFRICA

I

The great black shape below us
is the shadow of our balloon.
A fair wind drives it, casting
a pall upon native loon
and hippopotamus—
but what if the dark is lasting?

II

The antelope leap at hearing
our wind chimes on the air.
Do they fear what we bring in our flight?
Do the deaf snakes hear?
"Humans are nearing, are nearing,
bringing their circle of night!"

A WORKER AT THE WATERWORKS

He watched the water purling away.
No doubt it would soon be carrying off
loads of human excrement, with the lost
parts of bodies, dead cells, hairs,
bits and parts of burnt energy, the
stuff left over after the hard day's work,
after the argument, the loving in the
small bed while the kids slept fitfully.
There the tears of his beloved melted
into the blood, sweat, and tears of a city.

Off they go, he said, the domestic sewage,
and the storm runoff, to be wed and
to become the combined sewage; off it goes,
through flush tanks and scum collectors, through
grit chambers and sedimentation tanks,
through trickling filters and activated-
sludge units, through oxidation ponds
and the centrifuge, through heat coagulators
and into the incinerators, where, at last,
all our loves go up in smoke.

And the outfall works drop pure water,
cleansed, unsullied by any particle of humanity,
by any pitiful history of the human condition,
into the swaying receiving waters of river and sea.

LATE SLEEPER

She never woke without the smile
that shaped that rose, her pretty mouth.
She'd lift the telephone and dial
for breakfast; then she'd have her bath,
cheerfully free from righteous wrath.

There was no need to wait a while
to travel, study, learn a style:
her money made her polymath.
    She never woke.

After her bath she'd ride a mile
around the park, in single file,
with other girls of luck and wealth,
for poise, and skill, and better health,
and wonder what one *could* revile.
    She never woke.

ELEGY FOR A LATE TORNADO

I

No, Nature has no wrath, no, none at all, and you
are merely what you are, Tornado—or by some
counts twenty—touching down around this tarheeled state,
a thunderbooming menace innocent as pie,
the product of two airs, of heat and cold colliding
without intention in our Mother's general chaos,
O fearsome Mother of us all, who says take that
and see if you can take it, kid, or you're not mine.

II

Now we of social order must adjust insurance
and see what can be done about the fallen roof;
and too, some trees have fallen and a boy is dead,
and we must bury him, the poor unlucky lad
who stood too close to leaves while saws were lopping
    limbs
for safety's sake; and others, too, who died in homes
turned round as if they rode a carousel or flew
like helicopters up, foundationless on Earth.

III

How do we call the dead back? Well, She says we don't.
She says She doesn't care if we are fools enough to live;
and what are houses but the homes of hermit crabs,
delectable to cats, fish and furry felines both;
and what are we to Her, She says, sure not the best,

but who dare say She doesn't love us all? Tornado,
you were a special pet of Hers a day or two,
but now your short-lived reign of terror I record.

IV

And you were dead and now are gone and none of us
can show a thing but that some still endure, survivors
in pain and struggle and somewhat the stronger now
than otherwise, and though a small reward for hurt
reward it is, and in the aspect of eternity
the very thing that shapes the human race, and all
the injured creatures of the planet as they struggle,
not merely struggle—stronger, propagate—O Winds!

THE CAMPERS

He had given his family a very pleasant house. The house kept out anything he and his family did not care for, kept in heat, or cold, if air-conditioning happened to be required, and, for the most part, held the elements at bay. It even had a garage that protected his vehicles. Nonetheless, he loaded his recreational vehicle with items he thought he might need for his camping trip, then loaded his wife, children, and dog in it, and drove off into rough country. He parked by a stream and set to work erecting his tent, which extended from the back of his recreational vehicle. The tent wasn't nearly as pleasant as his house, the one he had left behind to come on this trip, but, for now, it would be the only house his family had. There were no amenities. His children complained about the lack of hot water, about having no outlets for their TV and their computer, about the primitive circumstances in which he had thrust them. His wife developed a rash, and did not know how to cook the few fish he caught. Tenderfeet, he called them. Then one night a bear came into the tent and ate his wife, children, and dog. He decamped as soon as possible. Back home again, he recognized that he had given his family a very pleasant house. He decided that he definitely preferred it to his tent. The house was clean and neat, and held no bugs, none to speak of, and the walls of the living room wore a pretty wallpaper, depicting the great outdoors, but with no bear smell and no blood dripping to the floor.

OVER THE MAGNOLIA

You want to know
what the moon
tells the wolf,
so at night
you lie in bed
and hold the crystal
ball you bought
at the novelty
store, hold it up
beside the moon,
which is right
outside the window,
over the magnolia,
and howl very
softly, so as
not to wake
anyone, growl
under the lips-
high blanket, and
beg mercy of
the moon.

DREAMSCAPES

I

Now go the seven wreaths of weeks:
sleep slips out like a moon-sucked sea.
The heaven-high haggard hero-rogue,
the cygnet, circles and he sinks
beyond the grindstone and the spur,
baptizing waters with bird-brogue.

II

Now go the garlands and the grave
down Time's counterclockwise lake
where good and evil are one law;
nor the lusty wives of leapyear rave,
but plumb the depths by plummet, wake,
and breathe the rose's claw.

MINIM

art
out of
the
small
end of
the
hose
like
a
water
saw
can
chisel
stone
or
cut
steel

like
laser
light
narrowed
to
pluck
bad
blood
from
an eye
can
be
very
useful
&
good

FLAG DAY

Main Street Parade

The turnout's thin as a mist.
A few piggy-backed babies seem
unconvinced of the holiday spirit
as they dribble ice-cream onto hats.

But they do love the volunteer firemen,
red-trucked, red-faced, and waving.
Wait, here comes the local high school,
and the students are all out of step.

But a boy bears Old Glory aloft,
and a girl the flag of our state.
Oops! Their band is an eldritch zoo.
Then a pickup comes, bringing the Princess

who some day will star in a movie.
But why is the sky turning dark?
Then the parade seems to vanish
as if put back in a box and away.

And we close for this year like last year,
with the thunder of strongly-held hammers
breaking the storm clouds apart,
and the long, rusty nails of the rain.

THE POET GAME

I'm looking for a good excuse to quit
  the poet game. But I've invested years
  and have accumulated such arrears
that newer portions of poetic wit
are ever needed just to compensate
  for my huge losses. Yet another sonnet
  mustneeds be penned to make a profit on it—
my work, that is—so I can pay the freight.

How could I know, when I began in gladness
  —I hadn't even heard of Wordsworth yet—
that I would end up with my poet's madness
  so certain that it wasn't worth a bet?
How could I know the age-old, old-age sadness
  of time and failure youth had never met?

SEE/SAW

Some artisan has molded
all these leaves out
of bright red clay and
baked them into this
mound of smoking ashtrays
on the lawn. I watch
my neighbor toss
his cigarette into
the burning mound,
and remember laws
against both smoking
and leaf burning
enacted here of late,
and think these may
be all the leaves
I see go up in smoke,
if virtue gets the best
of us, as it is wont
to do, until defeated
once again by our
rebellion, due in
turn eternally, and
here tomorrow if out
today. Our lives do not
so much improve as
see-saw with our wills,
and we clean up and
then we dirty up,
delighting in both
order and disorder
in their turns. I'd
wait for us to get it
right, if I had time.

LIGHT AS AIR

WHEEL OF FORTUNE

   On Wheel of Fortune, Sex, to lick its chops,
sends Vanna's highheeled little feet across the stage.
   She wiggles, turning cards. My old aunt thinks:
"I never looked like that, even at that age!"
   And so it goes, as Vonnegut has said; and, like the
     Wheel,
we turn and turn and wait—for what we wait,
   we wonder. Maybe the Jackpot Prize,
the house we always wanted, and, at its gate,

   a swanky Maserati! The Wheel clicks
and rolls and clicks. We count to ten.
   My old aunt saves her dough (but we say bread—
or maybe not). Click click! My old aunt says: "Well, then,
   where to?" And in the glitz of Vanna's Fortune Wheel
time stops. The nervous neon blinks with doubt:
   click click, and click click click, and here
we are! The universe turned inside out

   and, young and beautiful, or handsome male,
eating each other up, we drool, O hungry for the flesh.
   Who's who? Who's where? Again: the spinning
     Wheel,
the flashing lights, Vanna's target fanny, and fresh
   turnings of a card! O laugh, O laugh and laugh!
O scream! Once rated the most popular
   program on Earth, the Wheel of Fortune
itself comes back and back and back, bright star!

NEWS OF 45

Into his mid-life crisis
desperate man stalks wild
life brings home head of
thought for wall display
mounting it for worship
plenty yet more to come
proudly shows it to friends
who scoff saying some
body else got it for you
like hell they did shot
gun see all the holes
in it but its mine mine
mine proud of it autumnal
macho laughable necessary
joy so worry not thy heart
days of glory upon thy
wrinkled brow sparks
of plenty more to come
next better yet which
could be worse who
knows but plunge on
plunge on with no effort
for light takes you
smilingly home as you
stay & practice your
declensions sun-o
moon-a your conju
gations selvesyes
selvesalways selves
before selvesafter
glory glory glory
for my five & forty.

THE HONEY HOUSE

With its white picket fence and its little green lawn
and its rose bushes over here and over there in bud,
it was a picture book, a *Post* cover, a dream, of a house.
And it was theirs! But there *were* a lot of bees, weren't
   there?
It was the rose bushes, the wisteria, the dogwood, it was
the sweetness of their young love. She was pregnant—
bad to be stung by a bee she was trying to bat away, then
stung by another. She ran from the house and he came
   home.
Why, there was a beehive under the kitchen sink!
Then he saw that five bees had lit at the top of his paper,
which he shook, and he dodged but was stung just the same,
and the buzzing was deafening, he said, deafening.
So they called in the Masked Exterminator, who discovered
that the house was filled with hives, ten feet tall in the walls,
right up through the floors. Didn't you see the honey?
Now in full summer the walls had begun to drip, the floors
oozed honey. Yours, said the Masked Exterminator, is a
   honeyhouse.
It's true, said the bride, I have washed it up and hosed it
   down.
And suddenly all were attacked and ran from the house.
Upshot: bride thought groom a fool and divorced him,
groom sued broker, who sought out former owner,
who had moved to Alaska, with intention of recouping,
supermarket tabloids did a number of stories on the house,
and, after her abortion, bride was invited to pose for
   Playboy.

AGENT SONNET

for Alex Jackinson

"Why don't you write a novel, for God's sake,
   get down to something good to read, instead
of solipsistic verse? Give us a break!
   Write something worth a read at night in bed.

The public likes a song, a song in rhyme,
   not free-verse pouting about the poet's life
in chopped-up prose, a reader's waste of time!
   The reader wants a story full of strife!

The reader likes a good detective story,
or else a horror story, good and gory.
   The public likes a bit of gruesome fun.

The public wants some sex; to be a voyeur;
to let a woman be a man-destroyer
   while islanded romantically in sun."

OUT-PATIENT

I think about myself too much,
my hypochondria is showing;
I'm always sick with such-and-such,
I'm always glad my blood is flowing.

What's wrong with me I know too well:
I lack the necessary leaven—
my heart has skill to conjure hell
but my head is out of touch with heaven.

THE LADIES OF BURDETT

The ladies of Burdett
are straight tall wonders
as they think on men . . . .

Beside the country road
the grapes are plump,
the plums weigh down the springing boughs.

When Benjamin Franklin
invented bifocals
it was for the ladies of Burdett.

But this does not mean
that these wingless angels
of the consequential

do not, at midnight,
have bright red dreams
that give tone to their cheeks.

DETECTIVE STORY

Came in two hip nuns in unnunlike "funny"
disguise, and he who had been standing there,
sipping a pop, showed such interest—he
eyed them with eyes gone cold, studied what they were
in such strange dark habit and ivory-
embroidered cloaks—and so wondered, wondered

so plainly, as if he wanted them to know,
that they felt him there and turned toward
him, looking him over, eyeing him now,
wondering who this turkey was, some young cop,
some dude; but then, with bows, turned back to
order to-go burgers, containered pop,

straws sticking from eyed lids, and pulled rolls of bills
to pay with, flashing them; and, heeled, tapped
into the street, calling back, "You want girls?
Come on, then, boy!" Guffaws. And he followed them.
He kept his distance, though—for "speed kills"—
like a real cop, tailing them, shepherding lambs

to slaughter; for ahead there, in shadow, at
the far end of the street, waited Sam,
his partner. He'd signal Sam, by tipped hat,
to take the tail up soon, and he would drop back
to see what else was "going down," root
out some more crime, and then take in a flick.

SNOWBOUND

How the free spirit suffers his winter out in the
woods is his business, isolated alone in an unused
farmhouse rented from a farmer by a tall strange
city man with a beard like a board & a wife who
would sleep in it but has left for the winter her
husband alone to be hermit at his request, an artist,
poet & painter, needing neither wife nor child nor
sustenance but vision only,

that she go forth to the wicked city & fare there with a
former lover while he have visions during long mountain
downfall of flakes building to crescendo in white isolation, that there be firewood alone was his matter, that
chalk run smooth over blackboard & vision come summoned by white gods of sleet & snow & that that first
time should he die then the plan be known as faulted with
no firewood & the cold growing in his guts, that he
understand what he never understood, the seriousness of
his state, & learn to be a man once before claimed by the
white tongue, snapped like a spot from large blankness
making no orientation: be gone.

He feared nothing but the thought of no vision, not
the loss of his wife to another, nor the loss of his
life, nor the meaning of loneliness, but for the vision
forsaking all; was willing and willed that Death in a
white coat with bony knuckles knock: his wife in
wonder could not love her former lover but was
young and thrilled at her husband's exploit, leaving
the lover without chance as he regaled her with
delights on city nights of restaurants and theaters for
always she thought of her strange visionary husband
in the mountains alone turning whiter and whiter

like a snowbird of some extraordinary kind with
wings wide and eaglehead highbeaked proud &
coming down in spring with great talons spread
arresting her in midflight at subway entrance &
sweeping off up up and away to his glee-echoing
lair high on the spiked cliffs—

   meanwhile the wise farmer who owned the house had
snowploughed his way to the visionary's door & knocked
like whitecoated Life & found artist frozen but not dead,
who awakened to strains of hospital music & surrendered
his soul to it, thanking the gods but not any one in particular for the fact that only a few toes had had to be
removed—he liked his nurse, a warm vision in white.

THE SORROW OF YOUNG YEATS

When Algernon Swinburne died,
most poets doffed their hats,
but Yeats leaped up and cried:
"Now *I* am King of the Cats!"

THE FALLEN ANGEL

Angels have never been people,
so coming down to Earth was a pleasant surprise.
He landed on a river boat in Mississippi, heading north,
wearing a wonderful gray suit
with a waistcoat, and a tall gray hat,
his pockets full of Dix-notes.
He liked himself so much
he forgot what he was there for:
something to do with changing the future, he thought.
But, right now, well, he was too excited to think about that,
too filled with what must be human sensation.

He was on deck, and the river was foggy,
but he could see the bank, and a sign: Natchez.
The bank was filled with clouds of waving greenery.
From somewhere on board a band's gay
tunes rose in the air.
He began to beat time on the deck with his foot:
a real foot—and no wings!
He tipped his hat to the passing ladies,
who nodded from behind fans.
Some of the men frowned at him.
Were they jealous? Of him? He was joyous!
He gambled and won, gambled and lost,
gambled and won again.
The night in the saloon
was the most wonderful night of his existence.

He slept with a woman that night. She robbed him and
got lost in Natchez. He didn't mind.
No, not at all. It had been exhilarating!
He gambled again, cheated, and someone shot him.
He died and became a ghost.

He liked being a ghost much more than he ever had liked
being an angel. Now he had something to remember,
having forgotten why he had been sent down
as an angel in the first, blessed place.

THE COMPOSOGRAPH

Long before morphing, ah, the composograph,
which changed one's face into another's face,
a clever grafting on a photograph.

Now we can morph, and morphing makes us laugh,
but we could do the same, at slower pace,
long before morphing, with the composograph.

Old people might remember how a half
became a whole. There was no graphic race.
A clever grafting on a photograph

created, after all, half kid, half calf,
or otherwise some queen in dusty lace,
long before morphing. Was the composograph

worth keeping? I'd have its epitaph:
It was a simpler time and simpler place.
A clever grafting on a photograph

should be remembered on a cenotaph
for human ingenuity and grace.
Yes, before morphing was the composograph,
a clever grafting on a photograph.

A TALL ONE

Years ago, McSorley's Old Ale House
in New York City refused to serve women.

I, too,
wasted my time
in McSorley's
smokey Old Ale House
with no women
but once
sneaked a tall one
in wearing
a slouch hat
with her hair
stuffed under
in time to find
a combat zone
where a famous
British act-
OR had been
snug in steamy
old McSorley's
but, tables turned,
the bartender
in a sweat drawing
a round—
"Trevor was here
and had a fit"—
my tall friend
giggling like
a little girl
(he gave her
a doubtful look,
but served her

                    a Stout). My
                    elbow in her
                    slim ribs—
                    her new deep
                   voice, "Thanks!
                    and cheers!"

BLARNEY STONED

Read with Brogue

Ah, Dionysus, ya grapey divil deity,
ya'd lak ta have me back in Hellas
ta guzzle in the juice of yer depravity!
Ya know yer dirty bottled blood'll
keep me at yer bidden.
Ah puke it up and force it down lak cud,
but I'll tell ya straight, ya satyr goat,
tomorrow, ah swear, ah'm quitten!
Ya make me drink this soupy slop,
ah know ya do, ah know it!
Ya tease me on ta gulp the rot,
and sure'n hell ah show it.
But ya'll not beat me, goaty beast,
cuz ah tell ya straight, ya satyr goat,
tomorrow, ah swear, ah'm quitten!

SONG FOR HAND PUPPETS

Hannibal Handable was my good right hand.
Hannibal Handable was a one hand band.
Hannibal's friend was Lucy Left,
A Handable girl from a place called Weft.
Lucy Left was a very clever hand.
She did things Hannibal couldn't understand.
But Hannibal loved her just the same,
and was always glad when around she came.
Now Hannibal walked on the table one day,
And clever Lucy came his way.
Then Hannibal ran to the other side,
playing hide-and-seek and trying to hide.
But Lucy let him go around and come back
as if he were on his own little track,
and cried from her palm, "Boo!" and "Surprise!"
"I can't fool you, no matter how I try,"
Said Hannibal, clap-clapping with Lucy,
"There's not much that you don't see!
I think it's nice that you're so smart,
and I don't think we should ever part."
"Two hands are better than one," Lucy said.
"And I don't think we even *need* a head.
We're just fine all by ourselves.
Let's tipfinger like Handable elves."
And off they went, hand in hand,
clapping and snapping like a two-hand band.
"Isn't it wonderful just to be alive!"
cried Lucy, leaping in a happy high-five.

MONSIEUR ÉLAN

He insisted on life before death.
He went about waking people up,
refusing to let them sleep,
shouting "Rise and shine!"
He played a bugle call.
He was all for the sun.
Everyone began to hate him
and to shun him.
But he sought them out,
banging a tin drum,
commanding quick march.
He pursued them through life
like the spirit of life,
glad to be trouble.
Finally, finally, finally,
we attended his funeral
and went home to bed,
just dead.

WINDKU

The scholars in the
library heard one break wind.
None noticed the air.

THE MORAL OF FRANKENSTEIN

The instauration of a revenant
can prove very unpleasanant.

EDUCATION

Because he never went to college,
my father sold the Book of Knowledge.
Myself, I never went to school,
but did devote myself to pool.
Both of us ended on the rocks,
graduates of old Hard Knocks,
alums of Loving Kindness, yet
ignorant on how to get
along in life without degrees,
no forests for us, only trees,
yet publishing our poetry
in *Yale* and *Southern* and *Sewanee*.
Sometimes the editors write back,
Dear Professor, you're no hack,
we wish to publish "Ode on Birds"
in which we find such lovely words.
And I write back and say to them
I'm no professor, all the same.
I never even went to college,
but daddy sold the Book of Knowledge,
and I read it, growing up,
when he and I would share a cup
of sherry over Heraclitus
knowing nothing'd ever right us,
knowing nothing quite stands still,
that only changing always will
keep you up with changing things,
like that river on time's wings
that you can't step into twice
even if you'd pay the price.

Now that dear old daddy's gone,
I think I'll write about a swan.

BOD OF THE OLD MAN MOANED

as he swung one-handed over
the horse in the gym and amazed
the wonderful muscular women
and he leaped to the rings and swung
his gnarled and horny feet high and neat
between the ropes and discovered
that the stiffness was gone
from his shoulders and he hurled
the clubs in the air and began
to catch and juggle them and
the young women cried out and
cheered when he caught each club
one in the crook of his withered
leg O he wore only his jock
strap and it began to bulge
in a way that had not occurred
in decades he jumped and touched
his toes off to each side
and the women who had gathered
fainted together and got up
and asked him in chorus to
do it again and again and again
What an amazing old bod! cried
the beautiful young women
Indeed said the old man to
himself, What a bod, what a—
and bod of the old guy groaned
and bod of the old man was
just
    dead!

THE SAVAGE BREAST

I The Opera

This was some opera! The fat lady singing the aria was encased in red. Well, "encased" is a bit harsh. But she strode through thick yellow, syrupy golden yellow, like melted wedding bands. I liked it when she made a little fist, long red nails in a little fist, which she waved about her head with great passion. The opera was Wagner sung in Samoan. I could follow some of it—the search for the ring, everybody on stilts. The diva took a nosedive off her stilts but the tenor caught her on his horns. This was a cultural feast! Somebody just told me that the aria went something like: "I will pay you for some water." I studied the diva through my opera glasses. She had got back on her feet. The tenor's horn was crumpled. It must have been made of paper. Art is so tricky. Now just about everybody was on stage and caterwauling to beat the band. Cats in an alley. It was exciting. I felt that at any moment now something big was going to happen. There was a lot of blue smoke, and the diva strode right through it, unblinking, singing her heart out. "I will pay you for some water." It was my first opera, but you can bet I'm going back.

II The Bowel Organist

No concerti are written for the bowel organ. This is generally thought to be due to the fact that the instrumentalist has little control over his or her instrument. The bowel organ is expected to produce little more than flourishes, if well-tempered. Usually, the bowel organist is placed on a small separate stage, at some distance from the main body of the orchestra. At outdoor concerts, however, he or she is usually placed at the rear of the orchestra, back to the audience. As is an actor's, the bowel organist's instrument is him or her self. There is no school that teaches the bowel organ. The bowel organist is a lonely artist. From youth, he or she must practice alone. But now a bowel organist has come forth to present to the world his own composition, Opus One for the Bowel Organ, as he has dubbed it. And for the first time, the bowel organist places himself at the front of the orchestra. There is the tapping of the baton, as the orchestra prepares to support his prelude, a long high trumpet-like riff that engulfs the audience.

PEDANTIC PIECE

If you have no verbs,
you must *do* everything;
but, really, you must not:
not, for instance, *do* dope.

May I lend you a verb?
Do you wish to *use,
misuse, abuse,* to
inhale, inject, ingest,
or do you wish to *do,* dope?

Well, don't; don't *do* dope.
Do do something else.

VAN GOGH'S EAR

I have no friends
how can I have friends
I only know artists
arrogant egotistical
disagreeable people
like myself, so how
in the name of Van
Gogh's ear am I
supposed to have
any friends?

LUNACY

I
can't
wait for
two more
weeks if I
take it now
if I ate it now
I'd have got only
the half of it but
half is better than
nothing & I need my
fix of the moon. I
open the window &
reach for the moon-
pill & pull it down
& push it in & chew
the moist cheese of
it in the green cheese
of it & begin to
feel the effect
of the dog's moon
the wolf's moon
& chew & swallow
& swallow &
chew grinding
& swallow
& finally
HOWL
!

THE FINE ART OF HAUNTING

I

"Watch how," my teacher said, "when I tug, she tugs
right back, annoyed. She thinks she's caught on something,
then wonders, when she sees that nothing's there,
how she got caught—on what, on where? And now
she's baffled, for there's nothing near her sleeve,
no furniture nearby, no hooking chair.

II

And now she speaks to him. I think he's here, she says.
He thinks she's suffering guilt—There's no one here.
He pours champagne. She pulls her glass away.
She tells him that she feels your presence in the room.
Don't ruin the occasion, he tells her.
We've got his house and all his money and each other.

III

Yes, haunting is an art," my teacher said.
"You mustn't be too obvious, too crude.
They'll think it's all a trick, or caused
by natural tremors, earthquakes and the like,
and what you want above all other things
is to be certain that they know it's you."

A CONSIDERATION OF ANGELS

I IT MUST HAVE BEEN THE ANGELS

on the head of the pin who wrote the Bible
on the grain of rice, it must have been
a tulipful of minimalists who painted the rainbows
on the dew-drops, it must have been the microwave
that sang so hot from deep inside.

I know that the bee sees a different flower,
patterns and colors I can't see;
and I can imagine the million neon cells
of the octopus, that colorfully advertizes for love
or shyly vanishes before one's fascinated eyes,
or the corncobs of scent-cells in my sniffing,
trotting mutt's curious, streetwise nose.

I believe it had to have been
the angels on the head of the pin
who wrote the Bible on a grain of rice.

II INSTANT ANGELS

Thunder
    & lightning
        & downpour!

My clothes beat against me
like whirling laundry,

but I may never see angels again,
a myriad of instant angels

with transparent wings
appearing/disappearing

on the black asphalt
of the gleaming street,

all wings in a funnel,
like transparent butterflies

landing on black flowers;
but their long funneling wings

are of water.

III WINGS

Generally, children are not allowed to get tattoos, so the boy had wings drawn on his back with a marking pencil by his friend. He had a long, narrow back, so the wings had to be long and narrow, from his shoulder blades to his behind, where the pointed tips disappeared into his yanked-up shorts and came out behind his thighs. His friend objected that the pants would prevent the wings from opening, so, after a few moments of thought, the boy dropped off his pants and stood naked at the edge of the cliff. "How do you know this is going to work?" asked his friend. "It is going to work because these are not the wings of a bird," said the boy, "but of an angel." And he jumped and swooped down over the water and then swooped up again and flew into the clouds. "Goodbye," called his friend, the artist, and "Goodbye" called the angel, waving.

SONNET AT SIXTY-FIVE

Sixty-five orbits of the sun today
and, though I'm growing tired of this spacesuit,
which rag, as an unhappy by-the-way,
has lost its goggles and at least one boot,
so that I cannot see or even walk
as I once could, and have some trouble hearing,
and toothless too, and tongue-tied, cannot talk
without the noise of cranky broken gearing—

where was I?—tired of this spacesuit!—still I
am grateful that I have a suit to wear
at sixty-five, and wouldn't I be silly
if I preferred to lie in earth bone-bare
   to orbiting the sun again this year
   in this old-fashioned and bedraggled gear?

LIFE SURPRISED ME;
OR, BURROWING MOLES

*I only feared a little bit
that I might fail to make the grade,
for my Professor Gnome had made
the grade with even lesser wit.*

At first, I wanted for a theme,
like Yeats, then thought a campus idyll
(which Brits pronounce to rhyme with fiddle)
might be the thing to make my name.

"Publish or Perish," terrorized me,
so I worked late into the night,
and to my wife I would recite
my work in progress, "Life Surprised Me."

But then I thought too bold a title
might seem insensitive to some.
It must not shock, but seem to hum
(inaudibly at a recital).

"Burrowing Moles" seemed better to me
than "Life Surprised Me," loud and brutal.
My epic work must gently tootle,
or its strong echo might undo me.

*Because the heart is like a mole
that pads about beneath one's feet:
It has a pitter-patter beat,
but is quiescent on the whole.*

WHAT I DID ON MY SUMMER VACATION

This summer I flew to Trieste
to visit with Joyce, then
journeyed to Prague to find Kafka.
In Hamburg I had many a few
steins of beer with Thomas Wolfe,
and, because the Literary
Travel Agency rushed my itinerary,
soon found myself chugging through
the Chunnel and into Poet's
Corner at Westminster Abbey,
where I ran into a raging Dylan
Thomas. He hated the States
but loved Third Avenue, so
he said he would help me
paint London red, white, and blue.
Next morning we had vanilla
ice-cream in our beer
for our health's sake. Later
that afternoon Caitlin kicked
the stilts out from under his house,
so I thought it was time to leave
them there, under milk wood,
and get on to the relative peace
and quiet of Ireland, where I
visited with Pat Kavanagh,
who had come to regard comedy
as the "ultimate sophistication,"
which ordinary people, "do not
understand and therefore fear."
Pat believed that in tragedy
"there is always something of a
lie. . . comedy is the abundance
of life," etc., but I had to leave

him there, laughing at himself,
and life in general, and catch
the train on to Heathrow.
I landed in New York, where I
was met by Walt Whitman, who
was holding up a dishevelled Eddie
Poe, who greeted me with a wet kiss.
I got a manly hug from Walt. Then
I flew back down to Asheville to
present Wolfe's hometown with
his latest, *You Can't Go Home
Again,* which he gave me in
manuscript (much edited
by Max Perkins) and then drove
back to the College by the Lake
—and here I am, grading papers.

COCKTAILS FOR TWO?

John Ciardi
liked Bacardi
but drank Chianti
with his Auntie.

NOTICE TO MODERNS

You solipsistic sissies, male and female,
poets about the Me, Myself, and I,
should send yourselves, and then collect, your email,
and not pretend such jots are poetry.

"Poets are actors, and their books are theatres,"
wrote Wallace Stevens. Roethke spoke in tongues.
How many voices spoke through William Shakespeare's?
Create verse worthy of great scoptic lungs!

There is a gathering on a green hill
where scops will sing of everything they share.
In my imagination, with my will,
I try to see that time, and who was there.

Or in a book or on a stage I try
to tell of others, not Me, Myself, and I.

THE DECIDUOUS STRIP

This is the deciduous strip, primarily performed in November, when the trees throw off their lovely rusted leaves and make a carpet of them up and down the driveway and the lawn. The collapsed jack-o'-lantern, turned into pumpkin mush, past-perfect for pies, mouths his cigar and watches in cross-eyed glee from the top of the garbage can, a box-seat by the stage. The trees sway to the music of the wind. With their long slender limbs they tap the roof of the house for a more syncopated rhythm. Look! Look! Their limbs spring back naked! These leaves are better than boas! G-strings woven of last grass at the roots, and loyal pasties with twirlies in among the limbs. Now a crescendo from the orchestra in the sky, louder than Mozart sending Don Giovanni to hell, and then the diminuendo. Now the trees stand in the winter, naked to the world, bowing, and, as I turn away, dreaming of spring, they vanish into the wings of my imagination with a windy kick from one last, curvy limb.

THREE BY HERACLITUS

I

Offend yourself with mirrored knowledge
(where's that face you wore at college?)
and your sense of life's no-stasis,
thinking of various times and places,
recalling the endless grandmother summers,
remembering bees and thunderboomers,
and quote, "A boy's will is the wind's will."
All is flux, nothing stands still.

II

About to vacation some years ago,
it was yourself that you wanted to know,
so you left your wife behind and went
away to the mountains and set up a tent,
and re-read Walton, and cast your fly
as you did as a boy, long and high;
but something went wrong—and you got a fever.
You can't step twice in the selfsame river.

III

Discontent in retirement you stare at your land
(once wild but tamed by the work of your hand).
How long will it take to overgrow
when you are gone, you'd like to know.
You haven't the strength to do things twice.
It's all gone now, gone in a trice.
You're an old dog now, a dog with the mange.
Nothing endures but change, change, change.

POETRY AND THE POET

I Poetry

puts a foot
on the back
of philosophy
and a foot
on the back
of science
and enjoys
a wild ride
stuntrider
never failing
to note
a prominence
in the
passing scene
always
wise enough
to put
both feet
on one
when they get
too far
apart
patient
to see them
re-team
satisfied
with every sight
and sound, feeling
often
that the
eternal
factor
is the ride
itself
the rough
bucking ride
among the stars

II The Poet

In many moods
the poet broods
on dice and swans
or old bygones;
new turns of fate
in love and hate
or what wild words
are sung by birds.

THE FRUITS OF HIS THOUGHT DELIVERED TO HIS FAVORITE BARTENDER

The good man is like
the camel, George,
he standeth humped!
Drink not of the milk
of human kindness,
for it is binding!

Once a ladyfriend
tried to shut me up:
"Stop sounding like
a garrulous guru!"
she shouted.
"Be yourself!"
But then she thought,
and then she said,
"Oh, hell, you *are*
being yourself!"

She was looking
at *her*self in a
beautiful mirror,
and spoiling it.
"Art thou ugly?" I said.
"Not in the eye of the needle!"

OÖMANCERY

Oömancery is the magic of the universe
popping out of an egg.
I don't see why the universe should not
pop out of an egg, or into one.

I read with my morning coffee,
in the *New York Times,*
of a new theory of astro-physics,
providing for the possible

existence of multiple universes,
unknown to one another.
I don't see why there should not be
multiple universes.

I am so intrigued by the notion
that I fail to notice
that there are innumerable presences
in my house and that they are

attempting to tell me something.
I catch myself up and listen
but can only hear suggestions:
Mister Breeze, Mistress Boardcreak,

Master Bark, and little Miss Sigh,
speaking ineffably to me. Zounds!
Are their voices coming from my holy egg?
The light on the walls is

filled with dancing wings.
My egg is beautiful,

but not too beautiful to eat.
I swallow the soft-boiled universe

whole, and wash it down with coffee.
Now I am in one and have one in me.
The theory of multiple universes
has been proven to my satisfaction.

THE LAST WORD

Edwin Makepeace Thackery Schorb
wrote many words into his books,
drank too much beer, and lost his looks,
and then spun off this spinning orb.

We who knew him say that he
was quite mistaken in all he did;
others, however, from whom he hid,
called him a genius, readily!

What is the truth? Oh who may know?
Not I, who knew him when he was young!
Nor I, who wagged a flattering tongue!
Say this: He drank, and had to go!

BONJOUR À TOUS!

It's Earthgodown & the sun fringes the horizon, lightening
   the sky.

As the crickets fall silent & the new day sings through the
   birds,
as the squirrels chirp for conversation & business, I open
   my eyes
to light & the din of morning awakenings, glad to be alive,

full of pleasure at time that has given me these phenomena,
this morning variousness that includes the percolation of
   the pot

of coffee in the kitchen that my wife has beaten me to
   making—
& rise with the metaphysics of morning to a day gone by
that I shall remember with much fondness on the morrow,

should I awaken to yet another Earthgodown, Suncomeup
of a morning in the enchanted magic of eternity.

HANGING LOOSE, A MUSICAL SUITE

I THE FIDDLER

Played the devil's fiddle, stomping to it, shaking it out,
   full of corned blood, his boot down down down!
Days before the corn, his old bitch Lucy lay by his piston
   heel.
   Said later she smelled it, stayed by it, waiting
for the meaty bone; said later never done him no harm at all;
   said later not even a ghost of evil but Lucy got it,
old bloodhound bitch like red clay, wrinkled old lady
   hanging
   from her own bones—could make her moon-howl,
pointing his wild bow—do that at dances. Devil in a
   Baptist,
   playing the fiddle. Gradual as the mountains,
he found out how the devil got in. Fiddle under his spiked,
   gray chin, corn jug thumb-hooked and cradled on top
his elbow—capful for Lucy—then stomp stomp stomp:
   music
   through Blue Ridge pines!   Could choo choo it
so's you see smoke and steam, hear that wheezy accordion
   whistle;
   could conjure with it up a trainload of places
or turn you back home to the station of pines and blue
   smoke
   mountains, bring musical rain, or put the devil
in your heart, winking and drinking and stomping.
   Everybody loved
   him and his Lucy, including said devil, as the corn
     dropped
down into his right big toe. Said it hurt to stomp. But it
   don't

stop the fiddler. Don't nothing stop the fiddler! He was
one thing else than music; he was a man. Take more'n corn
going
through, dropping down in my right big toe, says at
the May dance, everybody seeing him stomp, ouch ouch
ouch on
his big red gray spiked old corned face. Devil
got in through the corn, slick as silk; got down in my boot,
but I'll stomp him out; give old Satan a head-
ache—stomp stomp stomp! But that corn went to killing
him.
His bow was flying! Went on like this, folks say,
a tad's five year, him stomping the devil in the corn and the
devil
stomping back. Said now he couldn't play no more if
he don't get rid o' that old devil. Takes him a broad wood
chisel
out back on a stump, sets his right foot up, sets
that chisel to his toe, and strikes down with a good hefty
hammer.
When he pulls back his foot, that devil in the corned toe
stays on the stump, says looka me, I'm off! Has brought
him
some fireplace soot and some gingham. Sticks that foot
in that black soot, to staunch the blood, and wraps it in
gingham
rags. Said never done him no harm again, quiet as a bone,
and he goes back to stomping in peace, rid of the devil. But
first, he throws that old corned toe to Lucy. Says:
I knowed you always wanted it. Now mind the nail, Lucy;
don't let
the devil get you, you drunk old droop-skinned hound
bitch, cuz I love you. And Lucy goes to lickin' that toe,
pops

it in, and goes to grinding up that devil in her old ground
   down
chops. And next time we see them, the fiddler and his
   drunk bitch,
   they both full of corn, and ready, now, for the dance!

II THE SOLD PIANO BLUES

Sold the piano,
I sold the piano,
   sold it to the husband of a blind soprano,
because I needed money
so I could pay the rent—
I needed money
so I could pay the rent—
   they had to make their living,
   I had to pay my rent.
(kept my guitar)

Sold that piano,
I sold that piano,
   the gap-toothed one that wobbled on three legs,
my poor piano,
   that made that sad soft sound
like when you're breaking eggs,
one dead pedal,
   many missing keys,
   its ivories all yellow and its broken knees.
Sold my piano,
oh I sold my piano
   and now I have to do a cappello blues.
(No, I don't—kept my gitfiddle)

Got no piano,

I sold it
   because I needed money so I could pay the rent.
Sold my piano
   and now I wonder where all that dirty money went
because I didn't pay the rent.
   I bought a month's supply of booze
   and now I sit and sing *a cappello* blues,
a cappello blues.
Ah... I sing the sold piano blues.
(good thing I kept my geetar)
I sing the sold piano blues,
sold piano blues...

III LATE NIGHT RAP OF SOUL AND BODY

When you speak, and fingers snap,
it's I who tell you what to rap.
I own your hands, I own your feet,
I own all your dancing meat.
You have no home but meat and bone.
You are not you in space, alone.
If my bones break, you cannot move.
How then, my Soul, do you show love?
I'd shake you till the last bulb blew
and with the dawn do something new.
Your Soul, who's master of his ship,
says bell your sails from toe to hip!
You'd have me break and die for fair
from endless wear and terrible tear.
But no, I'll sleep. What can you do?
If I am tired, then so are you,
and when I sleep, you too must sleep,
and in your universe must keep,
among your dreams, inside my head,

a restful quiet in our bed,
till we awaken, straight and narrow,
freshened, like a new-fletched arrow.

IV CABIN-FEVER BLUES

for Rodney Formon

Rain, rain, rain for forty days & nights—
  rain & more rain, dark rain days & nights!
But I can still remember bright white lights.

Rain, rain for forty days & not a beam,
  no, not a beaming smile of light! Jim Beam
keeps me afloat in all this flood, I deem,

Jim Beam, branch-water, music, memories,
  branch-water, music, memories, & sighs.
Outside the door the drenched cat cries & cries.

All dark outside the room & dark inside—
  It's so damned dark you'd think that I could hide,
& darkness is a thing that can abide!

I'll bring the cat inside out of the rain,
I'll bring him in to share my blues, my pain.

V BOWERY BLUES

O, it's sick green walls
  with a painted comet
and checkerboard tiles
  inlaid with vomit—

oh, if God made a fool
   you can bet I'm it,
old lady on the bum!

   O, it's "Cover your cough!"
      on a cardboard sign,
   and it's "def no credit"—
      ah, what a line
   for a biddy whose blood
      is ninety per wine,
   old lady on the bum!

O, its "The Big Boy Shot",
   that's the morning double:
for thirty-five cents
   it'll cure my trouble.
I sit down next
   to a tramp with a stubble—
old lady on the bum!

   O, it's the Salvation Army
      when I need a bed,
   or I just take my shoes
      and put 'em under my head
   and lie in a doorway
      and wish I was dead—
   old lady on the bum!

O, I'll die someday
   of this rotgut booze,
but what do I care?
   I got nothing to loose.
I loose all I have
   when I loose my blues!
Old lady on the bum!

VI SONG: ISRAFEL
Chorus by Patricia Schorb

There once was a king in the East
and a very good king was he.
He held a magnificent feast
and proclaimed all men were free.

Oh no, you'll never live to dwell
in the land of Israfel
where the golden flowers swell.
Oh no you'll never live to dwell
in the land of Israfel,
but my friend I wish you well.

But when the moon went away in the morning
the sun looked down to see
bodies and women in mourning
and not even the king was free.

Oh no, you'll never live to dwell
in the land of Israfel
where the golden flowers swell.
Oh no you'll never live to dwell
in the land of Israfel,
but my friend I wish you well.

This we learn from this king of the East:
a ruler can never impart
freedom to people at a feast,
for freedom resides in the heart.

Oh no, you'll never live to dwell
in the land of Israfel
where the golden flowers swell.

*Oh no you'll never live to dwell
in the land of Israfel,
but my friend I wish you well.*

VII PUB SONG

The jukebox unwinds a Piaf
　to us as we sit at the bar
trying to find some relief
　from a world where troubles are.

The bartender brings me my drink
　and I drink it without a remark.
Outside, the evening is pink
　with that pink that comes before dark.

"I regret nothing," sings Piaf,
　and the record drops dead in its box.
Now Piaf is free of the grief
　her glorious music mocks.

And drunk, I am free as a sailor
　to bless or not to bless.
Say, how can a man be a failure
　if he has no need of success?

VIII NOSTALGIC SONG

O darling, on this summer day
in Nineteen Hundred Two,
the parasol above your head,
your shadowed eyes of blue,

the way your yellow hair is piled,
the color on your lips,
the way you look at me and smile
and touch my fingertips—

all these conspire to make me dream
that we might fall in love:
yet what a jealous fool I am
when I touch your glove

and feel the prints upon that glove
of those hands of his,
and taste the ashes of old love
as we walk and kiss—

> O darling, were there others
> before Tom came along?
> O darling, have I brothers
> among the Coney throng?

> O darling, when we marry
> will you be true to me?
> O darling, let us hurry,
> let's hurry up and see!

IX THE RUBBER CHURCH

The church bulged with music,
  its clapboard sides were rubber.
Boom, went the church,
  boom, boom, boom,
and out of its steeple the shape of sound,
  like a gusting smoke,

came and scattered.
  Smacks of the hands,
smack, smack, boom,
  and the little church twisted,
shortened, its sides puffing,
  lifted, grew tall
grew skinny as its steeple
  that looked like a horn.
The fingers of feet on the piano floor
  stomped on the boards
while the wide-lipped windows smiled,
  puckered narrow,
and the little church bent,
  bowed before God.
Then the little church jumped,
  the little church gloried
in God-given life,
  and the voices lifted the roof
like a hat
  and the bats in the belfry
turned up
  and hung on tight
like parrots in the wind
  to the raised roofbeams,
Woosh, woosh, woosh,
  they turned up
and stood on the beams,
  crazy bats,
and when you came out,
  you came out singing,
swinging.

PART TEN

CONTRA MORTEM

In the midst of Life we are in Death.
Cranmer, Book of Common Prayer

NAMES OF THE DEAD

The names of the dead sail on.
They are like white seabirds against a white sky,
then black seabirds against a black sky.
Every so often you hear the flutter of wings.
Into your ear comes a name.
That was Kaufman, you say.
Then a vague picture appears in your head,
at the back or in the front, against the walls.
You shake your head.
Maybe you see a smile different from others.
Long, narrow teeth in front. Kaufman.
The names of the dead sail on
like seabirds over the moony sea.

A HUNDRED YEARS

Although the sea won't pose,
the picture that the boardwalk takes is clear.
In each ear, the old man says, he has a baby mouse
that squeals sometimes and makes the surf high-pitched.
A hundred years of being here, he says,
seems merely like a day, a day with many nights.
Once, he kept the old lighthouse, once, a tackle shop,
and once he was a fisherman himself, also selectman once,
but then he laughs and says he married twice.
Most of the Earth, he says, is sea,
most of a man is water,
and mother comes from *mare* and *meer* and others,
the sea we swim before our birth.
Once, too, he was a farmer,
and calved the cows inland, but not for long.
The sea must call him back, he must have the sea,
or the sea have him.
In a hundred years you learn a thing or two,
he says, but not so much as you might think.
Mostly it's the magic of it all.
You are born with that, you have that right away,
but then there's sex, and then there's all
that business in between that's meant to keep us going,
the race I mean, and you forget the magic
in the business, the busyness, he adds,
and you work hard, and you are tired a lot, and only see
   the sea,
as with your mind and not that sense the youngest have
that's gained again in age, when time's more free,
and you can feel the flow of life right on your skin.
You feel the wind, now, I don't doubt, but do you feel
the other thing? Do you feel the secret thing?
Do you feel the thing behind the wind?

Aldebaran was so bright last night,
I 'most could take it in my hand,
not so simple as a jewel, but a spiritual thing.
When I look at the sea, or at the stars at night,
I do not fear my hundred years as you might think.
They do not wish to go or stay.
They are always here with you and everything.

THE ROSES

The wishes live together in unease.
I see no stasis, but a perilous balance.
I watch as roses disassemble, petal
and petal, touched with darkened tips
and edges, and think of when they bloomed,
how determined their becoming,
how absolute. I have watched the gardens.
I have watched them carefully and long.

I think the wishes live together in unease.
Just when the turn comes, I'm not sure.
The roses hold and hold late in the year
but at some point surrender, at some point
you can't identify, it seems before you see it,
and you are looking, looking long and hard,
and then you realize that it has happened—
the roses wither, fall.

It's true that the wishes live together in unease:
the thing you knew was magic—you look again—
is just pedestrian. Is it because
you know more than you did, or have you lost
a knowledge you possessed? The wishes live
like twins who hate each other, jealous twins,
who want your only love. Live, says one, Die,
the other; and they stare across
your holy land like enemies, but finally
they compromise, and hold the ground they have.
And this can last most of a lifetime, like
the freshness of the rose that holds throughout
most of the summer and almost into winter.

THE SOULS

The Raleigh News and Observer Editor's Note: This poem, first published in the highly respected British quarterly "Stand," edited by Jon Silkin, which arrived on our desktop in late winter, was not intended as a 9/11 memorial poem. Yet, evoking as it does the thousands of souls who joined the "unsteady hum" a year ago, that is what it has become.

Outside on a green lawn a giant water-oak conducts a
   sunset.
   Some unsteady hum has summoned us out of our houses.
My ancient lady friend, who lives nearby, is jawing now,
   and wears
     an awed-holy expression as she says they are souls, yes
       sir.
And they are everywhere, they wade the dusky clouds, they
   are
     giant black-winged fruits hanging, falling, bouncing. The
       green
is black with them. And neighbors stare; they worry for
   their

cars and pickups. If they get into the red berries, it's hell on
   paint. Shoot them. No, they are beautiful. They are a
     menace.
Look out below! They rise and wheel, kaleidoscopic, inside
   rings
     of themselves. They set themselves against the sky, black
       on blue.
They caw. They are telling themselves, or us, something.
   They caw and caw, and what is it they are saying, so
earpiercingly, holes through your eardrums, through your
   brain,

as if lasered? Then they settle again, like a black blizzard
  of huge coal flakes. The souls come back to visit us, to
    tell
us that they know everything now. Now their sharp yellow
  beaks
    pierce the lawn. They are busier than worms, in a feast
of famishment, an ecstasy of appetite. Now, she says,
  the nonagenarian, I'll soon be with them, and then
it's always now for me like them. The souls have found
  their

bodies. I don't know which is which, but somewhere, there,
  is everyone who died, all the loved ones, and even the
    others,
the ones that nobody loved, they are all there now, she says.
  I stare as deep as I can see. They are every blessed
place—on roofs, looking down, in trees, on bushes, under,
  over, and around. Some seem to be waiting, some tug
at the turning-emerald lawn in the lowering light: and now

how do they know to rise suddenly, and become one wide
  black wing? How do they know to circle and circle in
    unison,
one boomerang black wing composed of so many blood-
  beating,
    sky-rowing black wings? How do they know when it's
    time
to fly along a horizon, rimmed with rising red? The souls,
  they know, they know! I think it must be out of some
    distant
folklore that the old lady speaks, eyes fixed, waving them
  goodbye.

WHERE ARE YOU?

What life does to us
is strange, too strange,
I suppose, for many to
think about. But I
think about it, about
how you were here,
right here with the
rest of us, and now
are not, are gone into
the ground and maybe
are waving in the grass,
or are sitting silent
there, being the rock,
or are looming up
and reaching out,
being the tree, or are
drifting easily down
the street, being
the leaves burning
and the smoke.

Where are you?
You cannot not be anywhere.
I want you to come back;
but you can't, I know.
I can fan the air
with my hands and
do no good. I was
sitting here, right here,
with you, and you were
saying or doing something
and I was not attending,
I was thinking my own

thoughts, but what
are they now? I
should have listened
deeply to you. I
should have recorded
your voice in my mind,
so that I could hear you
again and again until
I myself am smoke.

METAPHYSICS OF THE BIG WOMAN

The Big Woman is sweeping the floor.
There is dust in the corners, dust
in motes in light at the door
and whirling along the walls.

It has been twenty-four hours
since last she swept the dust;
but, to the dust, being small, it is more,
by some counts, ten billion years.

Quickly, she bends with a rag
and wipes a world from the world:
for all of the dust is shining,
radiant, with light from her source.

DESTRUCTION

In Florida a hurricane
came off the sea and
razed the town of
Homestead, in which
town lived a little
boy—in a mobile home,
a singlewide, on wheels—
whose hobby it was, he
told the reporter,
to build houses out of
cards. His mother worked,
his father had died, he
had no sister or brother,
no other, so when he came
home from school, second
grade, he would stack
cards, most beautifully,
the reporter gathered, up and up
and into the most wonderful
designs, so wonderful, he
said, that his mother
had photographed some of
his houses made of cards
(but the photos had been
blown away by the storm—
as well as everything else).
The boy said he could
stack some more, and
didn't care, his talent
remained, but frowned
and said, in a small voice,
that he felt sorry
for the wind.

CHRONICLE

Out of the mustard tang that filled my mouth
with the vivid day once when wind
brought itself riffling through my short golden mane
like the hand of God being the cub's mother's tongue
came that time when life was endless wonder
and listening to the wind take away laughter
as a chime with wings as little silver
stars afloat like darting butterflies
as sipping hummingbirds at one long meal
within that wind on such wide wings
as monarchs never know nor hummingbirds
but boys and girls flying their youth
wantonly was my dear time wasted
and now it is bells for a stopped watch
where I have ground my teeth out
my novel of ten thousand pages
empty as my mouth.

AND/OR
variations on a theme

1/The Invocation

I lean forward
feel my body
but become
my mind
soul
doing bidding
informed
to do
each does
must do
be
tran
scribing
in gregg
pitman
keeping
track
keeping
up
with
dictator
fired
for art
listen
the poem
is on
the way

thank
AND the
bugles
blow
in the
OR world

2/The Contemplation

AND
is making
what
AND knows
not OR

OR knows
what OR
makes
OR makes
what AND
knows
AND is
making

I make
this on a
field of
action
as I am
told by

my making
mind
AND's

can AND
make a
mistake
AND makes
everything
is OR's
best an
swer no
pangloss
served here
quack

3/Quark

an
atom
charging
angrily
around
is never trying
to find a place
to light
for it
getting there
is all the fun
the relatives
will be boring
its friends forgotten
atom doesn't care
it's a dare

a dare
let me go there
AND there
AND there
more AND
more
AND
atom
get hotter AND
hotter
barely holding
its particles
together
looping around
its own light
around AND
around
pulling away
from the pull
of its own
gravity
elliptical
like a man
with a beer
belly
then
thin again
so fast
in such a hurry
to be
where
it's
in
scape
heartbeating out

ballooning
shaking
shining
shooting
rocketing off
OR
barking
wagging
hissing
OR
knifing up
green through soil
pressing
in in
visible
no-stas
is to
renaissance
budding
blooming
blossoming
bursting
blowing out
up away
AND
starting again
AND again
AND again
heart pounds
head thumps
brain
pulses
communicating
message received
before sent

it seems
ions
zip zap
where's
time
here
see the
labanotation
of bird feet
in mud they
dance now
still as
they fly
away
see
the muddy
dance
see

AND see
them flying
being OR in
AND

it is all on the field
I feel it
the boy fielded the ball
how he felt when it hit
his glove
it was like light
like love

like ein's
grace

4/Envoi

gert
stein
sd
prose
is telling
poetry
naming
adamic
naming
a tree
a snake
parvis
parvis

AND
help me
I am
but an
OR

THE MAN WHO HATED CITIES

moved to a small town
which rapidly became a city
and moved to a smaller town
which began to become
a bustling city
and moved out to the edge of town
but the edge grew populace
and nearly became another city
and moved farther out
to the edge of the edge
which immediately started to grow
and become another city
and moved even farther out
to the edge of the woods
which were quickly being developed
and moved into the woods
among the darkening trees
and saw some hunters
and moved back farther
into the deepest part
of the already over-
crowded woods
and finally found
a cave in the side
of a hill deep
in the darkest part
of the woods
and lit a fire
which cast his shadow
on the walls of the cave
in the hill in the
darkest, deepest
part of the woods

and put out the fire
because now he knew
that it wasn't cities
or towns or crowded
woods or shadowed caves
that he hated
it was people
even himself
his own
shadow

MARKED MAN

He looks for Death
back over his shoulder,
some say too much.

He looks for Death
ahead on the hill there,
perhaps an inch.

KADDISH FOR MENKE KATZ

Be near me now; Time's weakened me; be
near me now; let me have my way once more.
Forgive, forget; you must remember me
now in my need. Come in the door,
sit down, relax, and let us talk
of all the silence listened for
these many years. I walk
alone in here and putter
weakly. I'm white as chalk.
Perhaps, I mutter,
in truth, it's I,
who could not utter
a cry,
must sigh . . . .
O
Menke,
with your sweet
mandolin and
thick-accented song,
your poetry of
burning villages and
brave forays beyond the pale,
of coming to America
and golden Lower East Side streets,
of the secret laughter at the center
of the most Holy Kabbalah, O Menke,
for you, dead at nearly ninety, I write
this Katzian sonnet. The body sleeps to free the soul.

OLD CHORISTERS

Singers
of our generation
are turning up
dead. A serial
killer
is injecting
them
with cancer
heart disease
and stroke.
This police
silhouette
of the killer
isn't made
of his head,
but of his
twisted mind,
made
of a brain
to answer
for his crimes
of torture
perpetrated
on so many
choristers.
With a rough
cat-tongue
he licked flesh
from bones
and made
the other
mercy-kill
to make
amends.
Look,
from
a high bridge,
as highway god,
he drops
stones on old bones!
Even the sap
of trees is worried
up the trunk
as the killer
waits
for an autumnal
weariness of
leaves.
I am
Time's agent
his tool
he brags.
Singers
of our generation
think that this
is a serial crime,
but have
no choice
but to
become ringers
and to pull
the ropes
and toll
the bell.

HOUDINI AND THE DYING SWAN

Where was he? Was it a tunnel?
But he had come to a wall,
a slimy, wormy wall.
He must break through.
He must break out.
He felt for a tool.

Naked, she lay back in the tub,
white as a white swan, long-necked
as a swan, thin as a silken thread,
her gloriously thick dark hair
piled loosely up, collapsing
onto her wide, sloping shoulders,
dark, water-dipped ringlets forming,
her swan's-down skin pinking,
steam misting her swan song,
her suicide with water and razor.

II

They concentrated. A glittering
company. Rich. Celebrated.
They waited for the great Houdini.
His monument was dark, unmoving.
The stars glittered, like the company.
Half a minute. They breathed
in short, shuddering breaths,
and waited. Houdini heard:
"Houdini, do not disappoint us,
for we must believe that Death
cannot take us, utterly."

Tearing at the wall, his long

yellow fingernails cracked off,
ricocheted; then he heard:
"I am dying, dying . . ." He drew back,
prepared to throw his body at the wall
--he must break through . . .

III

The steaming water in the marble tub
was streaked in ribbons of red.
She was going to die, that *he* would know,
her lover, what he had done.
He had killed beauty
in neglect and pursuit of money.
He would be sorry. Her long lashes locked.
It was like a dream, and she was falling,
falling over a dark sea, which now she struck.
The noise jolted her. It was like
breaking plaster, like tumbling bricks,
like an earthquake. Her eyelids rolled back
to see a mad-eyed specter
emerge from a great, gaping hole
torn through tiles. Her dizzy mind,
half-bloodless, saw the bloodless form,
and fainted. Houdini lifted her from
the marble tub and taped her wrists.
He put her in her bed and tugged
the bell pull. She was too beautiful to die.
A great grandfather clock obliterated
the last of midnight. A doorknob turned,
and he went back the way that he had come.

Houdini darkened into death.

DEATH ROW

for Piri Thomas,
author of Seven Long Times,
who knew them in Attica

In the Prison of the North,
in some Bismarck of winter,
the bars are ice, the walls
are iceberg tips, and the guards
steer past the cells on sleds of frozen water.
Whiteness at night, with shadows
behind each corner: thin cotton blankets
to teach us a lesson, another lesson,
one more than all the others.
But Death Row is not a place,
anymore than Purgatory,
it's a waiting period, and we stand
naked in it until, frozen, we fall,
we fall and break, we shatter,
we grit the floor like rice.
Fire here is the touch of ice—
we light our mentholated cigarettes
with a touch of ice, with our own fingertips,
our lost and blackened and found-again toes.
We light our smokes with our frost-bitten,
blackened toes and watch white paper
burning back, turning black, and a red spark
with its dark smoke vanish in the winter light.
This is what we get for being what we are—
monsters with ice-water in our veins,
cold-blooded killers of love, runaways.
The prison of the North does not contain us,
we contain it, got it young, most of us,

got it and walk about with it freezing up
inside us, got it and can't find warmth,
don't remember how, and the worst
of it is that we cannot even touch
one another or we shatter. Do you hear
that creaking sound? One of us
has tried to touch another,
the oh-so-lonely one we call
The Refrigerator, has tried to find a friend,
the friend he tried to find we call The Freezer.
The Refrigerator sought love so savagely
that he was iced in love's bipolar cell,
and now his durance on Death Row is done.

THE BIG CRUNCH

Upgathering, the dead are born again,
the dirt unshovels and the coffins rise
into the hands of backward walking men,
relieved, rejuvenating pallbearers.

A widow is again a married woman,
a wife, the mother of such lovely children,
these crying adults crying now like infants.
A hearse drives backward down a melting road.

From funeral parlor back to hospital
the warming body of her husband goes
by backward racing ambulance and crew,
who desperately try to save his death,

and watch in horror as his chest reopens,
and hear him laughing heartlessly at them.
They are too young to save him now and cry
at their own helplessness and nippled need.

Young, powerful again, he forges back
into the marketplace where he was born.
His girlish wife has lost her backward children,
forgotten them, but hopes to have some soon.

The objects of his life come rushing by;
his stature changes; and his wife is gone;
he vanishes inside his mother's womb.
The cemetery turns into a wood.

The world becomes a gas and joins the sun,
the sun becomes a part of many suns,
and suddenly the stars collect and vanish,
and everything is one again, just one.

THERE I AM

> *Everyman, I will go with thee...*

And there I go, stopping for a beer,
for several, and smoking too much.
There I am, laughing with the guys.
There they are, and we all look alike.
We tell one another about being in the service.
We tell one another about how bad the food was.
Some of us had never had better. There I go,
telling the same tired old dirty joke.
There I go again, for the umpteenth time,
and then I go, walking home to my wife.
I can see myself now. And there I am,
at the weddings, eating and drinking.
The tux is too tight now, the legs too short.
It's the same one I wore on the cake,
when I was the plastic man standing there
with the plastic bride in her white dress.
And there we are dancing at the VFW.
My stomach hangs over my belt.
And there I am with my gold watch.
And there I am with my first grandchild.
I am completely bald now. It's the chemo.
And I am thin again, my shoulders narrow,
but my hips have broadened; and there I am,
looking better than I have for years,
in my final repose, with the others looking at me
as if they had never seen me before,
calling me daddy and grandpa,
calling me husband, son, pal.

DEATH

What do I know about death?
It is a question one must
occasionally ask oneself
Death who are you what are you
No metaphor will do
because that is merely
a likening of one thing
to another thing, which
when it comes to death
is impossible, for
death being unknown
anything we should
choose would be
arbitrarily chosen
and therefore
would be a bad
metaphor nobody
being able to say
how close or distant
the vehicle
from the tenor
the subject being
death. How then
do we approach this
unsubject this
antisubject this
but you see
even here
is a metaphor
even here
we are at a loss
that we are asking
a question for which
the only answer
is death.

A REPLY

When the wind blows down the house we thank the Lord
    that we were out that day; or, when the sea
turns our mast under its swashing opaque belly,
    and we are thrown clear, we swim and pray
thanksgiving, thanksgiving, selfishly forgetting
    that, like so many bits of bait, our brothers
twirl downward in the darkness, being bitten and consumed
    —but when you say you are an atheist,
then qualify that you're a rationalist as well,
    you say to me your reason's on vacation.

For all we know, there *is* a God, a chemist,
    and we are the byproducts of experiment,
luckily unknown to the great creator,
    who, if that creator were to learn of us,
might draw from a vast laboratory a sterilizer
    and spray us from the surface of the earth.

We don't know what or why we are, my epistolary friend,
    only that we are and we can think,
and with this small equipment we can challenge existence,
    that it not best us for a time, at least.
For each of us can triumph for a time, even the unborn
    has spent some positive force in first
dividing against the inertia of matter, a tiny Knight
    against the Dragon of Death, or unaliveness,
a dust adumbrating itself against the odds.

WEBSITES

I LIFE.ORG

A virus has more organized life than a star, though a star has an order of appearance, star in the sky and star on stage, but I am speaking of organic life, though a star on the stage or a movie star has organic life, more, in fact, than the virus. This explanation is paradoxical, a seeming contradiction, but let it stand for something in the same way that anything can stand for something else, particularly among symbolists and surrealists. In the same sense that the paranormal is most normal, the surrealists are most real. But humans are coelenterates: my liver heaves, my bowels twist, squirm with excitement and lead their own lives inside me. I need a new part. It pulsates. It is not my friend, but perhaps we can get along, after a time. At first, other parts reject it, but eventually they are tamed. You are all working for me, I cry. We are our own liver, kidney, heart. I am not your heart. You have no heart. Your better half told you that. You have no other half. It is all a golden fiction, inspired by sex. Your sex organs aren't even your own—they do as they please. As the real estate agent told the homeowner who questioned him about an easement, you don't own property, you control it. You don't own yourself, and you barely control yourself for social reasons of benefit to you and to the group. Life is the opposite of what is burning out there in space, that celestial snow, those flickering fireflies, which, close up, are all titanic violence. Life is soft and squirms when you caress it, and it could rule the night of the stars, if given time.

II DEATH.COM

I think of Earth as a great piñata, stuffed with death. Traditionally, at the end of the party, you take a whack at a piñata and it breaks, spilling its contents. If you did that with Earth, the countless dead would be released and scattered into space, and, though the geologists and the astrophysicists would disagree with me, I say that what would be left would be a tenth the size of the present globe, a wrinkled, raisin-like, bag that no longer had an orbit or an axis on which to fall toward the sun or to do its wobbly spin. The dead from Earth's beginnings to the present, or what was left of them, would float off into space, much as the stars, the galaxies are floating off, away from each other, red-shifted, and growing lonelier and lonelier. But perhaps there is something to meet somewhere out there. Perhaps the universe has a bright side. The darkness of the void wouldn't bother the remanents of the dead, they are used to it. They are as blind as they were when they lived, for we see with our minds not our eyes. So the whole thing is for the living. Death. Commercial. Stand in the midst of life and look at them go, to bones, to smoke, to ashes; then rejoin the matter of the universe yourself; the universe that, if it were capable of hope, could only hope to live.

THE TOWN DUMP; OR, LILY

1880-1901

A Carolina Sinner

From the galling stones dumped down to fire
from the edge of the purifying fire and into it
starcrossed at night in the raging beams

from all things house from all things home
fried fish and olive oil and a halo of smoke
church bell cup and anchor cast from hearth

for him that John that love and lust was life
from town by galling stones and loving wives
by where the mill-freight siding runs with

bells and beams that light the night and halo the fire
Lily the lovely jealoused stoned and trampled
for the sun's sake inside her and her son

from her evil life in a small room to the edge
of town where a thousand shoes kick and fail
to shine but turn black and smoke like tar

that holds wings serpent and dragon of flight
for the loved Lily now bannered and pitched
sword ax lance and club Lily the peacock lamb

and dove Lily lion of love crowned king
though woman for the androgynous skull
and in her castration birthing the phoenix

her son rising from the burning feathers
for always flight at Kill Devil Hill
with angels and strangers upward in smoke

OLD WOMEN, PAUSING

Old women, pausing, standing midblock on a hill
or midlevel on subway steps, waiting for breath,
their shopping bags hanging from toughened hands,
their eyes back in girlhood, perhaps, or ahead,
on the next meal, the contents of the bags
cooked and served, their honor again earned,
exist away from where they are, the grade or incline
slowly flattening, reversing, as their hearts calm
and their breath comes slower, more peacefully;
and so they stand, with the stillness of statues,
black-coated, black-shod, eyes straight ahead,
wisps of pale hair riffling slightly with the breeze,
waiting for breath, ahead of or behind where they are.
—So all of us, ahead of or behind where we are
or separated from what we are, not complete,
having left part of ourselves behind,
not having done that which we hoped to do,
not having attained to that which we hoped to attain,
all like old women, standing midblock on a hill,
waiting for breath, ahead of or behind where we are.

THE TERRIBLE SHADOW

Mind free of the terrible shadow of death, the child, who had gathered itself in the womb and could no longer remember its long genetic history, nor the gunmetal black un-time before it, sprang forth and grew until a time came when a whisper of futurity touched its quivering nerves; but still, mind free of the terrible shadow of death, felt by its mother and father, the child played in a place of organic magic, eating gummy worms and studying the dirt forming under its nails; now, mind free of the terrible shadow of death, the child attended the properly appointed and appropriate schools at each required stage, suffering often, but often joyful beyond adult reason—a bright kite flew, an airplane left a jet trail, a rainbow appeared out of the blue—and the shadow began to form, the terrible shadow of death. Mind no longer free of the terrible shadow of death, the child wrinkled like an overripe fruit, grew old, felt the terrible shadow of death, and died; then, no more mind, the child became the shadow.

THE NURSING HOME

There are more women than
men in the nursing home and
more men than old doctors.

Staff doctors visit once a
month. The few old men do
very little but sleep. Two

or three of them occasionally
gather outside in clear
weather for a smoke, which

is allowed them. I suppose
those in charge feel that
it can make no difference

now, and it brings the old
men a little pleasure. I
sit and chat with them

sometimes. Perhaps "chat"
is a bit too lively a word
to describe what passes for

conversation during these
puffing sessions. A lot
of low grunting goes on.

There is one old man who
is afflicted with bone
cancer and who says, in

high good humor, that his

guarantees have run out.
He was a travelling salesman

in women's wear, and still
remembers how much he loved
women. Many of the women

have become little girls
again. They carry dolls
about with them, mostly

rag-dolls, I suppose so
they can't injure themselves
when they squeeze them.

To see these toothless,
balding old ladies, frail
as twigs, clutching these dolls,

is heartbreaking. Oh, to love
something! It's still there.
It has been in them since

they were little and had dirty
knees and bows in their hair.
Some recognize me now, and,

when I give them a wave,
they wave back. It's a
wonderful feeling to make

contact, but it is difficult
to tell how much they know.
The care-givers are kind and

efficient. They are mostly
young, and apparently try
to imbue the old with some of

their zest for life, but
of course the old know all
that already—or knew and have

forgotten it. I wonder,
can the young reverse their
situations with the old

and see themselves looking up
at such fresh faces from the
vantage of bed or wheelchair

or walker? I am too young
to join the old here in the
nursing home, this metaphor

(or is it the tenor of a
metaphor?) for the last days,
but I am too old

to feel the buoyancy of the
young; so, at least for the
context of the nursing home,

I have arrived at yet another
awkward age. After visiting
my mother, who is only partly

present, I go out and sit
with the old men and have a
smoke. We hope for clear days.

THE LOSS

When the blackbird stood on the chimney and called,
poking her beak at the clear blue ice of the sky,
I watched from inside the frame of an old wooden house
across from the once two-chimneyed house where she stood,
heard her cry crack the ice of the sky that day
from the wrongest of chimneys, the wrongest.
The bricks lay scattered next to the house.
The big nest of hay had blown away.
The ugly babies now lived in the barn,
but for one, who had drowned in the well.

LEADBELLY

for the musical ghost of Blind Lemon Jefferson

    Leadbelly, grim with your Cajun accordion,
with your harmonica blues, with your knife
    flicking down the twelve strings of your guitar
—*the Rock Island Line was a mighty good road*—
    bowing, scraping, white-suited trainman . . .
made your pride sick, but you sang,
    fast, strong, quiet, like a driven
demon, like you had to get it out
    before a razor dumped your guts
on a blood-mud taphouse floor,
    or some drunk crazy rednecks
nailed you up like Christ, in a dangerous world
    for anybody but most America for a black
poet of low-down places and sky-high loves.

    Leadbelly, thirty years hard time murder,
six and a half, sang your way out, ten more, intent,
    then Alan Lomax and his bro, John, folklorists—
makes you laugh inside at night—white boys,
    playing—but they get you out again and in
the Library of Congress, that grinding
    voice part now of something big, like
storm darkness, like that lifething,
    love, always beyond somewhere or
crying deep inside, in a dark place,
    yeah, big like music, big like that gal you
call Irene! How many Irenes, you think?

    Even the Lomax bros, even them white boys,
they know Irene—you driving them through
    New York traffic, them folkloring in back and you
being their folkloring black chauffeur.

    You drink sharp liquor in Harlem, play
with Woody Guthrie, Sonny Terry, Brownie
    McGhee, the Headline Singers—radio too,
Hollywood and *Three Songs by Leadbelly*,
    a French tour . . . . You show 'em your razor
stretch marks, your shotpitted pot.
    Good night Irene I'll see you in my dreams . . .
all that good hot mean hard American life
    and Lou Gehrig's *amyotrophic lateral sclerosis*.
It's *The Midnight Special*!   Fade me, Death!

AN ANTIQUARY OF THE FUTURE

We have nothing like it, dating, I should say, from the mid-Twenty-first Century. Look at those hairdos. The clothes. They just don't make them like that anymore. Here, shake it. It won't break. It can't go away anymore. It is all told. But you see, they still have a touch of the old moonglow? And look at those sunbelt tans. Notice that when you shake it, no snow drifts, only it glows with a kind of sunlight and there are white puffs of cloud in that light blue background. Clearly, it was a beautiful day. But it rained later, see, and the sky turned dark blue, and then nearly black, so that you can hardly see the lovers, and, when it lightens again, time after time, they are different, older and sadder, but kinder. Then shake it again, and there they are again, full of young lust, full of hormones and mean selfhood of the worst sort. It's sad. Dates back to the ancients, the primitives. What's it worth? You can't put a price on a dream like this. It's a classic.

ELEGY FOR THE LEADER BIRD

This compass-headed bird,
                      dead-reckoning South in Fall,
arcing its bloody breast
                      above the roof and cawing
some kind of bold farewell
                      to higher air and leaderless
V'd fliers off on it,
                      was shot (we saw and heard),
and staggered in the sky,
                      dripping blood and guts
down on the lobstered roofers
                      working in the sun.
It sang its downfall swan
                      song silently, now, spread
its wings, and then, as silent
                      as its eyes, it lay
resting on the roof,
                      face up, and looked at clouds,
(and some sweet heaven we
                      could almost see); but soon
pain shook it like an angry
                      nurse, so one good roofer
struck head from body with
                      a spade, merciful severance,
and catwalked off, bloody
                      spade dragging on the tiles,
a man of dirty duty,
                      unlike the murderer
of song, the wanton boy-
                      in-man, who pellet-shot
the bird (the shot we heard);
                      and this once musical,
most bright and beautiful,
                      small dust was part of all.

ANTHOLOGIES ARE SAD

Impressed by smoking-ember music,
as I have always been, drinking gin,
and reading the poets of the past—
who are in anachronistic pain
as if alive, striving, thriving
today—I think of today's.

I have a new anthology,
one including me,
with, alas, dates.
Most have only births and dashes,
a few the flying ashes,
the smoking music, of the past—
dates that say, *At last! At last!*

What then of Berryman
and those other merry men
and women who were human—
in pain and joy—alive?
In the anthologies they thrive,
possessing their due dates!

So now I turn a page,
afraid to find my final age;
and, though my last is but a dash,
I feel the flutter of ash.

OLD ICARUS

Grandchildren turning
their faces from
drooling kisses
to avoid
what you have
become:
teeth like graveyard
stones, sunken cheeks
pockmarked
(where once,
as a boy,
the feathers went),
wens, wild hairs.

The wax your father poured
has melted
and the feathers,
plumes he placed so carefully,
flew, fell,
and you fell
into the sea
but did not drown,
owning a future,
as you did,
long enough
to hug your grandchildren
close and have them
turn away.

MEMENTO MORI

When these blow-dried twigs
finally fall, or are deracinated,
tangled in some last, accomplished comb,
or in the glib fingers of a lover
fine-boned and sharp-nailed enough

to play tweezers, the scarred skin
will gleam nakedly in the mirror,
burnished by sun and overhead bulb
and, quick as life, we shall have been
transformed into a meditative monk,

skull-capped and burnoosed, who
belongs to the Monastery of Maturity,
and bears on his weary shoulders,
silently, to his last small cell,
his own *memento mori*.

DEATH AND THE MERMAID

This mermaid is a virgin,
dreaming her last dream,
her upper half human and
milk-breasted, with seaweed-
tangled but human hair,
not an elderly patient
on display in a cave of plastic,
hearing the susurrus of the sea
in her own harsh breath.
She kicks, kicks open
her blanket-bandaged,
fish-tailed lower half
in her bound dream,
as the second tide
smacks hard on the rocks
a mile from the sanitarium
and foams in. *Life*, she cries,
in a siren sound, *life, life,*
under her plastic hood,
but Death dreams back
with a huge, curlicue wave
and spindrift, and the
cave-water rises, floating her up
on her forked, fish tail, where
she stands, breasts floating,
dark, tangled hair sparkling with
water-jewels, and leans forward,
into the tide, away
from a woman's world
of men, and reaches her
glistening long arms out
to take in the rising sea,
her only lover at the end.

THE DIAMOND MERCHANT

> *A diamond is forever.*
> —B. J. Kidd

The buoys of memory have faint bells, noticed in the night.
I have left these chiming seamarks for the time of my return.
They ring out there, but faintly, so faintly I can hardly hear.
I think they want me to remember the severances of the
   soul,
if soul is more than mere electric tissue. If Death is king
and I do not reclaim what I have jettisoned, it goes to him.
I do not want the king to have my life. Therefore, each
   night at sea,
I must set out to find the ringing buoys and haul aboard
the lagan realities, for now my aging body, my emotional
   mal de mer,
lend renewed reality to the cold, damp camps. One
   numbered friend
should wear a wedding ring, another was engaged, and yet a
   third,
below and silent, had eyes like Tavernier blue diamonds set in
   Fabergé
eggshell by the master. I cannot put a name to the smiling
   face I see,
but she existed, who is now the faint dream of a
   denouement.

    Shalom alekhem   *Shalom alekhem*

So now I sail all night to find them and their symbols, to
connect with them whatever seems appropriate, their rings,
their eyes, their ways: but not alone to find the persons
but to find the meanings of the persons to myself, the
   electric
mind, before the king should claim them from my life.

HOPE AND THE BIPOLAR POET

O make me at last an Immortal born for this life,
so hard when the wind like a horse that has eaten of loco
    weed
kicks in the shining green meadow of death that is the bright
    day
beyond which the galaxies turn in dark matter like great
    carousels
with mad imagery rising and falling along their white ways,
all celestial combustion and anger as if there were truth in
    the gods
and I had come from their birth to mine that happened in
    heat
in the bowels of the ship of the universe powered by
    diamonds,
dead glitters of light burnt in the sky. O Heraclitean Fire,
forgive one who has not known the one pinch of peace
held in the index and thumb of the chef who concocted this
    stew,
brew that biology seeks in its crystals that fall like the fall of
    each phylum
down the great day of time, no matter all time be an infinite
    cloud,
O Fire have mercy and snuff out the wick of your running
    black wax
and spare me the waste of beginnings, evolutions, and ends.

Stop, for the fire at the center of self is the fire at all
    distances,
emanation and flow like the oceans of life serve likewise the
    Heraclitean Fire
though the walking world is of mercury sulphur and salt, sex
    sun and sand,
yet the fire heats the shards till they melt, reshaping them-

selves in their clay and
thereby a new entity is formed bearing the heart's evergreen
   name of Hope.

ALLEGORICAL FOUNTAIN

Upon the Rock of Insolence
stands the Accuser,
a child. He is looking at the Accused,
pointing a finger,
shouting in a voice of watery music
that he himself
will never grow up.

The accused
has round eyes of love
for the Accuser.
He would walk back down
the leaden years
to be at his side
upon the Rock of Insolence.

GIN RUMMIES

To find a friend one must close one eye.
To keep him—two.
    —Norman Douglas

for Rodney Formon

Friday nights, a fry-cook,
arms scarred by sizzling fat,
Rodney bangs on my door.
We like to drink together,
shoot the breeze, and laugh.
Drunk enough, we sing!
It's karaoke with CDs scattered
on the table, improvisational
shandygaffs and combinations
you can't enjoy with your relations.

It's good to have a drinking buddy.
I've used up two already—
one who fell down a flight of stairs
and one, who was much older,
who died of his warrior life.
But now I've got Rodney,
who is very different from the others.

The other two were quite and somewhat
intellectual, and where the one
could talk history or science, art,
music, or just about any subject
in just about any language and come back,
being polyglot, and polymath,
even polymorphic, after hooch,

the other was a man of action,
a war hero with many medals
tucked away in drawers locked
by indifference, but still would tell of
weapons, arms and the man, and such
with fervor—my Heraclitus—
and also with disgust, with
fatalism, believing nothing
changes in man's fighting nature,
disposed to think the worst;
but enthusiastic over chess,
which he played in earnest
as if he were at war again.

But Rodney is another sort:
He knows I write but will not read
a word I write, nor much else either,
but likes the Internet so much
he slides crabwise in thought,
toward what depth of cyberspace
I often cannot fathom until *zing*
I see it for myself, or am I drunk?

I see with Rodney that the other two,
complimented first my young and then
my middle-aged delusions
of a deeper self-knowledge
than available to most. Yes, Rodney
shows me to myself, or shows me
to my youthful ghosts, as ego-fed,
but did and does this unintentionally,
whose wonderful indifference makes me shrink
like a cock in the cold, and chug my drink.

THE THIN DISEASE

> *Note: In Africa, AIDS is often*
> *referred to as the thin disease.*

Nearly seven feet tall, a skeleton
made of giant bird bones,
a bird-cage rib-cage,
his heart a little pulsing
robin, Kwame from Ghana
on the old Gold Coast
was my best friend.

Kwame had to reach down
to tap me on my red head. "Dutch,
we're going to cadge some drinks.
You do the talking.
Tell them I'm King Quazi
of oilrich offshore Quaziland,
and I can't speak English.
Tell them my kingdom is ten miles long
and a quarter mile wide, including beaches."

Kwame had purple-grey skin
and was so thin he looked like the shadow of a pole,
but his head was large and noble,
with cheekbones carved in slate,
and royally crested with a pompadour
befitting the son of a son of a king
from the ancient West African Empire,
though he was always church-mouse poor.

We worked on the New York docks,
off-loading ships, on-loading trucks.

He wasn't very strong. He drank a lot
and bled from the rectum when he worked.
They had to cut the grapes away.
Like a daddy longlegs and a flat red beetle,
we wobbled to a bar near St. Vincent's,
a knot of stitches still in his new tight ass.
He could ignore the pain for the booze.

He put his arm over my shoulder.
"Dutch, I'm going to die.
I've got the thin disease.
I'll never go back to Ghana."
"Sure you will. You'll go back."
There were good times yet.
But he died. He died.
He died. The white bed
was empty but for a wave-crested,
welted head, and limp hoses,
some of which were black
and leaked their fluids.
Ghana was far away, a dream,
but I was there, near, here,
his friend, holding his hand,
our funny different fingers
entwined, though pulling apart.

SPRING AND THE BLACK HOLES

When green things grow, in glowing spring,
I attend to nature for a time, dreaming
that there is meaning, something, beyond
what I can tell, not merely the Heaven and Hell
of whirling galaxies, not Byron's dreamless sleep,
or merely to be part of the dust that swirls,
and someday to be sucked in, as by
a celestial vacuum cleaner, a black hole,
into a what? another universe, still dust?
A what? The soul must be my vademecum
or life and spring become intolerable.

But I am trapped, caught in the trap of life,
the spring of death. Yet it's not death
which is the worst pain of my soul:
it's *rerum natura*, it's the black holes,
it's the not knowing, not being allowed,
which *is* allowed even in bright spring,
even in prime spring when green things grow.

And suppose there is no dreamless sleep? Suppose
we wake somehow to feel again
and what we feel is endless pain,
pain of time and space being born,
birthpang of stars, the spaceless yet infinite
pain of the black holes, where time, perhaps,
runs backward, or, worse, does not run at all,
but leaves your shadow magnified stiff,
frozen forever, upon its lip,
while every molecule, still
sentient, is smoked and rayed apart,
while still, while still, though somewhere else,
green things grow, in glowing spring.

THE ORBITING X

Hallelujah! saw X twenty-two thousand five-hundred
miles off blue Earth, heavenly luminous body, nebulous,
long-tailed, fiery Cross, cross Heaven like a comet,
airless incandescent meteor-Messiah, whirling Aether,
leagues-arcing rainbow-halo of lights, rolling, rolled
into one long-suffering, fragmented Star, returning &
returning. The ecumenical others, crew of *All Faiths*,

bound out for the dead red planet, Mars, doubters, saw
the Unidentifiable Flying Object, too, but cautioned:
a star-cluster, an optical illusion, looking really
more like a scimitar, caduceus, fylfot, The Wisdom Tree,
a whirling glowing Saucer! Hallelujah! he cried at
the infinite night. The links of stars, like bars,
crossed everywhere. . . and beyond them, galactic webs,

far glittering spiders climbing space. In this vastness,
this immensity of lights, his soul seemed unmeterable,
or an impertinence imprisoned in endlessness. The others
kept bitten-tongued silence in face of this—this what?
Vision? Hallucination? Madness? What should they
bear witness to? It was too late to abort Mission Mars,
too late to turn back. The dead red planet loomed ahead.

MICE ON A MUDBALL

I The Futurist

And then we must replace you, Death, for you must go
with the combustion engine down the tube of time
and all will laugh at you as they do now at blimps
and bleeding, flapping wooden wings for flight and
   leeches
on the back for purifying blood, for in the future, Death,
hiatus will replace you, the storage called cryonics,
the deep freeze, or some such method to define
and discipline ourselves, to give a shape to time
and render meaningful our lives as you do now,
O wisdom-wasting Death, when life is lived poetically,
in many stanzas, each building on the last, developing
its theme, so that an open-sequence poem of life
is lived and not a golden drop of honey-wisdom wasted
that cost us generation after generation,
O Future, in long darkness climbing into you.

II The Mall on the Moon

At the Meat Market in the Mall on the Moon, there are no cuts of dead animals, only meat, muscles and organs, developed from cells in a dish. Rumps, shanks, and livers that have never had a body. Vegetarians are in a state of consternation. Should such meat be condemned? But no animal died in its production. The meat is developed without nervous connection, so there has never been pain. There has never been life, in a sense, for none of this meat has had a head (sorry, brains are not manufactured). Should something be done? It is alive, in a sense, but its life must be a profound dimness, an almost nothingness. The Modern Meat Packers Association insists on a nothingness. Skin, and fur, of course, are developed (grown) in the same manner. There are no animals, merely yards of skin and fur, fur of all kinds: mink, ermine, seal, sable. But you do not buy them at the Meat Market in the Mall on the Moon, you buy them at the Fur Coat Fair in the Mall on the Moon, where you can also purchase birdless feathers, and alligator shoes from alligator skin grown without legs or heads on huge trays in factories in Orlando and Miami. Horns and tusks of all kinds can be bought, whole or powdered, at the Horn and Tusk Shop in the Mall on the Moon, and not one horn or tusk, whole or powdered, has had a concomitant animal: no elephant has been poached, no deer has been slaughtered for its antlers, no moose has been shot, no wild boar has been knifed, arrowed, or clubbed. But they are all represented at the Horn and Tusk Shop in the Mall on the Moon.

BECAUSE

in the port-cities they have found everything out and
Aristotle-like have put everything into categories
and the unicorn is an ungulate because they say so
because the fine-print of the unreligious sun says we circle it
it is not for us but we for it because the moon hit us
and bounced off instead of was born of our first spin
because the ninth planet is an invading comet caught
and because there is no now and there never has been

because we look upon ourselves in savannas past
knuckling to water because we see the white lemming's hole
in the snow smashed down by hooves and hear its pitiful
chirp of counter-aggression because the avalanche
indifferently buries the contested world of the snow
valley because stars die because we believe in facts
and because the deluge led to the ark because because
and because we bury our dead and dig up their bones

because the unsoundness of our judgments lead to sound
judgment and because facts are facts and we must reckon
and because the sea is cruel and because time flies
because the wind blows down our houses and because
we remember the snow hare and the hawk because
because the dove is taken in air by the eagle
and because space is either empty or full of dark matter
because galaxies hold for a long time their pinwheel-shapes

because time and space are curved and we can blow our-
    selves up
and because we blow ourselves up constantly and because
it makes us wonder because doesn't it mean something
because we are riding a mud-ball through space because
we were born here and because we have categories and

because we dig up our bones and dogs dig our bones up
and because we are not even safe in pyramids because
we dig ourselves up and look upon our own bones

THOSE WHO DIE IN THEIR SLEEP

When the mind is wakeful
and the eyes are shut,
ears buried in their pillows
hear the song and
then it fades behind them
as on a distant shore,
and some drown then
and can never hear again
the song of the dreaming mind
singing its own mystery,
but now the song of the non-
life of the non-mind, of
the stars wheeling to Nowhere,
of time ending, snuffing out
the stars, one by one, the song
of all that has never known
of its own existence.

THROUGH THE LOUPE

Great quiet things reside in viewpoint, if we think oddly enough. The leaf of grass, of course, when a child—how it looks to the ant like a frond. Life lied by size, pen lied by ink, later, everything lied, alas, and we grew up and filed it all away in Can't, or Won't, or in Beside-the-Point. We had a drink, and scratched our head, or ass, whichever itch went wild, because we were the parent now, and saw our children deride our uncertain augenblick with their sweet sass. Oh, we were foiled! But we toiled on. Our errands made us errant. We had failed, groom and bride, to remember the link between the parts and the mass, the link that was being spoiled—the lost current that powers the ride we take to the brink of life. Things pass, they pass quickly, as on oiled marble, in a torrent of time, while we in the loge pride ourselves, missing, like women in mink in the looking-glass, missing the opera, coiled, apparent, in the pearl.

HEART FAILURE

I have made my moon landing at night
by way of the emergency ward,
on the strong black arm of a nurse.
My wife is the other woman,
and between the two women I enter,
seeing, reflected in glass, my red car
half up on a curb, and mal-angled,
the glare of the high beams showing
my terrified wife's confusion.

There is no air in that car,
there is no air in the night,
but there is air in the hose that the nurse
claps to my turning-blue face,
and strength in her arms that are used to
the harsh struggles that have plagued her existence,
strength that I finally can share in.

I lie in a gown in a room,
and the silent killer says nothing.
He signalled, I guess, with red flags.
I paid no attention. I'd developed
an elephant's hide, an armor for the arrows
of insult that poor boys endure.
From childhood, when I was raw,
and my nerves could actually bleed,
I worked on this suit of armor,
oiled it and flexed it and shined it,
but now it belonged to them,
the doctors who probed me with wonder.
"Didn't you notice a thing?
You sound like a sidewinder, rattling."

"I thought I'd caught cold in the chest."
But I had no desire to know
because I had no desire to stop.
I could see that they thought, "What a fool!"
All but the black nurse, who knew
how the poor slid the slippery slope
that poverty, stress, and high blood pressure
grade for the struggling-upward.
She pulled at my ear, and said, "Tough guy!
He don't take no crap from his heart."
She knew how the pressure builds up,
as you climb in the ignorant ghetto,
until you would break, or be broken.

"How you doing, baby doll? Better?"
"Yes, but now I'm embarrassed."
—embarrassed at being so weak,
ashamed of my heart that can fail,
ashamed to have such a heart—
no lionheart, no Coreleone, I.
But they tell me it's stress that's at fault:
the heart is okay, the tests show.
The angel nurse flattens my hair,
pulls at my ear, and says, "Go!—"

THE URN

Containing the Night Thoughts of a Sexagenarian

It is this heavenly tale, that the child in one could wish for,
that keeps me awake tonight, on the eve of my sixtieth year,
fearing death and wishing for grace, not knowing what
either is, or even if either is, though the unbreathing
stillness of bodies has me fairly convinced of the
former, and of the latter I have seen so little as to
doubt what I have seen as aberrant, some twist in the
air and light that, so full of desire for the magic of
exemption, I have deluded myself, half knowing
I lied, half believing my own white lie. But by
sixty I've come to believe that the only grace
is the goodness of the rational mind, and the
only evil the old instinctive animal brain, the
knob of the cerebellum, seeking its own satis-
factions of food and sex and selfhood, the
ultimate isolate one, that yet does not
understand that we are together in this
flowing, amazing hologram, with
or without a creator that may or
may not care; that, come alive, we
have every right to judge the nature
of existence, for, however arrived
at, our brains are analytic, not made
to hunker down in obeisance to
riddling gods, nor to any phantom
that hides in a cloud of unknowing.
For we have one another and have
courage and the hope of courage
and the practice of courage,
to help us, and, when the
wind is calm, and

the waters lean down
for the moon, we have
lonely senses to share till
at last our time has run out. Now,
as I think in the night, somewhat afraid
of the day that will see me another year older and
that much closer to death, I mark the speed of time
that has seen me, a moment ago, a child walking home from
school, or a man going off to harm's way, or this or that or
the other, and think of these things that we have, of others
and courage and love, of human intelligence used as it plainly
was meant to be used, and I think that I'll sleep and awaken
less anxious than I was considering a heavenly tale, for in the
realist reality, the closest thing to the truth, there is finally a
peace of mind that is a grace in a sweet surrender. It is the
heavenly tale that the child in one should wish for. *It* will
allow me to sleep in the night of my sixtieth year.

PROVENANCE OF AN OLD POET

for Stanley Kunitz

Today he strolled the park,
seeing babies and their bright
new mothers, and he thought
of death, but not depressingly,
just as a fact of life, because
birth makes the old mark
how time is running out.

Then, too, he thought of provenance—
proof of birth, the papers
going with an antique,
or work of art—which was the word
which prompted him to start
a park-bench verse to relatives,
friends, and to the world in general
—distant friends, he guessed
you could call them, just to say
how far back his parchments go
—to Europe, Asia, Africa, even
to the great Oneland, Gaea,
and perhaps beyond—it could be
that they started at God's waving hand,
and came down from Bango.

All this youthful joy
has made him think of how,
when he was young,
he loved to go dancing
to the Big Bands.

He could dance the legs off ladies
who were willing to swing
until the stars came out
and the dawn star shown once more.
These young mothers were like them.

Well, as the great globe goes,
tonight will bring him
the Starlight Ballroom back,
with enough documents,
validations,
certificates,
provenance,
viz., tickets,
to allow him to dance
between the starry poles
in a not unfriendly universe.

TOWARD THE END

One long winter at Revere Beach in Massachusetts,
with snow banked up two feet or more at the door,
I read Karl Marx's romantic tales from Dickens.
I discovered that the essence of that big tome
was somewhere in the first fifty pages,
where Marx gives out with his theory of value,
i.e., that the labor that is put into something
invests it with value. A flattering fallacy.
I had worked as a laborer much of my young life
and knew that if two hundred men moved a pile of shit
weighing two hundred tons two feet from its original
location—it was still a pile of shit.
Shovelling shit was something I knew about,
something you don't learn much about in the
reading room of the British Museum,
so Marx was a big disappointment to me.
And was it true that if God did not exist
everything was permissible, as in *The Brothers
Karamazov*? I went through the *Great Books
of the Western World*, the *Cambridge Ancient Histories*,
etc., etc., and in the end came to the conclusion
that all learning is meant to teach only one thing:
how little one knows. Now, in the face of the Great Dark,
I know that I know nothing—well, little of importance,
a few apparent facts, a wet paper bag full of information,
so, toward the end, now, though still seeking to understand,
I only read poetry or look up at the mysterious stars.

CURTAL SONNET

Goodbye, myself, whom I have loved so well,
   when you are not around me, I'm alone,
  but then there's not a me to be around,
alas, not even one for heaven or hell,
   unless you count a carcass, broken bone
  under a sunken lid under a mound,
or ashes in a box, or in a breeze,
   instead of slow decay beneath the ground.
    Goodbye, myself, without you I shan't groan
but be my bravest, like those lonely trees
  that fall without a sound.

NOTES ON EARLIER WORKS

FOREWORD

A first book by a forceful new poet, THE POOR BOY, by E.M. Schorb furnishes memorable images of life in the streets and boroughs of the city. With a keen eye for the realistic detail, by turns ironic, lyrical, at times grotesque and macabre, Schorb presents his candid testimony in a terse and modern idiom, in language that is original, personal and, occasionally, experimental. An artist still growing and developing, he has the power to share with us his pity, rage, compassion and moral indignation.

Among his most effective poems in this collection are *Obituary*, on his father's death by fire; *Night Life; The Kite; Dirge for the Dead Students* at Kent State University, which has been set to music and is as compelling a manifesto as Zola's *J'Accuse!* The title poem, *The Poor Boy*, was awarded second prize in the international John Keats Poetry Competition of 1973; chosen from among some 1500 entries from 30 countries, it offers the following statement:

> *I know, for I have foraged in the lots*
> *of blackened cities looking for a prize*
> *of red discarded unbroken flowerpots*
> *to place my plants, to brighten eyes.*
> *I've shined a thousand shoes along the streets*
> *of coughing cities all across this land.*
> *A child, I'd enter taverns and retreats*
> *the like of which to others would be banned.*
> *Oh, I know poverty, unhappiness;*
> *such things I know, I have no need to guess.*
>
> *And yet a sturdy strength comes out of it,*
> *that's undeniable; but at what cost!*
> *The strength of street-bred children is their wit*
> *and nerve; nobility is lost*

> *in the hungry race of mongrels for a bone,*
> *and Honor hangs his head before the scene.*
> *The heart of the street urchin is a stone*
> *ground more with each engagement, until mean.*
> *We learn to fight and hate, but not to love,*
> *no matter who says so. We learn to shove.*

As may be surmised, Schorb writes from a wide range of experience in the workaday world, having been a shoeshine boy, a stevedore, a waiter, a U.S. Marine. "I can't remember all the jobs I've had," he remarks. Yet he also observes: "You can never use autobiography in literature until time has deepened the experience so that it suggests something greater than itself."

In choosing the poems for the present volume, he sought to give the selection a sense of unity, but found this a challenging task. "My method is changing," he states in an informal letter. "I have tried to retain poems that had likeness, not a mere seeming likeness, but the deep true likeness that results from intention and method . . ." Schorb does not hold with critics who claim that a poet used this style or that style or that his style has changed. "The sensibility, which is the style, remains the same," according to Schorb. "The style is what does the using: the method is what is altered." His favorite artist is Picasso, because Picasso never forgot that art at its best is a process of working toward something unknown. "He didn't repeat himself. He didn't imitate even his own best work, though occasionally he did imitate the best work of others. . ."

Commenting on the marginal position of the poet in the modern world, Schorb observes: "It's sad to think that an *athlete*, whose comparable talent may not be superior to that of a *poet*, is paid in thousands and hundreds of thousands of dollars, while all over the world a poet is paid, if not in derision, then most certainly in small change . . . . The law of supply and demand, no doubt. The greater the quality the less the demand, it seems, for great quality implies an investment of the self, an employment of the mind at its energetic best, to be appreciated. Not many are capable of such an investment, fewer are willing to make it; hence, poetry generally goes begging. If the world were set right, poets would earn more than presidents. Their minds give the ultimate life to language, and language, as used by great poets, gives the ultimate life to the mind, thence to the heart, a metaphor for all secrets . . . ."

Thus Schorb suggests his own poetic credo.

If the modern poet is no longer a legislator to the world, neither acknowledged nor unacknowledged, merely ignored, he may still perform a vital service to the more thoughtful remnant of humanity as a candid witness to scenes in the universal arena. Schorb has observed the streets of Manhattan, as Juvenal studied the tenements of Rome, as Hogarth drew the alleys of London. He has searched for clues to the mystery of man's inhumanity to man; he has weighed what he found in the scales of good and evil; and he presents us with his findings in his true witness book.

—Cornel Lengyel, Editor/Publisher
Dragon's Teeth Press

FOREWORD

What strikes me most about the poems in *Words in Passing*, E.M. Schorb's largest collection to date, containing work from four decades, is their subtle musicality and intellectual range. They demonstrate that Mr Schorb is a poet of great skill and keen wit, a rare formalist whose iambs do not thump and whose ear is attuned to a most intriguing symphony. They hearken back to the great poems of the first half of the twentieth century, to the masterpieces of Robert Frost, John Crowe Ransom, Wallace Stevens, W.H. Auden and William Dickey. They bespeak the presence of a major American poet, one whose mastery of forms is unparalleled and whose voice is resonant, passionate and true long after his book is returned to the shelf.

—Leo Yankevich, Editor/Publisher
The New Formalist Press.

Thoughts of Houdini free a poem aimed at the heart of Death

All E.M. Schorb knew was that the poem was going to be about Houdini. He'd been watching a TV program about the magician and about how Houdini was going to try to come back each year on the anniversary of his death.

Schorb wondered: So where was Houdini when he wasn't around? In a tunnel?

The question interested him enough that he wrote it down. For Schorb, writing it down means going into his study, which holds three computers. One computer is for business—Schorb is a real estate broker. One computer is broken. And the old computer, the 10-year-old computer, the one that's been on continuously for all those years, is his poetry computer.

In the poetry computer he typed: "Where was he? Was it a tunnel?"

Then, Schorb went about his business, the business of being Schorb the broker, the poet, the husband, the father.

That same evening, Schorb returned to the computer, and he added more lines: "Where was he? Was it a tunnel? / But he had come to a wall, / a slimy, wormy wall."

As he write, the story began to present itself to him, Schorb says.

The poem, "Houdini and the Dying Swan," appeared first in The Sewanee Review and appears now in Schorb's third and latest collection, *Murderer's Day,* winner of the 1998 Verna Emery Poetry Prize, sponsored by Purdue University Press.

To think about Houdini surviving death is, in essence, to consider one's own mortality. For, as Schorb says, if anybody could come back, if anybody could do it, it would be the great magician.

So the fact that Houdini hasn't come back must mean he's been distracted by something en route. What could that be? Schorb wondered.

Enter into Schorb's imagination the image of a woman in a tub, contemplating suicide.

"Naked, she lay back in the tub, / white as a white swan, long-necked / as a swan, thin as a silken thread, / her gloriously thick dark hair / piled loosely up, collapsing / onto her wide, sloping shoulders, / dark. water-dipped ringlets forming, / her swan's-down skin pinking, / steam misting her swan song, / her suicide with water and razor."

Part II of the poem depicts another scene: the "glittering company" awaiting Houdini's return. They are "rich," "celebrated." Houdini hears them say: "Houdini, do not disappoint us, / for we must believe that Death / cannot take us, utterly."

And there, of course, is the heartbeat of the poem, the universal question: *Does* death take us utterly?

In Part III, Schorb returns to the woman in the marble tub. She is dying, the water streaked now "in ribbons of red."

But a noise jolts her, a noise "like / breaking plaster, like tumbling bricks, / like an earthquake."

It is, of course, Houdini, breaking through to her through the tunnel, and he "lifted her from / the marble tub and taped her wrists."

"He put her in her bed and tugged / the bell pull. She was too beautiful to die. / a great grandfather clock obliterated / the last of midnight. A doorknob turned, / and he went back the way that he had come. / *Houdini darkened into death.*"

At last, Schorb had answered his own question. Indeed death does *not* take us utterly.

I choose this poem out of a collection full of excellent poems—poet Heather McHugh in a blurb calls this a "feisty book, a confident book, and in its own way, a furiously festive one"—because it helps to illustrate the elusive process of making poetry, how meaning can quicken from the stray and specific to the deep and universal.

It is not easy for a poet to reconstruct this process because during the writing, Schorb, like many writers, experiences an "out-of-world" feeling, "a little removed," he says, "trance-like, hypnotized."

Schorb says he thinks it's important for a poet to be unique, identifiable. And if he or she is not, he says you suspect them of not having achieved their vision.

What does achieving vision mean?

"I believe when a poet makes full contact with whatever that is in the subconscious—that ultimate nerve center—then they cannot speak with another's voice.

"When the poet reaches that center of the psyche, then, as Polonius says, 'You cannot be false to any man.' The words come only as you can say them."

What are the best circumstances for the poet to make that full contact with the psyche?

"It's a rather passive state of mind," says Schorb. "It's somehow connected to the idea of negative capability. You have to allow yourself to be free and the connection begins to happen. You can't sit down and bang on the typewriter and make a poem come out of what you've banged away. You have to finesse it."

Schorb has finessed his own way into the deep, and the poems in *Murderer's Day* will challenge both your mind and your soul. They will also make you laugh with joy at the mind's swift and graceful flight into wit and fancy.

—Dannye Romine Powell, Editor,
Book Page, *The Charlotte Observer*

Poet in the Shadows

Judged solely on the basis of honors received, and prizes won, the poetry of E.M. Schorb would hold a high place in the estimation of his contemporaries. This poet's work, published in over sixteen volumes of verse and prose, has taken awards in many categories and from a wide range of competitions. We began publishing his poems in our second issue, but Schorb's material has appeared in more than seventy journals worldwide over the last four decades.

Nevertheless, Schorb remains fairly unknown, largely because his work is not a part of what I call Mainstream Mediocrity—that is, the great flood of child-friendly pabulum and amorphous emoting that constitute "poetry" today. His work is sharp, clear, well-structured, and solidly in the formalist camp. There is still a patent and active prejudice against the formalist revival and its practitioners—one which works to keep many good poets in the shadows despite their achievement.

This is why it is gratifying to have a major selection of Schorb's work in this fine printing from The New Formalist Press. Nearly two hundred pages of excellent material are gathered here from numerous hard-copy and on-line venues. The poems are divided into several thematic groups ("Souls," "Love," "Trouble," and others), but these are just convenient and non-rigid gatherings. There are surprises and delights in each section.

I love the kaleidoscopic range of reference that Schorb demonstrates in these many poems. He can move easily from an appreciation of the French photographer Eugène Atget to his own brief encounter with Marilyn Monroe; and from a whimsical speculation on the drinking habits of the scholarly translator John Ciardi to a dreamy evocation of Vanna White on *Wheel of Fortune*. He comments on the zoological observations of Jane Goodall, the songs of Edith Piaf, and an imaginary interaction between Rodin and Balzac. And there are literary allusions galore: Heraclitus, Skelton, Kipling, Swinburne, Housman, Yeats, Wallace Stevens, William Empson, William Carlos Williams, Frost, Berryman… here is a poet who has not just read widely, but woven his readings into the fabric of his own art.

In addition, Schorb can use history and mythology in an arresting and novel manner. His poem "Paris Recidivist," written in the voice of the Prince of Troy, is an up-to-date and cynical macroeconomic account of the causes of the Trojan War, ending with a cavalier dismissal of Helen as a silly, deluded woman who mattered not a whit in the struggle. "Letters Home" is an epistolary recounting of the death of an R.A.F. pilot in 1943. The dialectical "Blarney Stoned" is addressed to Dionysos, Greek god of drunkenness, by an inebriated Irishman tottering between alcoholism and vowed sobriety. The sonnet "Caesar and Cleopatra" is a very succinct report on how a bemused Caesar was seduced into an affair that led to the destruction of the Roman Republic.

There's much more than this: poems of joy and pain, of terror and anger, of political protest, of satiric commentary, of family re- membrance. Schorb is also at home with antique poetic templates like the pastoral eclogue, the elegy, and Skeltonic verse. But rather than sing his praises abstractly, I prefer to give some quoted verses to demonstrate the man's skill. Here are the five lines ending "Elegy," written for a late friend:

> Merely the blanket statement, tragic gesture,
> As when some friendly hand is flung aloft
> Above the crowd, remains to keep; a vesper
> Of evening memory; a prayer I coughed
> To save your life that wasn't saved by me.

Notice the way the governing verb in this five-line section (*remains*) is postponed to the third line, and even there it is placed exactly in the middle, followed by an extended apposition to the sentence's subject. Then there is the unusual singular form *vesper*, which brilliantly pulls the reader's mind towards the suggestion of evening and twilight while also, by felicitous homeophony, hinting at the word "whisper." This is language as used by a wordsmith of top-notch ability.

I also like Schorb's straightforward description, in more-than-vivid English, of teenage lovers petting in the bushes. These lines are from "Hot Teen Hogs," which appeared in TRINACRIA # 6:

> They rub the blue out of their bluejeaned crotches.
> They rip the teeth out of their red-hot zippers.
> They fan the flames, and then curl up like kippers.
> At last they check their charioteering watches.
>
> They tell each other where to meet next week.
> They shake their leather jackets free of gunk,
> and she with red nails combs her ducktailed hunk,
> as he wipes damp mascara from her cheek.

The metaphor of "charioteering watches" is striking, the way every new trope should be. Have you ever thought of speeding chariots when you glanced at your watch and noticed how late it was? Now you will. Sure, there's a reference to

Marvell there, but the personified Time is replaced by a more mundane wristwatch. The imagery of leather jackets and red nails and "ducktailed hunk"? If you were alive in the 1950s you'll know exactly what Schorb is talking about.

There's an amazing poem, "The Big Crunch," composed as if a human life were running backwards like a reversed film strip, and clearly designed to be a sardonic comment on the "Big Bang" theory of cosmology. And Schorb is not afraid to make thundering judgments on the evil and stupidity of the human race, when he speaks of us in the poem "As Good As It Gets":

> we, who are madder than the maddest hatter,
> our every word a snippet of mad song;
> who've served the heads of people on a platter,
> or blood in a tureen for Sunday soup!

But even this indictment of our race is qualified by his asking, in the same poem, if in fact our cruelty and savagery are perhaps necessary requirements for the preservation of our lives and identity:

> Karl Barth said we were no damned good. Yes, he
> shared Jeffers' view of humankind. Karl Barth
> was probably correct, if we agree
> to measure by his standard. But what hearth
> was ever won or kept by kindness?

This is the sort of brutally honest question that a sentiment-soaked and Pollyannaish western world had better start asking itself, instead of wallowing in suicidal altruism towards our enemies.

Schorb can write concisely, or extensively. There are many short pieces in this collection, but also ambitious long ones, such as the moving "Obituary" on the life and death of his father. He gives us part of an unfinished musical drama, "Candy Butcher," and the strange "White Stallion," an amazing tale told by a blind Irish seer about a magical horse and the futile attempts to capture it. In every instance these poems are unpredictable and intriguing. Schorb never falls into the hackneyed or the formulaic traps that are the occupational hazard of the formalist poet. He can pen a firm and metrically precise line, but when his subject matter requires it he will release his line from any imposed demands, and write as the flow of inspiration dictates.

Schorb has an excellent touch with simile, as when he ends a poem by saying:

> …till we waken, straight and narrow,
> freshened, like a new-fletched arrow.

When he speaks of "gold-nugget bees," he has created a likeness that you will never forget. And nevertheless he can also dazzle with descriptions that have neither simile nor metaphor, as in the octet of his sonnet "The Fashion Show":

> The slim young women float their subtle curves
> before a fashion-conscious audience.
> Diaphanous enough to tickle nerves,
> their gowns lift off them in a breezy dance
> as left leg forward forces right hip out,
> and small breasts, bra-less, bounce beneath a gauze
> of punctuated pink. Their red lips pout.
> Their veteran eyes, dark shadowed, seek applause.

It's a pleasure to read a poet whose vocabulary goes beyond the fourth-grade basal reader. Schorb has no fear of difficult or strange words, which he uses with skill and confidence. He also has a playful streak that comes out in unusual coinages such as *leucomelanous* (which I assume from its Greek roots to mean "white-and-black") as a way to describe salt-and-pepper hair; and he uses *firnificated* (probably from the rare *firn*, or fallen snow) to speak of white birch trees in a winter storm. Can't you just hear the little dorks in the workshops screaming about "elitism" and "democratic accessibility"?

Schorb's relative lack of celebrity might have something to do with the demanding nature of some of his work (and I emphasize *some*, because much of Schorb is as lucid and straightforward as a clock chime). This is not only an injustice, but also an example of the ludicrous hypocrisy that dominates contemporary po-biz. Vapidly opaque free-verse garbage is printed everywhere and celebrated, and its partisans defend its impenetrability with various asinine theories. But when a poet like Schorb writes a piece that might require a second reading, or—Heaven forbid!—a trip to the dictionary, then all of a sudden we hear murmurs about how "difficult" a poet is, and how "unfair to his readers." In other words, you can write off-the-wall surrealist and experimental crap if you are published in *Poetry*, but you'll be chastised for elitism and ignored if you write discursively lucid poems that demand actual thought and attention.

I can't resist quoting one poem in its entirety, Schorb's Shakespearean sonnet "Notice to Moderns." It encapsulates practically the whole critique of confessional verse that new formalists have been making for the last thirty-odd years:

You solipsistic sissies, male and female,
poets about the Me, Myself, and I,
should send yourselves, and then collect, your email,
and not pretend such jots are poetry.

"Poets are actors, and their books are theatres,"
wrote Wallace Stevens. Roethke spoke in tongues.
How many voices spoke through William
   Shakespeare's?
Create verse worthy of great scoptic lungs!

There is a gathering on a green hill
Where scops will sing of everything they share.
In my imagination, with my will,
I try to see that time, and who was there.

Or in a book or on a stage I try
to tell of others, not Me, Myself, and I.

Notice the wonderful adjective *scoptic*, created from the Anglo-Saxon *scop*, or poet. Here Schorb calls our errant literary clerisy home, urging a return to genuine poetic praxis in place of the narcissistic whingeing that has become *de rigueur* in our Mainstream Mediocrity. In isolation, this poem would be no more than a shot in the dark. But embedded in a collection as powerful as this one, it carries great force, and is more than just a word in passing.

—Dr. Joseph S. Salemi, Adjunct Instructor in Liberal Studies
   New York University, Publisher/Editor, *Trinacria*

BY WAY OF INTRODUCTION

Fiat Lux! is what a light-verse collection should be: it entertains a variety of forms, it does not eschew silliness, but it also doesn't give in to chaos or predictable jokes. It's an erudite book even as there are poems about autodidacts, and—the best and most Seinfeldian part—it tells you things you feel you should have known but have never taken the time to think about—for example, that ghosts require training:

> "Yes, haunting is an art," my teacher said.
> "You mustn't be too obvious, too crude.
> They'll think it's all a trick, or caused
> by natural tremors, earthquakes and the like,
> and what you want above all other things
> is to be certain that they know it's you."

Schorb uses the familiar as both subject and model. "Late Night Rap of Soul and Body" is a modern answer to Yeats, who took himself far too seriously anyway, and "A Tumble for Skelton" gives poor old John a tunning of his own. "News of 45" (the age, not the president) evokes e e cummings in its punctuationless juxtaposition of images.

Most surprisingly, there are prose poems in here that are quite funny. "An Experiment in Governance," pushes absurdity to the point that it's completely believable in our present bizarre moment. "Last Exit to East Hampton" reads like a concentrated drop of Dorothy Parker's "Lady With a Lamp," with a dash of West Egg thrown in for flavor.

The diadem in this book can be found in a series of seven sonnets collectively titled "Symbols." Each poem addresses a

Christian symbol, from the cross to the lamb. While this may sound very serious, the application of a light-verse touch actually enhances the explanations. Among these poems, "The Fish" tests the capacity of the form and finds it roomy enough for two entirely separate stories. The octet gives the history of the symbol, tying it, eventually, to the Spanish Inquisition. The sestet compacts the story of St. Peter into six lines, finishing the etymological loftiness of the first stanza with the homeliness to which all Christian symbols should remain tethered. That this homeliness is wrapped in a pun is kind of perfect:

> St. Peter was a fisherman, they say,
> and one day caught a sole and then another
> and soon his bobbing boat was full of fish.
> All soles, he said, are one another's brother
> (most women were excluded in his day),
> And, rinsing it with wine, he cleaned his dish.

The rest of this book engages the literary, the bawdy, and the surreally urinary (trust me on that one). Beyond its obvious skill, the feeling that comes through most clearly is a respect for the versatility of light verse—the forms it can be found in and the subjects it will accommodate.

—Barbara Egel, Author and Scholar
Light Magazine

Straddling Two Worlds

by way of introduction

The schoolboy's definition of poetry, "Lines that don't come all the way out to the edge of the page," doesn't fit most prose poems, certainly not E. M. Schorb's. Attempts have been made to refine the definition, claiming that poetry, whether in short-falling lines or solid blocks, tends to abound in verbal music, imagery, metaphors and other figures of speech. A typical prose poem (or, as some call it, piece of "lyrical prose") has to look like prose with right-hand margins, while providing the satisfactions of poetry. It is a slippery kind of literature. As Peter Johnson, editor of the magazine *The Prose Poem* has put it, "Just as black humor straddles the fine line between comedy and tragedy, so the prose poem plants one foot in prose, the other in poetry, both heels resting precariously on banana peels."

Naturally, then, writers of prose poems have trouble staying upright. They will be tempted to put on poetic airs, lest readers doubt they are poets, throwing in wildly colorful images, exaggerating metaphors, making grandiose statements, coining new words where old words would have sufficed. Lately I noticed these tendencies in some less impressive prose poets while serving as a consultant to an anthology of prose poems, reading work being considered for it. Many a writer waxed cutesy, thinking that that was what poets do. Not one to call a spade a spade, he'd call it a potato-uprooter or an earth-displacer, or something.

Well, you won't find those assininities in the work of E.M. Schorb. It helps, of course, that he is a genuine poet, outstanding among the better ones. It may also help that he is a born storyteller, for many of his prose poems convey strong narratives, sometimes bizarre reversals of reality: a man whose new carpet turns overnight into a wetland full of snakes, a dog show in which dogs lead their masters and mistresses past the reviewing stand to be judged, a church made of rubber whose walls can bulge to accommodate its music, the day a gigantic head appears in the sky and starts devouring the sun. Such dreamlike recitals grab us from the start and refuse to let go.

Gathering together all of Schorb's work in this genre, *Dates and Dreams* comes at a timely moment in his career. He has voiced his intention to move on to other things, but of course there's no telling what his Muse will goose him with in times to come. Anyhow, this book now gives us the opportunity to look back on his rich accomplishment in prose poetry. I don't know of a living poet working in prose poetry who has accomplished more.

Schorb is aware that he labors at the present end of a long tradition. Literary historians usually trace the beginnings of this form back to the French Symbolists, notably Baudelaire and Rimbaud. In naming an earlier collection *Manhattan Spleen*, Schorb pays homage to Baudelaire, whose prose poems in *Paris Spleen* performed a comparable urban tour. Leading bards of other countries have carried on the tradition: Pablo Neruda, Rilke, Octavio Paz, and countless Americans.

To be sure, we can find passages we can call prose poetry in many classic works of prose from Burton's *Anatomy of Melancholy* to *Moby Dick*. But if you want a bountiful supply at your fingertips, without having to ransack a library, here it is. Besides, you'll find in these pages a generous selection of Schorb's unique drawings—strange, witty, and memorable, like the prose poems from the same hand.

—X. J. Kennedy

INTRODUCTION

EMANATIONS FROM THE PENUMBRA. Schorb is a prize winning poet having gained recognition and awards several times over so it was with some trepidation I approached this work with the intention of presenting it at our "Poetry Life & Times" site. It opens with a quote: "Penumbra: The Gray area where logic and principle falter"– it is in fact a corpus of poems, two hundred pages of them, written by a writer/poet,– by that I mean, a person who writes extensively and writes poetry as well. Schorb has an excellent, polished and sophisticated technique in whatever manner he approaches a poetic theme and in *Penumbra* these are many and varied emanations. He is of course a writer/artist who hails from the USA and he covers widely from its socio historico background, everything from workers rights, the broken war hero to the persecution of blacks by whites.

Part 6. titled the same as the name of the collection, starts -/ *Poets of my generation are turning up dead. A serial killer is injecting them with cancer heart disease and stroke* / and ends / *My generation think that this is a serial crime, but have no choice but to pull the ropes and toll the bell* / – but as much as there is pessimism and cynicism, there are as many shades of mood together with a host of erudite literary reference ranging from Empson, Scott Fitzgerald, Ezra Pound to Aristotle and Donne to name but a few. The fact that during the time I received and was reading this work, I also happened to be reading the classic "Paterson" by William Carlos Williams, I couldn't help but find similarities and the recognition how a modern poet like Schorb has emerged out of the influences of such a great work in contemporary North American Literature. Carlos Williams set a trend for commentary on the mundane and current affairs in the city, whilst expanding into pure lyricalism, and this is what happens in Schorb's work, at least as I experienced it. In particular, I found a quote in "Paterson," which Carlos Williams had seized upon, which I thought was entirely applicable to Schorb's work in *Emanations*. I quote it here, {recognizing the harmony which subsists between crabbed verses and the distorted subjects with which they dealt – the vices and perversions of humanity, as well as their agreement with the snarling spirit of the satirist. Deformed verse was suited to deformed morality} – *Studies of the Greek Poets*, John Addington Symonds Vol: 1. I could go on, the pathos of love, nihilism, spirituality are all covered by the poet and often brought out via descriptions of small scenic events like theater clips crafted into a free and flowing verse where the poet is speaking as often as not through another's voice or persona——though sometimes we find self depreciation as in "The Last Word" at the end of Part 4. / *Edwin Makepeace Thackery Schorb / Wrote many words into his books /..../ Was quite mistaken in all he did /.../ What is the truth? Oh who knows? / Say this: He drank and had to go!* / Let's hope he's not gone forever and comes back. It's impossible really to select favorites from such a ranging work but I liked especially "The Isle of Langerhans". Written in vertical inter-facing columns, it makes the reader work hard at reading it and I think that's important in modern poetry, why should poetry be made easy for the reader to read, it's the struggle that counts. And here we present at PLT the particular poem Schorb has selected, "Because," originally published in *The Iowa Review*.

—Robin Ouzman Hislop, Editor
Poetry Life and Times

Life and Opinions of Doctor Bop the Burnt-Out Prof and Other Poems

"My old man was a Moishe Kapoyr if you ever saw one." Well, yes, as it happens, I did see one: *my* old man. How many readers will respond to those initial words of Schorb's book just as I do? I am willing to guess: most. Those who haven't felt as an insult to reason the crazy contradictions in the mind of their dad (or of their mom, as the case may be), belong to the few free from Œdipal conflict. That's why it is a powerful opening: willy-nilly, it draws you in. And what follows will not disappoint:

"Well, my old man respected
education, but, having very little, was jealous
of those who had it. He claimed fluency in five
languages, all of them Yiddish. 'Polymath,'
I said, and he said, 'I learned to count on the streets
of New York, making change from what I peddled.'"

Schorb has perfect pitch, and if the above is not proof enough, here's more:

"When I was taking my masters at Columbia,
my old man, the meshugge maven, said:
'What do you care for a super goy like Donne?
You said he was a pirate once. I bet
He would come and pull the pale and
Take the whole *shtetl* away with him.
And then you say, Dean of St. Paul's—
What would he care for the likes of us?"

That's all part of the first poem. In the second, "Grooves of Academe," we listen to the Burnt-Out Prof, who, having spent his youth contending with his old man's meshugas, is now, as Dr. Bop, overwhelmed by the crazier meshugas of the newer generations, which is the fate of us all. His curmondgeonness is served in bitter portions like this one:

> "1736: Patrick Henry was born. That was also the year
> that Fahrenheit died and Hogarth produced his 'Good
>   Samaritan.'
> None of these things seem to have had much 'impact,'
> (now there's a word that I would ban) and,
> while I wend my way through this historic traffic,
> toward an historic college that no longer
> recognizes history as a legitimate subject,
> I notice that the leaves are down and tumbling
> in the wind along the road to higher learning."

Why should not old men be mad? Or as my grandmother used to say, *meshuga af' toyt*, crazy to death? The downfall of historical consciousness has given way to these unanimous, unbearable pretentions to moral superiority. Remember? Trust me, trust no one over thirty.

Or the portions may be more on the sweet side, wet and shiny with ironic nostalgia, caressable like a backbone arching cat, as in "Spine and Spirit," which is dedicated to Vicki, Schorb's cat:

> ". . . The slinkiest person I ever saw
> I saw at Minsky's burlesque in Newark when I was
>   sixteen.
> I think Senator Long may have met her there,
>   backstage."

Blaze Starr appears to be the artistic name of the slinky burlesque dancer, who, in the memory of the old poet, is linked not only with Senator Long but, somehow, with Marie Curie, the physicist. This may be because the latter died of aplastic anemia, a disease of the bone marrow, hence, in particular, of the spine. Who knows. But here are the last few lines:

"i.e. Senator Long's backbone and Blaze Starr's slinky
spine: and imagine those two vertebrates going at it.
And what about Madame Curie's curious chemistry?
I must agree with Pascal. I must assert the primacy of
 spirit
and to hell with the backbone; but that would mean
that one must have some backbone in order to assert
the primacy of spirit, a backbreaking thought."

I'm not sure about the third line above: all of a sudden, *in mitten drinnen* (my grandparents speak again), without rhyme or reason, we are offered a bit of alliteration. But the rest is right and convincing.

Backbreaking though it is, the primacy of spirit, Schorb tries to give himself courage and spine in the "Ballad of the Burnt-Out Prof," almost as heart rending as that other *Ballade des pendus* by old Villon:

"Old Duracell, old Mazda-man
You've got to keep the light—
It's growing dim inside you
but that's no time to hide you—
there's just a chance you might
say something shedding light.
Old Candle-wick, old Burnt-Out Prof
(who calls himself the Bop)
old hairy ears and snout,

> *Tochis afn tish!*
> you gouty worn-out lout—
> oh, call yourself a name, old cuss—
> because you weren't the best,
> and yet you know it doesn't matter,
> no, not in the least."

I do not believe those last two lines above, yet I know they are true: it really doesn't matter. After my father's death at 56, we discovered a sheet of paper he had written not long before, titled, "*El fósforo habla*" (the match speaks). The match is lit, about to burn out—like Bop, Old Candle-wick, or like my dad—but while there's a tiny bit of flame in me (the match says) I can set the world on fire. From nihilism to terrorism, from zero to infinity.

You will enjoy this book. Like Heinrich Heine, Schorb is sad and full of fun.

—Ricardo L. Nirenberg
Editor, *OffCourse*

Schorb has been writing some of the best American poetry for decades.

—Jim Barnes

"The Journey," together with some fine ancillary poems, is a major work by one of our most challenging and surprising poets: a profound exploration of dream that seeks to fathom the nature of reality. Stunningly beautiful passages of verbal music seem to leap off the page. In his long career, E.M. Schorb has never given us anything more ambitious, more likely to last.

—X.J. Kennedy

Schorb goes after the very essence of poetry, the vivid image, the arresting phrase, the original fusing of words. Labels bother him not at all. "The White Stallion" is not a poem, ballad, or a narrative epic—it is Americana, a classic!

—Alex Jackinson

Absorbing, Engrossing. A passionate, triumphant, tragic look at the Twentieth Century, played out by the aging remainders of a family, driving to their inevitable end. "American Mobile" is the Great American Poem.

—Pat Mullan

A story-teller's gift for selecting and relating the points he wishes to make, combined with a dramatist's flair for moving the points into place, make many of Schorb's poems memorable, as in "Obituary."

—*ETC., A Journal of General Semantics*

To be a first-class poet requires a fluency of language, mastery of a vocabulary sufficient to express seminal, original thoughts set down with rhythm, with imagery, and with descriptive evocation that communicates flawlessly with the recipient of the poetry of verse. Such is the case with the poetry of E. M. Schorb.

—Paul T. Vogel
Midwest Book Review

You're the real thing—the way you're able to write on such an enormous variety of subjects and though the forms change the voice is consistent. [Because] the writing is rooted in the daily lives of actual, or in some cases, mythological characters, you can get away with a measure of mystery. I like you best when you're a little mysterious, or maybe more than a little. Have you got a new book out or on the way? I'll look for it!

—Philip Levine
Excerpt from a Letter

The poems of E.M. Schorb shine calmly even as they buzz with energy; are connaissant with the world and yet transcendent of it; make something deeply funny and yet highly sad--given a world and a time and a good mind's eye. This is the work of a mature intelligence, its ironies unadulterated by cynicism, and its swells informed by understatement.

—Heather McHugh
Award Citation

I am always happy to drop everything—pretty nearly—when I make the acquaintance of a new poet as good as E.M. Schorb.
—James Dickey

Schorb's poetry is rich with humor and an almost gestaltic sense of clarity; this unique voice allows him to maintain a tonal unity while moving through a variety of forms.
—Raymond Thibodeaux
New Delta Review

Schorb draws from science, art, literary history, and popular culture, balancing these subjects in a thoughtfully conceived and organized book. Lurking behind all is the danger and violence of life—call it man's and nature's inhumanity to each other—which Schorb handles maturely, without cynicism, and often with a humor that places him somewhere between Marvin Bell and Kenneth Koch.
—Todd Verdun
The Carolina Quarterly

E. M. Schorb demonstrates that the world of prose poetry has no boundaries of form, theme, or style. His prose poems both give us metaphysical fancies and reveal the unexpected in the ordinary. Schorb walks through the world with wonder; in his pieces, dogs can drag cadavers home, sinister objects can hang from clotheslines and, like Schorb himself, poets in their wanderings can step into the lives of other people.
—Jack Anderson

www.ingramcontent.com/pod-product-compliance
Lightning Source LLC
Chambersburg PA
CBHW021349290426
44108CB00010B/161